POSTTRAUMATIC STRESS: NEW RESEARCH

Posttraumatic Stress: New Research

Guida D. Kume
Editor

Nova Science Publishers, Inc.
New York

For permission to use material from this book please contact us:
Telephone 631-231-7269; Fax 631-231-8175
Web Site: http://www.novapublishers.com

LIBRARY OF CONGRESS CATALOGING-IN-PUBLICATION DATA

Posttraumatic stress : new research / Guida D. Kume, editor.
p. ; cm.
Includes bibliographical references and index.
ISBN 1-60021-078-3
1. Post-traumatic stress disorder. I. Kume, Guida D.
[DNLM: 1. Stress Disorders, Post-Traumatic. WM 170 P8587 2006]
RC552.P67P6755 2006
616.85'21--dc22 2006005671

Published by Nova Science Publishers, Inc. ✣New York

CONTENTS

PREFACE

Posttraumatic Stress Disorder, or PTSD, is a psychiatric disorder that can occur following the experience or witnessing of life-threatening events such as military combat, natural disasters, terrorist incidents, serious accidents, or violent personal assaults like rape. People who suffer from PTSD often relive the experience through nightmares and flashbacks, have difficulty sleeping, and feel detached or estranged, and these symptoms can be severe enough and last long enough to significantly impair the person's daily life. PTSD is marked by clear biological changes as well as psychological symptoms. PTSD is complicated by the fact that it frequently occurs in conjunction with related disorders such as depression, substance abuse, problems of memory and cognition, and other problems of physical and mental health. The disorder is also associated with impairment of the person's ability to function in social or family life, including occupational instability, marital problems and divorces. PTSD is associated with a number of distinctive neurobiological and physiological changes. PTSD can be treated by a variety of forms of psychotherapy and drug therapy. This new book presents leading research from around the world.

Posttraumatic life change was investigated in a sample of nonrecent sexual assault survivors in chapter one. An average of 16 years postassault, most survivors identified positive changes that had resulted from the assault, particularly in the domains of self (e.g., increased assertiveness), spirituality (e.g., spiritual well-being), and empathy (e.g., concern for others' suffering). Negative changes in beliefs about the fairness and safety of the world also were common, however. Controlling for recent life stressors and personality, positive changes were associated with fewer symptoms of depression, anxiety and Post Traumatic Stress Disorder (PTSD) and greater life satisfaction. Self-reported positive changes generally were related to personality, social support, coping, and control appraisals in hypothesized directions. Coping and control appraisals (particularly control over the recovery process) mediated the relations among personality and social support and positive life change.

Human beings have always experienced disasters. A disaster may be brief, but its psychological effects may last for many years. These psychological effects are increasingly well-documented.

Disasters affect not only those immediately involved, but also those who know the victims. This is perhaps particularly so when the victims are children. Commonly when adults hear news of disasters they ask first: What about the children? (Saylor, 1993). Of course, typically it is worse for the parents.

In chapter two the definition and classification of disaster and the effects of disaster on survivors and their relatives will be discussed.

Trauma management requires a multidisciplinary approach. This includes treatment of physical injuries involving different organ systems. At the same time, it is essential to prevent and treat the behavioral and psychological sequelae of trauma. These problems not only affect patients but also their family members and the caregivers.

The causes of psychological disturbances in trauma patients may include pain, sudden and unexpected events, various life-saving procedures and interventions, trauma ward and ICU environment, sleep and sensory deprivation, medications, fear of loss of body function or death, damage to CNS or underlying medical diseases. Helplessness, humiliation, threat to body image and mental symptoms are some problems specifically concerning these patients. The patients react to these stressors by various defense mechanisms like conservation withdrawal, regression, anger, denial, anxiety, depression or grief reaction. Some of the patients develop delirium or more severe problems like acute stress disorder or post-traumatic stress disorder. A number of scales have been used for assessment of post-traumatic psychological symptoms. Various physical, pharmacological and psychological interventions to prevent or manage such problems have been described. Problems and management of specific patient groups e.g. patients with burns, spinal cord injury, traumatic brain injury and amputation are also highlighted.

The experience of having a seriously injured relative in hospital is a source of intense psychological stress for family members. They demonstrate symptoms of denial, fear, helplessness, confusion, depression and sometimes even post-traumatic stress disorder. Two way communications between clinical staff and families, hope for survival, support and reassurance from the personnel, proper counseling of relatives and some organizational changes have been found to be helpful.

The healthcare professionals involved in the care of trauma patients are also under threat of developing psychological problems. Stressful working environment especially in the critical care units; repeated exposure to very sick, disfigured or dying patients; need to communicate with patients' relatives and face their emotional reactions are some of the factors which trigger emotional and psychological reactions in the caregivers.

In conclusion, as presented in chapter three, knowledge of psychological problems along with their prevention and management in patients, families and caregivers is an important aspect of trauma care.

Posttraumatic stress disorder (PTSD) is a condition that has a lifetime prevalence of approximately 7.8%. It is defined in DSM-IV as an anxiety disorder in which a person has been exposed to a traumatic event, involving either witnessing or experiencing threatened death or injury or witnessing or experiencing threat to physical integrity. The response to the traumatic event must involve fear or horror. In PTSD, the patient develops symptoms in three domains: reexperiencing the trauma, avoiding stimuli associated with the trauma and experiencing symptoms of increased autonomic arousal. Exposure to stress can have numerous pathophysiological effects. In order to understand the neurobiology of PTSD, it is important to establish animal models of PTSD, in which different aspects of this disorder may be studied. Some of these models include inescapable footshocks in a shuttle-box, exposure to a predator, underwater trauma, and early stress models. Exposure of animals to these situations may lead to behavioral changes such as maladaptive responses to stress, avoidance, and increase in responsiveness to external stimuli in a stressful context. The authors broach endocrine changes in the HPA axis, biochemical alterations in neurotrophic factors, cytokines, and neurotransmission at serotonergic, noradrenergic, glutamatergic and

GABAergic synapses. The use of biochemical peripheral markers is discussed in chapter four, as well as limitations and contributions of the current investigation into this psychiatric disorder.

Chapter five deals with trauma and PTSD in general outpatient psychiatry, its prevalence and aetiology, the long-term consequences of unrecognised PTSD and the benefits of focusing on trauma in treatment.

Chapter six aims to review existing literature on posttraumatic stress following train disasters. It is organized according to primary, secondary and quaternary victims, with emphasis placed on the latter. Following their exposure to a train disaster, the link between quaternary victims' subjective experience of the train disaster, death anxiety, personality traits, coping styles, posttraumatic stress reactions and general health problems will be described. The chapter will end with some suggestions on future research on victims exposed to train disasters.

In: Posttraumatic Stress Disorder: New Research
Editor: Guida D. Kume, pp.1-22
ISBN 1-60021-078-3

Chapter 1

POSITIVE LIFE CHANGES FOLLOWING SEXUAL ASSAULT: A REPLICATION AND EXTENSION

Patricia Frazier,* Amy Conlon, Michael Steger, Ty Tashiro, and Theresa Glaser
University of Minnesota, Minneapolis, MN

ABSTRACT

Posttraumatic life change was investigated in a sample of nonrecent sexual assault survivors. An average of 16 years postassault, most survivors identified positive changes that had resulted from the assault, particularly in the domains of self (e.g., increased assertiveness), spirituality (e.g., spiritual well-being), and empathy (e.g., concern for others' suffering). Negative changes in beliefs about the fairness and safety of the world also were common, however. Controlling for recent life stressors and personality, positive changes were associated with fewer symptoms of depression, anxiety and Post Traumatic Stress Disorder (PTSD) and greater life satisfaction. Self-reported positive changes generally were related to personality, social support, coping, and control appraisals in hypothesized directions. Coping and control appraisals (particularly control over the recovery process) mediated the relations among personality and social support and positive life change.

INTRODUCTION

Surveys of community samples (e.g., Breslau et al., 1998) indicate that most individuals experience some kind of major traumatic event in their lives. It thus is not surprising that the psychological effects of trauma have been the focus of much research attention. Most

* Patricia Frazier, Ph.D. Department of Psychology, University of Minnesota, N218 Elliott Hall, Minneapolis, MN 55455; Phone: 612/625-6863; Fax: 612/626-2079; Email: pfraz@umn.edu

research has focused on negative consequences, such as Posttraumatic Stress Disorder (PTSD). However, a growing body of research demonstrates that many survivors report positive life changes following various traumatic events. This phenomenon is referred to by several names including posttraumatic growth, stress-related growth, and perceived benefits or benefit-finding (Tedeschi & Calhoun, 2004). Common areas of growth reported by survivors of various traumas reflect changes in three general life domains: changes in one's sense of self (e.g., increased strength and maturity), changes in relationships (e.g., increased closeness to others), and changes in spirituality or life philosophy (e.g., increased sense of purpose in life) (Tedeschi & Calhoun, 1995). Additionally, trauma survivors often report an increased sense of empathy with others' suffering (e.g., McMillen & Fisher, 1998). While not denying the distress associated with traumatic events, posttraumatic growth research reflects the potential for traumatic events to serve as the impetus for positive transformation.

Although sexual assault is a relatively common traumatic event that has a high conditional risk for PTSD (e.g., Kessler, Sonnega, Bromet, Hughes, & Nelson, 1995), few studies have examined posttraumatic growth following sexual assault. In two previous reports we have investigated the prevalence, timing, and correlates of posttraumatic growth among recent sexual assault survivors (Frazier, Conlon, & Glaser, 2001; Frazier, Tashiro, Berman, Steger, & Long, 2004). One goal of our previous research and the research reported here is to broaden the scope of events examined in the posttrauma growth literature, which has focused heavily on individuals struggling with health concerns. Additionally, unlike many studies on posttraumatic growth that have focused exclusively on positive changes, we have assessed both positive and negative life changes (e.g., negative changes in self worth), which provides a more comprehensive picture of the aftermath of the traumatic experience (McMillen & Fisher, 1998). We first briefly review the results of this initial longitudinal study, and the goals and hypotheses of the present study.

Our Previous Longitudinal Study of Sexual Assault Survivors

Because of the limited data on sexual assault survivors, in our first paper (Frazier et al., 2001), we focused primarily on documenting the prevalence of various self-reported positive and negative life change in recent survivors. With regard to prevalence, the majority of the survivors in this initial study reported positive life changes, even as soon as 2 weeks postassault. The most common positive life change at all time points (2 weeks, and 2, 6, and 12 months postassault) was increased empathy for others' suffering. Positive changes in the domains of self (e.g., ability to be assertive, ability to recognize strengths) and spirituality (e.g., greater life appreciation, closer to God) also were common. Nonetheless, negative life changes also were reported frequently. For example, across all four time periods, the majority of participants reported negative changes in beliefs about the fairness and safety of the world and the goodness of other people.

A second goal of the first paper was to assess the time course of perceived positive and negative life changes. One assumption in the literature is that the number of positive life changes reported will increase over time, as the term posttraumatic "growth" implies (see O'Leary, Alday, & Ickovics, 1998, for a review). Using hierarchical linear modeling (HLM), we found that on average positive changes increased and negative life changes decreased over time. However, there was also significant individual variability in the time course of self-reported positive and negative life changes. In other words, not all individuals followed the typical pattern: Some survivors reported fewer positive changes and more negative life changes from 2 weeks to 12 months postassault.

Our third goal in this first paper was to assess the relations among positive and negative life change and standard measures of posttraumatic distress (i.e., depression and PTSD). Individuals who reported more positive life changes reported lower levels of depression at both 2 weeks and 1 year postassault, and fewer PTSD symptoms at 2 weeks postassault. Those who reported more negative life changes reported more symptoms of depression and PTSD at both time periods. Changes in self and spirituality were more strongly related to the distress measures than were changes in empathy, relationships, or beliefs about the world. In addition, the relations among negative changes and distress were stronger than those between positive changes and distress (see also Joseph, Williams, & Yule, 1993; Lehman et al., 1993). Finally, because there were individual differences in patterns of positive and negative change over time, we compared individuals with different patterns in terms of 12 month distress levels. These analyses revealed that those who reported higher than average levels of positive change at both 2 weeks and 12 months were less distressed than those with lower than average levels at both time periods. In addition, those who reported higher levels at 2 weeks but not 12 months (i.e., those who "lost" their positive changes) were as distressed as those who never reported positive change (i.e., those who reported lower than average levels at both time periods). Thus, finding benefits early and maintaining them over time appeared important to the recovery process. Conversely, those who reported higher levels of negative change at both time periods were more distressed than those who never reported negative change. There also was a trend for those who reported fewer negatives over time (lost negatives) to be less distressed than those who reported higher levels of negatives changes at both time periods.

In our second paper based on this first longitudinal study (Frazier, Tashiro, et al., 2004), we examined factors that were related to self-reported life changes, focusing on positive life changes.[1] As described above, our first paper highlighted the importance of both early reports of positive change and patterns of self-reported positive changes over time for later distress levels. Thus, the purpose of this second paper was to assess factors associated with reporting positive life change soon after the assault and with individual differences in patterns of self-reported positive changes over time.

Several researchers have developed models of factors that may either facilitate or hinder positive life change following traumatic events (see O'Leary et al., 1998, for a review). These include personal resources, environmental resources, and the individual's coping strategies and appraisal of the event. In this second study (Frazier, Tashiro, et al., 2004), we assessed the relations among variables in each of these categories and both early reports of positive

[1] As described in the Method section our life change items assess both negative and positive life change. In the first paper (Frazier et al., 2001), we created scales representing the total number of positive and negative life changes reported. In the second paper (Frazier, Tashiro, et al., 2004), we scored the items on a continuous scale so that higher scores represent more positive life changes and lower scores represent more negative life change. To be consistent with this more recent work, in this paper we use the scoring system used by Frazier, Tashiro, et al. (2004). The correlation between the two scoring systems (number of positive changes reported and total scores on the scale) is .91.

change and changes in self-reported positive life changes over time. The specific correlates measured in each category were: personal characteristics (prior sexual victimization, ethnicity), environmental resources (social support), coping (approach, avoidant, and religious), and control appraisals (behavioral self-blame [past control], control over the recovery process [present control], and taking precautions to prevent future assaults [future control]). The environmental, coping, and control appraisal measures were gathered at all four time points. The significant correlates of early (2 week) positive change were higher early levels of social support, approach coping, religious coping, and control over the recovery process. With regard to predictors of patterns of change over time, the trajectories of social support, approach coping, religious coping, control over the recovery process, and taking precautions were all positively associated with positive-change trajectories, suggesting that, within individuals, increases in these variables were associated with increases in self-reported positive life changes over time. Avoidant coping and behavioral self-blame trajectories were negatively associated with positive-change trajectories, suggesting that decreases in avoidant coping and behavioral self-blame were associated with increases in self-reported positive life changes over time.

Consistent with Schaefer and Moos' (1998) model, we also assessed whether the significant relations between any of the personal (i.e., ethnicity, prior victimization) and environmental (i.e., social support) resource variables and positive change were mediated by coping and control appraisals. None of the personal resource variables were significantly related to positive life change, although social support was significant. The potential mediators (i.e., variables related to both social support and positive life change) were approach and avoidant coping, taking precautions, and control over the recovery process. Regression analyses revealed that control over the recovery process was the strongest mediator of the relation between social support and positive change trajectories. In other words, the primary reason that increases in social support were associated with increases in positive life change was because increases in social support were associated with increased control over the recovery process.

Although this first longitudinal study provided useful data regarding posttrauma life change among sexual assault survivors, it was limited in terms of the make-up of the sample and the range of variables examined. First, all participants had reported to an emergency room following the assault and hence were not necessarily representative of most sexual assault victims. Moreover, the study focused exclusively on recent assault victims, which precluded investigation of long-term changes resulting from sexual assault. Second, the outcome variables were limited to measures of distress, which is an important limitation given that posttrauma growth tends to be more strongly related to positive well-being than to distress (e.g., McMillen, Smith, & Fisher, 1997). Finally, some potentially important correlates of growth were not assessed, such as personality traits.

These limitations were addressed in the current study in which we examined self-reported posttrauma life change in a sample of nonrecent sexual assault survivors recruited through a random phone survey of community women. Specifically, the current study was designed to replicate Frazier et al.'s (2001) findings regarding the prevalence and types of positive and negative life change among sexual assault survivors and the association between posttrauma life change and distress. These earlier findings also were extended by examining the relations among positive life change and a broader range of outcomes, including life satisfaction and perceived health, and by accounting for the effects of recent life stressors and personality in these relationships. We also sought to replicate Frazier, Tashiro, et al.'s (2004) findings regarding the correlates of positive life change, and extended this work by examining additional correlates. The research questions are explained more fully in the following sections along with the study hypotheses.

PREVALENCE AND TYPES OF POSTTRAUMA LIFE CHANGE

Consistent with our previous research on sexual assault (Frazier et al., 2001) and other traumatic events (see Linley & Joseph, 2004, for a review), we predicted that the majority of participants in the current study would identify positive life changes resulting from the assault. Changes in empathy, self, and spirituality were expected to be the most frequently endorsed areas of positive change, whereas changes in beliefs about the fairness and safety of the world were expected to be the least common type of positive change and the most common type of negative change reported.

POSITIVE LIFE CHANGE, DISTRESS AND WELL-BEING

Also consistent with Frazier et al. (2001), we expected more positive change to be associated with less distress (see also Linley & Joseph, 2004). Based on previous research (e.g., McMillen et al., 1997), we also expected positive change to be more strongly related to measures of well-being (i.e., life satisfaction) than to measures of distress (i.e., depression, anxiety, PTSD). We also assessed perceived health because sexual assault often is associated with significant health concerns (Frazier, 2002). Self-reported growth is associated with better health outcomes (e.g., Affleck, Tennen, Croog, & Levine, 1987), including better immune functioning (e.g., McGregor et al., 2004), and we expected a positive relation between self-reported positive change and perceived health in our study as well.

In examining the relations between positive life change and adjustment (i.e., distress, life satisfaction, perceived health), we controlled for the effects of both recent life stressors and personality. Given that most participants in the current study had been sexually assaulted several years previously, it seemed important to account for the contribution of recent life events to current adjustment. Similarly, because variability in adjustment may be accounted for partly by basic personality traits (Watson & Hubbard, 1996), we examined the associations between positive life change and adjustment controlling for both neuroticism and extraversion. These are considered the "Big Two" personality traits and have received the most attention in the stress and coping literature (Watson & Hubbard, 1996). Although we hypothesized that accounting for these variables would decrease the strength of the correlations between positive change and adjustment, we anticipated that self-reported positive life change would still account for unique variance in distress, life satisfaction, and perceived health.

CORRELATES OF POSITIVE CHANGE

The final research question concerned identifying significant correlates of self-reported positive change. As mentioned, conceptual frameworks tend to view the process of posttrauma growth as emerging from several conceptually distinct classes of variables, including personal characteristics, environmental resources, and appraisal and coping responses (e.g., O'Leary et al., 1998). Schaefer and Moos (1998) further hypothesized that the relations among personal and environmental resources and growth are mediated by appraisals and coping. A brief review of the literature linking these variables to posttrauma growth follows.

Personal Characteristics

In our earlier study of correlates (Frazier, Tashiro, et al., 2004), neither of the personal characteristics we assessed (i.e., ethnicity and prior victimization) were associated with positive life change. Thus, in this study we assessed basic personality traits, which may be more important determinants of responses to stressful life events. In their recent review, Tedeschi and Calhoun (2004) concluded that two basic personality qualities (extraversion and openness to experience) are associated with the tendency to grow following trauma. Although neuroticism was not associated with perceived growth in their research (Tedeschi & Calhoun, 1996), it was negatively related to growth in another study (Evers et al., 2001). In addition, positive reinterpretation coping, which is related to posttraumatic growth (e.g., Mohr, Dick, Russo, Likosky, & Goodkin, 1999), has been linked to lower levels of neuroticism in several studies (see Watson & Hubbard, 1996, for a review). We thus predicted that participants higher in extraversion and openness, and lower in neuroticism, would report more positive life changes.

Environmental Resources

Models of posttrauma growth typically include environmental resources, such as social support, as factors that account for variability in the extent to which individuals report positive change. As mentioned, Schaefer and Moos (1998) hypothesized that social support may be associated with outcomes because it is associated with more adaptive coping and event appraisals (see also Tedeschi & Calhoun, 2004). More specifically, supportive others can help individuals process their thoughts and feelings about a trauma, which is necessary for finding benefits in it. Although social support measures have varied, positive relationships between support and growth have been found in several studies (see e.g., Armeli, Gunthert, & Cohen, 2001; Evers et al., 2001; Park, Cohen, & Murch, 1996; Revenson, Wollman, & Felton, 1983) as well as our own prior research (Frazier, Tashiro, et al., 2004). Thus, we expected social support to be related to more self-reported positive changes.

Coping and Event Appraisals

Coping resources and event appraisals play a central role in many theories of positive change (O'Leary et al., 1998). With regard to coping, in general, individuals who engage in more active approach-oriented coping (which involves processing thoughts and feelings about the trauma) are hypothesized to be more likely to report positive changes following a trauma, whereas those who engage in more avoidant coping (which involves avoiding thoughts and feelings about the trauma)should report fewer positive changes (Schaefer & Moos, 1998). Several studies support these hypothesized relations between positive change and various approach-oriented coping strategies (Aldwin, Sutton, & Lachman, 1996; Collins, Taylor, & Skokan, 1990; Cordova, Cunningham, Carlson, & Andrykowski, 2001; Evers et al., 2001; Mohr et al., 1999; Park et al., 1996). In the Park et al. study, approach coping strategies explained more variance in positive life change than any of the other categories of variables (e.g., personal resources, social support). However, results for avoidant coping have been more mixed. Specifically, avoidant strategies have been negatively related (Aldwin et al., 1996), positively related (Collins et al., 1990), and not related (Park et al., 1996; Mohr et al., 1999) to reporting positive change.

A recent review and critique of the broader coping literature recommended that researchers assess "core families" of coping rather than the higher-order dimensions (e.g., problem vs. emotion focused, approach vs. avoidance) typically used to measure coping (Skinner, Edge, Altman, & Sherwood, 2003). They identified five "clearly core" families (i.e., cognitive restructuring, problem solving, support seeking, distraction, avoidance) and four additional "strong candidates" (e.g., social withdrawal, emotional regulation/expressing emotions, rumination, helplessness). Thus, in this study we assessed the same forms of coping as Frazier, Tashiro, et al. (2004), which are all either "clearly core" (i.e., cognitive restructuring, [problem] avoidance) or "strong candidates" (i.e., expressing emotions, social withdrawal) but examined them separately rather than as combined measures of approach and avoidant coping. We expected cognitive restructuring and expressing emotions to be associated with more positive life change and problem avoidance and social withdrawal to be associated with fewer self-reported positive life changes.

Although Schaefer and Moos (1998) focused on approach and avoidant coping, another coping-related variable that appears to be related to positive life change is religiosity. A religious worldview may help survivors to make sense of and find meaning in a traumatic event. Various aspects of religiosity are positively related to positive life change following traumatic events (Aldwin et al., 1996; Calhoun, Cann, Tedeschi, & McMillan, 2000; Park et al., 1996; Tedeschi & Calhoun, 1996), including sexual assault (Frazier, Tashiro, et al., 2004; Kennedy, Davis, & Taylor, 1998). We expected greater use of religious coping to be positively related to self-reported positive life change in this study as well.

Several aspects of event appraisals have been studied in relation to posttraumatic growth (see Linley & Joseph, 2004, for a review). The event appraisal we studied was the perceived controllability of the event, in part because of the centrality of perceived control in theories of trauma recovery and PTSD (see e.g., Foa, Zinbarg, & Rothbaum, 1992). There are various aspects of a trauma over which survivors may feel that they have control, including the occurrence of the trauma (past control), the current impact of the trauma (present control), and whether they will experience future traumas (future control). In their review of the literature on perceived control and trauma, Frazier, Berman, and Steward (2002) found that these three aspects of control had differing relations with measures of posttrauma distress, with present control being the most adaptive. They hypothesized that survivors who feel that they have more control over the recovery process (which is one aspect of present control) may be particularly likely to report positive life changes posttrauma. Indeed, this was the only form of control related to positive life change in a study of bereaved individuals (Frazier, Steward, & Mortensen, 2004). Control over current symptoms (another form of present control) also was associated with reporting more positive life change in a study of arthritis patients (Tennen, Affleck, Urrows, Higgins, & Mendola, 1992). With regard to the other types of control, Tedeschi (1999) hypothesized that self-blame (which can be thought of as control over the past event; see Frazier et al., 2002) would hinder positive change, but that a sense of future control would be associated with reporting more positive changes. In our previous longitudinal study (Frazier, Tashiro, et al., 2004) past control (i.e., behavioral self-blame) was negatively associated with self-reported growth whereas present control (i.e., control over the recovery process) and future control (i.e., engaging in behaviors to try to prevent future assaults) were associated with more self-reported growth, and we expected the same relations here.

In sum, we predicted that the following variables would be associated with reporting more positive life changes after a sexual assault: higher extraversion and openness, lower neuroticism, greater social support, more use of cognitive restructuring and expression emotions and less use of problem avoidance and social withdrawal as coping strategies, greater use of religious coping strategies, less behavioral self-blame, and greater perceived control over the recovery process and future assaults. In addition, when any of the personal (personality traits) or environmental (social support) resources were associated with self-reported positive changes, we assessed whether those relations were mediated by coping strategies or control appraisals. The following conditions must be met to establish mediation: (1) the predictor variable (e.g., personality) must be associated with the outcome variable (positive change); (2) the predictor variable must be associated with the mediator (e.g., coping); (3) the mediator must be associated with the outcome variable, after controlling for the relation between the predictor and outcome; and (4) the addition of the mediator variable must significantly decrease the association between the predictor and outcome variable (Kenny, Kashy, & Bolger, 1998). The data are consistent with complete mediation when the relation between the predictor and the outcome is not significantly different from zero when the mediator is added to the model. Partial mediation occurs when there is a significant reduction in the relation between the predictor and the outcome when the mediator is added but that relation is still significantly different from zero.

METHOD

Participants and Procedure

Participants initially were contacted through a random phone survey regarding stressful life events completed by 894 women (response rate = 72%) residing in Hennepin County (which includes Minneapolis, MN and its immediate suburbs). Of these 894 women, 198 (22%) reported having been sexually assaulted (defined as nonconsensual sexual intercourse involving threats or physical force) and 190 (96%) agreed to participate in a follow-up study that involved completing a mailed questionnaire regarding the assault for which they were paid $25. We received 135 completed follow-up questionnaires (response rate = 71%). Comparisons between participants (n = 135) and nonparticipants (n = 63) revealed no significant differences in race, education, income, relationship status, or age. Data from this sample also have been used in two prior reports (Frazier, Mortensen, & Steward, in press; Frazier, Steward, & Mortensen, 2004).

Respondents ranged in age from 18 to 78 (mean = 39 years). Most (79%) were Caucasian, 16% were African Americans, and the remaining 5% represented other racial groups. The assaults had occurred an average of 16 years previously (range = 1 month to 62 years). The modal education level was "completed some college" (36%), and the modal income was $20,000-$30,000 (26%). Fifty-seven percent of the sample was employed full-time and 59% were married or in a long-term relationship.

Measures

Posttraumatic Life Change

To identify specific aspects of life that had changed as a result of the assault, participants completed a 17-item life change measure. Respondents rated each item on a five-point scale (1 = much worse now, 2 = a little worse now, 3 = no change, 4 = a little better now, 5 = much better now). Items were grouped to reflect the four domains of positive change most often identified in previous research: changes in self, relationships, life philosophy/spirituality, and empathy. Additionally, three items assessed changes in beliefs about the world (e.g., safety), which were expected to change primarily in a negative direction. For analyses of correlates of positive change, we used the 14-item scale used by Frazier, Tashiro, et al. (2004) in which scores on the 14 items dealing with change in self, spirituality, relationships and empathy are totaled so that higher scores indicate more positive change. The alpha coefficient for that scale in this sample was 91.

Psychological Distress

Distress was assessed via measures of depression, anxiety, and PTSD, commonly reported sequelae of sexual assault (Frazier, 2002). Subscales of the Brief Symptom Inventory (BSI; Derogatis, 1993) were used to assess depression (6 items; $\alpha = .88$) and anxiety (6 items; $\alpha = .85$). Participants indicated the degree to which they were distressed by each symptom (e.g., feeling blue) over the past month. Responses were made on a 5-point scale (0 = not at all to 4 = extremely). Past research has demonstrated the reliability and validity of the BSI as a measure of psychological distress (Derogatis, 1993). A 17-item checklist developed for this study was used to assess the symptoms of PTSD listed in the DSM-III-R (APA, 1987). Participants were asked to check the symptoms they had experienced in the past month (e.g., "I often have bad dreams about the rape"). The internal consistency reliability coefficient (Kuder-Richardson 20) for the 17-item checklist was .86.

Life Satisfaction

Life satisfaction was assessed with a 9-item measure developed for this study that asked respondents to rate their degree of satisfaction in various life domains within the past month (e.g., "work," "relationships with family members," "life in general"). Responses were made on a 5-point scale (1 = very dissatisfied to 5 = very satisfied; α = .72).

Perceived Health

Perceived health was assessed via the General Health scale of the Medical Outcomes Study Health Survey – Short Form 36 (SF-36; Ware & Sherbourne, 1992). The General Health scale consists of 5 items that assess perceived health (e.g., My health is excellent; I am as healthy as anybody I know) on 5 point scales. The SF-36 in general, and the General Health scale in particular, has excellent psychometric properties (see e.g., Stewart, Hays, & Ware, 1988). The alpha coefficient in this sample was .85.

Personality

Neuroticism, openness, and extraversion were assessed using subscales from Saucier's (1994) Mini-Markers, a self-report measure based on the Big Five model of personality. Respondents rated (1 = extremely inaccurate to 9 = extremely accurate) the extent to which adjectives related to extraversion (e.g., energetic), openness (e.g., imaginative) and neuroticism (e.g., moody) described them at the present time. The 8-item subscales were used to assess extraversion and neuroticism and 3 of the 8 items were used to assess openness. The alpha coefficients were .83 (Extraversion), .78 (Openness) and .85 (Neuroticism).

Social Support

Social support was assessed with two items. Respondents rated the helpfulness and caring demonstrated by individuals who provided support following the assault (0 = not at all to 10 = very) and the amount of support they had received since the assault (0 = no support to 10 = a lot of support). The social support index was the average of these two ratings (α = .79).

Coping

The Coping Strategies Inventory (CSI; Tobin, Holroyd, & Reynolds, 1984) was used to assess the coping behaviors used in dealing with the assault in the past month. Tobin et al. provided evidence of the predictive, criterion-related, and structural validity, and of the internal consistency and stability, of the CSI. The CSI contains eight 9-item subscales that measure various forms of problem and emotion focused approach and avoidance coping. Four subscales from the CSI were chosen that capture coping behaviors considered "core" or "strong candidates" by Skinner et al. (2003). These include cognitive restructuring (CR) (e.g., "I tried to get a new angle on the situation"), expressing emotions (EE) (e.g., "I found ways to blow off steam"), problem avoidance (PA) (e.g., "I went along as if nothing were happening"), and social withdrawal (SW) (e.g., "I avoided being with people"). Two items that are confounded with distress (Stanton, Danoff-Burg, Cameron, & Ellis, 1994) were removed from the expressing emotions scale. All items were rated on a 1 (Not at all) to 5 (Very much) scale to reflect the extent to which each strategy was used to cope with the assault in the past month. The alpha coefficients for the four scales were as follows: CR (.90), EE (.87), PA (.78), and SW (.85).

Ten items assessed religious coping thoughts and behaviors. These items were adapted from other measures of religious coping, including the Religious Coping Activities Scale (Pargament et al., 1990), religious problem-solving styles questionnaire (Pargament et al., 1988), and the religious coping subscale from the COPE (Carver, Scheier, & Weintraub, 1989). Sample items include "I sought God's help in dealing with the situation," and "I took control over what I could and let God help me with the rest." All items were rated from 1 (not at all) to 5 (very much) in terms of how much they were used in handling the stress of the assault. Coefficient alpha for the religious coping scale was .93.

Control Appraisals

Three scales from the Rape Attribution Questionnaire (RAQ; Frazier, 2002) were used to assess the extent to which survivors attributed the assault to their past behaviors (5 items), felt control over the recovery process (4 items), and reported engaging in behaviors to try to prevent future assaults (5 items) in the past month. Respondents rated the behavioral self-blame items on a 1 (never) to 5 (very often) scale using the following stem: "How often have you thought: I was assaulted because...[I used poor judgment]." Items for the other two scales were rated from 1 (Strongly Disagree) to 5 (Strongly Agree). Sample items include "I know what I must do to help myself recover from my assault" (control over the recovery process) and "Since the assault I try not to put myself in potentially dangerous situations" (taking precautions). All items were judged by a panel of experts to be good indicators of the constructs (see Frazier, 2003, for more information, including all scale items). The alpha coefficients for the three scales were .88 (behavioral self-blame), .78 (control over recovery), and .66 (taking precautions).

Past year Life Stressors

Participants in the random phone survey were asked whether they had experienced a list of 7 stressors in the past year (e.g., relationship loss, non-life threatening illness). The stressors were taken from the Potential Stressful Events Interview (PSEI; Kilpatrick, Resnick, & Freedy, 1991). These data were used to create a variable representing the total number of previous year stressors experienced (range = 0 to 6, $M = 2.60$, $SD = 1.53$).

Results

Prevalence and Domains of Life Change

Participants reported an average of approximately seven positive changes and four negative changes resulting from the assault (see Table 1). Increased empathy for others in similar situations was the most commonly reported positive change. A considerable percentage of respondents also reported positive changes in self such as increased assertiveness and a greater ability to recognize their strengths. Similarly, positive changes in spirituality were frequently reported (e.g., appreciation of life and spiritual well-being). Slightly less than one-third of respondents reported that their relationships with friends and family had changed positively as a result of the assault. Positive changes in beliefs about the fairness and safety of the world were reported by relatively few participants, whereas a substantial proportion reported negative changes in these beliefs. Negative changes in mental health also were common. The average score on the 14-item positive life change scale used in the following analyses was 3.52 (SD = .85), which again reflects that survivors perceive more positive than negative life change.

Table 1. Percentages of Respondents Reporting Positive and Negative Change in each Domain

	% positive change[a]	% negative change[b]
Self		
Ability to be assertive	60	20
Ability to recognize strengths	61	11
Sense of self-worth	41	28
Sense of personal control	46	33
Ability to take care of self	54	16
Beliefs in own judgments	37	37
Mental health	33	44
Mean	*47*	*27*
Relationships		
Relationships with family	31	21
Relationships with friends	29	20
Mean	*30*	*20.5*
Spirituality		
Appreciation of life	56	13
Sense of closeness to God	43	11
Sense of purpose in life	42	18
Spiritual well-being	47	19
Mean	*47*	*15*
Beliefs		
Goodness of people	16	32
Safety of the world	11	48
Fairness of the world	8	44
Mean	*12*	*41*
Empathy		
Concern for others in similar situations	78	3
Number of changes		
Mean	6.94	4.15
Standard Deviation	5.10	4.27

[a] Percentage answering 4 or 5 for each item [b] Percentage answering 1 or 2 for each item
N = 123 due to missing data.

Correlations Among Positive Life Change and Distress, Life Satisfaction, and Perceived Health

Correlations among the positive life change scale and measures of distress, life satisfaction, and perceived health are shown in Table 2. Interpretation of the strength of these correlations followed Cohen's (1992) effect size conventions (.10 = small, .30 = medium, .50 = large effect). Survivors who reported more positive life changes reported fewer symptoms of depression, anxiety, and PTSD with correlations in the medium to large range (r's = -.37 to -.51). There also was a large correlation between positive life change and life satisfaction (r = .49). The correlation with better perceived health was significant but small (r = .18). All correlations were reduced after controlling for previous year stressors and personality although they remained significant (except perceived health).

Table 2. Bivariate Correlations and Partial Correlations Among Positive Life Change and Adjustment Measures

	Positive Life Changes[a]	
		Controlling for Current Stressors and Personality[b]
Depression	-.51‡	-.32‡
Anxiety	-.38‡	-.18*
PTSD symptoms	-.37‡	-.22*
Perceived Health	.18*	.05
Life Satisfaction	.49‡	.32‡

n's = 116 to 130 due to missing data.
* $p < .05$ ‡ $p < .001$
[a] 14-item positive life change scale [b] Neuroticism and Extraversion

Correlates of Positive Life Change

Mean scores on the various personal, environmental, coping, and appraisal variables are in Table 3 and their correlations with self-reported positive life change are in Table 4. The correlational analyses revealed that reporting more positive changes was associated as hypothesized with less neuroticism, more extraversion, more social support, more cognitive restructuring and expressing emotions and less problem avoidance and social withdrawal, greater religious coping, and more perceived control over the recovery process. These correlations generally were in small to medium range (r's = .19 to .44). The strongest correlates were neuroticism (which was negatively associated with self-reported positive life change) and perceived control over the recovery process. Contrary to predictions, three variables - openness, behavioral self-blame, and taking precautions – were not associated with self-reported positive change.

Table 3. Mean Scores on Personal, Environmental, Coping, and Appraisal Variables

	Mean	SD
Extraversion	5.80	1.44
Neuroticism	4.56	1.64
Openness	6.72	1.87
Cognitive Restructuring	2.45	1.08
Expressing Emotions	2.19	.98
Problem Avoidance	2.51	.87
Social Withdrawal	2.73	1.02
Religious Coping	2.39	1.14
Social support	5.69	3.00
Behavioral self-blame	2.45	1.20
Taking precautions	4.13	.69
Control over recovery process	3.85	.83

N's = 112 – 133 due to missing data

Table 4. Correlates of Self-Reported Positive Life Change

	Positive Life Change[a]
Extraversion	.27[†]
Neuroticism	-.43[‡]
Openness	.04
Social support	.31[‡]
Cognitive restructuring	.19[*]
Expressing emotions	.22[*]
Problem avoidance	-.23[*]
Social withdrawal	-.31[‡]
Religious coping	.35[‡]
Behavioral self-blame	-.09
Control over recovery process	.44[‡]
Taking precautions	.06

n's = 109 to 128 due to missing data. [*] $p < .05$ [†] $p < .01$ [‡] $p < .001$ [a] 14-item positive life change scale

Mediation Analyses

We next assessed whether the coping and appraisal variables mediated the relations among any of the personality or social support variables and positive life change. As shown in Table 3, all three personal and environmental resource variables – extraversion, neuroticism, and social support - met the first criterion for mediation (a significant relation with positive life change). The second criterion is that these predictors are significantly related to the proposed mediators (coping and control appraisals). Analyses assessing this second criterion are in Table 5. Behavioral self-blame and taking precautions were not included because their bivariate correlations with positive life change were not significant. Based on these analyses, social withdrawal and control over the recovery process were tested as potential mediators of the relation between both extraversion and neuroticism and positive change. These two variables, along with expressing emotions, problem avoidance, and religious coping, were tested as mediators of the relation between social support and positive change. To meet the third criterion for mediation, the mediator variable must be significantly related to the outcome with the predictor variable in the equation. Three of the above variables did not meet this criterion. Specifically, expressing emotions, problem avoidance, and social withdrawal were not related to positive life change when social support was included in the model.

Table 5. Correlations Among Predictors and Mediators

	Predictors		
	Extraversion	**Neuroticism**	**Social Support**
Mediators			
Cognitive Restructuring	.07	-.15	.03
Expressing Emotions	.14	-.06	.28†
Problem Avoidance	-.10	.17	-.38‡
Social Withdrawal	-.28†	.31‡	-.39‡
Religious coping	.11	-.16	.28†
Control over recovery process	.18*	-.36‡	.27†

n's = 100 to 128 due to missing data. $^{*}p < .05$ $^{\dagger}p < .01$ $^{\ddagger}p < .001$

Table 6. Mediation Analyses

	B	SE B	β	Goodman's test
1a. Predictor: Extraversion	.17	.06	.29†	
1b. Predictor: Extraversion	.13	.06	.22*	
Mediator: Social withdrawal	-.21	.08	.25†	1.92*
2a. Predictor: Extraversion	.16	.05	.27†	
2b. Predictor: Extraversion	.11	.05	.20*	
Mediator: Control over recovery	.41	.08	.40‡	1.89+
3a. Predictor: Neuroticism	-.26	.05	-.47‡	
3b. Predictor: Neuroticism	-.23	.05	-.41‡	
Mediator: Social withdrawal	-.16	.07	-.19*	-1.77+
4a. Predictor: Neuroticism	-.22	.04	-.41‡	
4b. Predictor: Neuroticism	-.15	.04	-.29‡	
Mediator: Control over recovery	.34	.09	.33‡	2.34*
5a. Predictor: Social support	.09	.03	.34‡	
5b. Predictor: Social support	.07	.03	.27†	
Mediator: Religious coping	.19	.06	.27†	2.06*
6a. Predictor: Social support	.08	.03	.31‡	
6b. Predictor: Social support	.06	.02	.21*	
Mediator: control over recovery	.35	.09	.36‡	2.34*

N's = * to *. $^{*}p < .05$; $^{\dagger}p < .01$; $^{\ddagger}p < .001$.

The analyses testing the final criterion for mediation for the six remaining sets of variables are presented in Table 6. For each test, two regressions were performed, one in which positive life change was regressed on the predictor alone and one in which positive life change was regressed on the predictor and the mediator. The significance of the drop in the relation between the predictor and positive life change when the mediator was added to the model was assessed using Goodman's test (see Frazier, Tix, & Barron, 2004, for more information). For all six tests, the relation between the predictor and positive life change was smaller when the mediator was in the model but in all cases the predictor was still significant, which suggests partial mediation. The drop in the relation between the predictor and positive life change was significant in four cases and marginally significant in two cases. Focusing on the significant mediators, social withdrawal partially mediated the relation between extraversion and positive life change and perceived control over the recovery process partially mediated the relations among both neuroticism and social support and positive life change. Finally, religious coping also partially mediated the relation between social support and positive life change.

DISCUSSION

One goal of the present study was to compare the prevalence and types of posttraumatic life changes reported by a sample of nonrecent sexual assault survivors to that reported by a sample of recent assault survivors who had reported to the emergency room following the assault (Frazier et al., 2001). Despite the differences between the two samples, the prevalence of positive change is remarkably similar across the two studies. The mean number of positive changes reported in the current sample an average of 16 years postassault (6.94) is comparable to that reported at 1 year postassault by Frazier et al.'s sample (6.34) although the average number of negative changes reported is slightly lower in this sample (4.15 vs. 6.12). When scored as a 14-item life change scale, the mean in this sample (3.52) also is similar to the mean at 12 months in our initial study (3.24; Frazier, Tashiro, et al., 2004). That survivors report areas of growth many years postassault is consistent with the view that positive changes resulting from traumatic experiences are not simply mechanisms for coping with the immediate effects of the trauma (Tedeschi & Calhoun, 1995). However, as mentioned later, researchers need to take greater pains to establish the validity of these self-reports.

The frequency of the various types of changes reported in the current sample also is quite similar to that reported by Frazier et al. (2001). Across both studies, increased empathy is the most common positive change. After increased empathy, the three most common positive changes years after the assault are in the areas of self (increases in assertiveness and ability to recognize personal strengths) and spirituality (greater appreciation of life), which also is consistent with Frazier et al.'s findings. Positive changes in relationships were slightly less common among the nonrecent assault survivors than among the recent assault survivors. This suggests that the impact of a trauma on relationships may fade over time whereas the impact on the self and spirituality may be more enduring. Alternatively, unlike the participants in Frazier et al.'s study who sought help immediately following the assault, women in the current sample may not have told anyone about the assault and thus their relationships may not have been as affected.

The most common negative changes reported by survivors in the current study are with regard to beliefs about the safety and fairness of the world. Again, despite differences between the two samples, these also were the most commonly reported negative changes in the previous study (Frazier et al., 2001). However, negative changes in beliefs are less common an average of 16 years postassault than in the year following the assault. Nonetheless, that a substantial proportion of nonrecent survivors continue to report negative changes in their views regarding the benevolence of the world is consistent with other findings that basic assumptions about the world can remain shattered for years posttrauma (Janoff-Bulman, 1989).

The relations among positive life changes and traditional distress measures also are quite similar to those reported by recent assault survivors (Frazier et al., 2001). Specifically, sexual assault survivors who report more positive life changes also report less depression, anxiety, and symptoms of PTSD. The magnitudes of the relations also are similar (with the exception of the relation between positive life change and PTSD symptoms at 12 months postassault in the previous study). These relations remain significant even when the effects of personality and current life stress are controlled. The current study thus provides stronger evidence linking positive change to distress by demonstrating that these relations are not accounted for by recent life stressors or personality. They also suggest that measures of positive life change provide incremental validity in explaining posttrauma distress.

The current study also extended Frazier et al.'s (2001) findings by examining self-reported positive life change in relation to life satisfaction and perceived health. As predicted, positive life change was associated with higher levels of life satisfaction, and this relationship remained significant when previous year stressors and personality were taken into account. Thus, rather than simply experiencing lower levels of posttrauma distress, individuals who report posttrauma growth may actually experience enhanced life functioning (see also McMillen & Fisher, 1998). Survivors who report more positive life changes also report better health, although this relation is not significant once the relations among personality and current life stress and positive change are accounted for.

The final purpose of study was to replicate and extend Frazier, Tashiro, et al.'s (2004) findings regarding the correlates of self-reported positive life change, which can help inform developing models of the posttrauma recovery process. We first discuss the relations among the coping and appraisal variables and positive life change, followed by a discussion of the personal and environmental resource variables and whether their associations with positive life change are mediated by the coping and appraisal variables.

First, as predicted, both cognitive restructuring and expressing emotions are associated with more self-reported positive change whereas social withdrawal and problem avoidance are associated with fewer self-reported positive life changes. This is consistent with the findings from our previous study in which the combined approach and avoidant coping scales were positively and negatively associated with positive change, respectively (Frazier, Tashiro, et al., 2004). It is interesting to note that in this study social withdrawal has the strongest (negative) correlation with positive life change and that it is the most frequently reported coping strategy, even though the assaults had occurred many years previously on average. The specific social withdrawal items most frequently endorsed involved keeping one's thoughts and feelings to one's self and not letting others know what was going on. This suggests that even many years after the assault survivors may still be coping with the assault but feel reluctant to talk with others about it. Other studies also report high rates of avoidant coping in rape survivors (Santello & Leitenberg, 1993; Valentiner, Foa, Riggs, & Gershuny, 1996) and more avoidant coping with regard to sexual assault (Santello & Leitenberg, 1993) and sexual abuse (Coffey, Leitenberg, Henning, Turner, & Bennett, 1996) than with regard to other events. Finally, greater use of religious coping also is associated with more positive life change, consistent with our prior research (Frazier, Tashiro, et al., 2004) and other studies (e.g., Park et al., 1996). In fact, it is more strongly related to positive life change than cognitive restructuring or expressing emotions, and is as common as these other more widely discussed strategies.

With regard to event appraisals, we assessed three aspects of the controllability of the event: behavioral self-blame (past control), control over the recovery process (present control), and taking precautions to prevent future assaults (future control). The only form of control associated with positive life change is perceived control over the recovery process. Similarly, this form of control was most strongly associated with positive life change in our previous research (Frazier, Tashiro, et al., 2004), perhaps because the present is in fact more controllable than the past or the future. Perceived control over the recovery process also was the only form of control associated with stress-related growth in a sample of bereaved women (Frazier, Steward, & Mortensen, 2004) and was the strongest correlate of distress in other analyses using data from the two sexual assault studies described here (Frazier, 2003; Frazier, Steward, & Mortensen, 2004). Other aspects of present control, such as control over physical symptoms of disease, also are associated with positive life changes (Tennen et al., 1992). The differences in the relations between past, present, and future control and self-reported growth underscore the importance, highlighted by several authors (e.g., Frazier et al., 2002; Skinner, 1996), of carefully defining the targets of control efforts.

With regard to personal resource variables, in our first longitudinal study the variables we assessed (ethnicity and prior victimization) were not associated with positive life change. Therefore, in this study we examined three personality variables that we thought might be more related to positive life change. Specifically, individuals higher in extraversion and lower in neuroticism reported more positive life change. Both Tedeschi and Calhoun (1996) and Evers et al. (2001) also reported positive relations between extraversion and positive change. Only Evers et al. found a significant relation between neuroticism and positive change, which was the strongest relation in our study. We did not replicate Tedeschi and Calhoun's finding that greater openness is associated with positive life change. Additional analyses suggest that the primary mediators of the relations among extraversion and neuroticism and positive life change are social withdrawal and control over the recovery process. Specifically, extraversion is associated with positive life change because extraverts are less likely to withdraw from others and more likely to perceive that they have control over their recovery process. The opposite is true of individuals higher in neuroticism: they are more likely to withdraw from others and less likely to perceive that they have control over their recovery process.

Finally, as in our previous study, the environmental resource variable we assessed was social support. Consistent with our own past research (Frazier, Tashiro, et al., 2004) and other studies (e.g., Armeli et al., 2001; Park et al., 1996) individuals who have more social support following the assault also report more positive changes. The mediation analyses suggest that individuals with more social support report more positive change because they use more religious coping and perceive more control over the recovery process. In our previous study, the significant mediators of the relation between social support and positive life change were approach and avoidant coping, taking precautions, and control over the recovery process.

Thus, the only consistent finding across the two studies is that control over the recovery process mediates the relation between social support and positive life change.

The conclusions that can be drawn from our data must take into account several study limitations. First, although our goal was to examine posttrauma growth in a sample of nonrecent assault survivors, the large amount of time that had elapsed since most participants were assaulted leaves open the possibility that responses were affected by retrospective bias. Second, given that we did not have data on pre-trauma functioning, we could not assess actual life changes but instead relied on self-reports of posttrauma life change. Because most data on posttraumatic growth consists of self-reports, concerns increasingly are being raised regarding the validity of these self-reports and whether they reflect actual life changes (see e.g., Wortman, 2004). Third, including only women in our sample precluded examination of gender differences in posttrauma growth, which have been reported in other studies (e.g., McMillen & Fischer, 1998). Fourth, given the cross-sectional nature of our data, the direction of the relations among the variables cannot be determined and other models may fit the data (Frazier, Tix, & Barron, 2004). For example, it may be that religious coping is associated with positive change because it is associated with greater social support rather than the other way around. Finally, our sample was too small to conduct structural equation modeling (SEM) analyses, which is the preferred method for testing mediation (Frazier, Tix, & Barron, 2004). Sample sizes of at least 200 are recommended to have sufficient power to detect mediation effects. Because our sample was smaller than that, we may have underestimated the extent to which the coping and appraisal measures were mediators in our study.

Despite these limitations, our data contribute to the growing body of research on posttraumatic growth by replicating the finding that growth is common even among survivors of traumas involving intentional harm, like sexual assault. Our data also show that self-reported positive changes are associated with traditional distress measures, even after controlling for the effects of recent stressors and personality, which suggests that measures of such changes have incremental validity in explaining individual variability in posttraumatic distress. Self-reported positive life changes also are associated with greater life satisfaction, after controlling for these other variables. Finally, our data on correlates of positive life changes help to fill out the network of relations between these changes and other important constructs in the stress and coping field. For example, our data indicate the importance of assessing specific aspects of perceived control, particularly control over the recovery process, and religious coping, which is a form of coping often overlooked in psychological research.

References

Affleck, G., Tennen, H., Croog, S., & Levine, S. (1987). Causal attribution, perceived benefits, and morbidity after a heart attack: An 8-year study. *Journal of Consulting and Clinical Psychology, 55*, 29-35.

Aldwin, C. M., Sutton, K. J., & Lachman, M. (1996). The development of coping resources in adulthood. *Journal of Personality, 64,* 837-871.

Armeli, S., Gunthert, K. C., & Cohen, L. H. (2001). Stressor appraisals, coping, and post-event outcomes: The dimensionality and antecedents of stress-related growth. *Journal of Social and Clinical Psychology, 20,* 366-395.

Breslau, N., Kessler, R., Chilcoat, H., Schultz, L., Davis, G., & Andreski, P. (1998). Trauma and posttraumatic stress disorder in the community: The 1996 Detroit area survey of trauma. *Archives of General Psychiatry, 55*, 626-632.

Calhoun, L. G., Cann, A., Tedeschi, R. G., & McMillan, J. (2000). *Journal of Traumatic Stress, 13*, 521-527.

Carver, C., Scheier, M., & Weintraub, J. (1989). Assessing coping strategies: A theoretically based approach. *Journal of Personality and Social Psychology, 56*, 267-283.

Coffey, P., Leitenberg, K., Henning, K., Turner, T., & Bennett, R. (1996) The relation between methods of coping during adulthood with a history of childhood sexual abuse and current psychological adjustment. *Journal of Consulting and Clinical Psychology, 64,* 1090-1093.

Cohen, J. (1992). A power primer. *American Psychologist, 112*, 155-159.

Collins, R. L., Taylor, S. E., & Skokan, L. A. (1990). A better world or a shattered vision? Changes in life perspectives following victimization. *Social Cognition, 8,* 263-285.

Cordova, M., Cunningham, L., Carlson, C., & Andrykowski, M. (2001). Posttraumatic growth following breast cancer: A controlled comparison study. *Health Psychology, 20,* 176-185.

Derogatis, L. (1993). *Manual for the Brief Symptom Inventory*. National Computer Systems. Minneapolis, MN.

Evers, A.W.M., Kraaimaat, F.W., van Lankveld, W., Jongen, P.J.H., Jacobs, J.W.G., & Bijlsma, J.W.J. (2001). Beyond unfavorable thinking: The illness cognition questionnaire for chronic diseases. *Journal of Consulting and Clinical Psychology, 69,* 1026-1036.

Foa, E., Zinbarg, R., & Rothbaum, B. (1992). Uncontrollability and predictability in Post-traumatic Stress Disorder: An animal model. *Psychological Bulletin, 112*, 218-238.

Frazier, P. (2003). Perceived control and distress following sexual assault: A longitudinal test of a new model. *Journal of Personality and Social Psychology, 84*, 1257-1269.

Frazier, P. (2002). The scientific status of research on rape trauma syndrome: Rape trauma syndrome, § 13-2.0. In D. Faigman, D. Kaye, M. Saks, & J. Sanders (Eds). *Modern scientific evidence: The law and science of expert testimony, 2nd. Ed.* (pp. 117-143. St. Paul, MN: West.

Frazier, P., Berman, M., & Steward, J. (2002). Perceived control and posttraumatic distress: A temporal model. *Applied and Preventive Psychology, 10,* 207-223.

Frazier, P., Conlon, A., & Glaser, T. (2001). Positive and negative life changes following sexual assault. *Journal of Consulting and Clinical Psychology, 69*, 1048-1055.

Frazier, P., Mortensen, H., & Steward, J. (in press). Coping strategies as mediators of the relations among perceived control and distress in sexual assault survivors. *Journal of Counseling Psychology.*

Frazier, P., Steward, J., & Mortensen, H. (2004). Perceived control and adjustment to trauma: A comparison across events. *Journal of Social and Clinical Psychology, 23*, 303-324.

Frazier, P., Tashiro, T., Berman, M., Steger, M., & Long, J. (2004). Correlates of levels and patterns of posttraumatic growth among sexual assault survivors. *Journal of Consulting and Clinical Psychology, 72*, 19-30.

Frazier, P., Tix, A., & Barron, K. (2004). Testing moderator and mediator effects in counseling psychology research. *Journal of Counseling Psychology, 51*, 115-134.

Janoff-Bulman, R. (1989). Assumptive worlds and the stress of traumatic events: Applications of the schema construct. *Social Cognition, 7,* 113-136.

Joseph, S., Williams, R., & Yule, W. (1993). Changes in outlook following disaster: The preliminary development of a measure to assess positive and negative responses. *Journal of Traumatic Stress, 6*, 271-279.

Kennedy, J. E., Davis, R. C., & Taylor, B. G. (1998). Changes in spirituality and well-being among victims of sexual assault. *Journal for the Scientific Study of Religion, 37*, 322-328.

Kenny, D. A., Kashy, D. A., & Bolger, N. (1998). Data analysis in social psychology. In D. T. Gilbert, S. T. Fiske, & G. Lindzey (Eds.), *The Handbook of Social Psychology* (4th ed.). New York, NY: Oxford University Press.

Kessler, R., Sonnega, A., Bromet, E., Hughes, M., & Nelson, C. (1995). Posttraumatic stress disorder in the national comorbidity survey. *Archives of General Psychiatry, 52*, 1048-1060.

Kilpatrick D., Resnick H., Freedy J. (1991*). The Potential Stressful Events Interview. Unpublished instrument.* Charleston, SC: National Crime Victims Research and Treatment Center, Department of Psychiatry, Medical University of South Carolina.

Lehman, D., Davis, C., DeLongis, A., Wortman, C., Bluck, S., Mandel, D., & Ellard, J. (1993). Positive and negative life changes following bereavement and their relations to adjustment. *Journal of Social and Clinical Psychology, 12*, 90-112.

Linley, P.A., & Joseph, S. (2004). Positive change following trauma and adversity: A review. *Journal of Traumatic Stress, 17,*11-21.

McGregor, B.A., Antoni, M.H., Boyers, A., Alferi, S.M., Blomberg, B.B., & Carver, C.S. (2004). Cognitive-behavioral stress management increases benefit finding and immune function among women with early-stage breast cancer. *Journal of Psychosomatic Research, 56,* 1-8.

McMillen, J.C., & Fisher, R. (1998). The Perceived Benefit Scales: Measuring perceived positive life changes after negative events. *Social Work Research, 22*, 173-187.

McMillen, J.C., Smith, E., & Fisher, R. (1997). Perceived benefit and mental health after three types of disaster. *Journal of Consulting and Clinical Psychology, 65*, 733-739.

Mohr, D., Dick, L., Russo, D., Likosky, W., & Goodkin, D. (1999). The psychological impact of multiple sclerosis: Exploring the patient's perspective. *Health Psychology,18*, 376-382.

O'Leary, V., Alday, C., & Ickovics, J. (1998). Models of life change and posttraumatic growth. In R. Tedeschi, C. Park, & L. Calhoun (Eds.), *Posttraumatic growth: Positive changes in the aftermath of crisis* (pp. 127-151). Mahwah, NJ: Erlbaum.

Pargament, K., Ensing, D., Falgout, K., Olsen, H., Reilly, B., Van Haitsma, K., & Warren, R. (1990). God help me: (I). Religious coping efforts as predictors of the outcomes to significant negative life events. *American Journal of Community Psychology, 18,* 793-824.

Pargament, K. I., Kennell, J., Hathaway, W., Grevengoed, N., Newman, J., & Jones, W. (1988). Religion and the problem-solving process: Three styles of coping. *Journal for the Scientific Study of Religion, 27,* 90-104.

Park, C. L., Cohen, L. H., & Murch, R. L. (1996). Assessment and prediction of stress-related growth. *Journal of Personality, 64,* 71-105.

Revenson, T. A., Wollman, C. A., & Felton, B. J. (1983). Social supports as stress buffers for adult cancer patients. *Psychosomatic Medicine, 45*, 321-331.

Santello, M., & Leitenberg, H. (1993). Sexual aggression by an acquaintance: methods of coping and later psychological adjustment. *Violence and Victims, 8,* 91-104.

Saucier, G. (1994). Mini-Markers: A brief version of Goldberg's unipolar big-five markers. *Journal of Personality Assessment, 63*, 506-516.

Schaefer, J. A. & Moos, R. H. (1998). The context for posttraumatic growth: Life crises, individual and social resources, and coping. In R. Tedeschi, C. Park, & L. Calhoun (Eds.), *Posttraumatic growth: Positive changes in the aftermath of crisis* (pp. 99-126). Mahwah, NJ: Erlbaum.

Skinner, E. (1996). A guide to constructs of control. *Journal of Personality and Social Psychology, 71*, 549-570.

Skinner, E., Edge, K., Altman, J., & Sherwood, H. (2003). Searching for the structure of coping: A review and critique of category systems for classifying ways of coping. *Psychological Bulletin, 129,* 216-269.

Stanton, A., Danoff-Burg, S., Cameron, C., & Ellis, A. (1994). Coping through emotional approach: Problems of conceptualization and confounding. *Journal of Personality and Social Psychology, 66,* 350-362.

Stewart, A., Hays, R., & Ware, J. (1988). The MOS short-form general health survey: Reliability and validity in patient populations. *Medical Care, 26,* 724-735.

Tedeschi, R. G. (1999). Violence transformed: Posttraumatic growth in survivors and their societies. *Aggression and Violent Behavior, 4,* 319-341.

Tedeschi, R., & Calhoun, L. (2004). Posttraumatic growth: Conceptual foundations and empirical evidence. *Psychological Inquiry, 15,* 1-18.

Tedeschi, R., & Calhoun, L. (1995). *Trauma and transformation: Growing in the aftermath of suffering*. Thousand Oaks, CA: Sage.

Tedeschi, R., & Calhoun, L. (1996). The posttraumatic growth inventory: Measuring the positive legacy of trauma. *Journal of Traumatic Stress, 9*, 455-471.

Tennen, H., Affleck, G., Urrows, S., Higgins, P., & Mendola, R. (1992). Perceiving control, construing benefits, and daily processes in rheumatoid arthritis. *Canadian Journal of Behavioral Science, 24,* 186-203.

Tobin, D. L., Holroyd, K. A., & Reynolds, R. V. C. (1984). *User's Manual for the Coping Strategies Inventory*. Athens, OH: Ohio University.

Valentiner, D., Foa, E., Riggs, D., & Gershuny, B. (1996). Coping strategies and posttraumatic stress disorder in female victims of sexual and nonsexual assault. *Journal of Abnormal Psychology, 105,* 455-458.

Ware, J., & Sherbourne, C. (1992). The MOS 36-item short-form health survery (SF-36): I. Conceptual framework and item selection. *Medical Care, 30,* 473-483.

Watson, D., & Hubbard, B. (1996). Adaptational style and dispositional structure: Coping in the context of the five-factor model. *Journal of Personality, 64,* 737-774.

Wortman, C. (2004). Posttraumatic growth: Progress and problems. *Psychological Inquiry, 15,* 81-92.

In: Posttraumatic Stress Disorder: New Research
Editor: Guida D. Kume, pp.23-80
ISBN 1-60021-078-3

Chapter 2

TRAUMA: PSYCHOLOGICAL ASPECTS

Mahmoud Mirzamani[*]
Baqiyatallah Medical Sciences University,
University of Social Welfare and Rehabilitation Sciences, Tehran, I.R. Iran

ABSTRACT

Human beings have always experienced disasters. A disaster may be brief, but its psychological effects may last for many years. These psychological effects are increasingly well-documented.

Disasters affect not only those immediately involved, but also those who know the victims. This is perhaps particularly so when the victims are children. Commonly when adults hear news of disasters they ask first: What about the children? (Saylor, 1993). Of course, typically it is worse for the parents.

In this chapter the definition and classification of disaster and the effects of disaster on survivors and their relatives will be discussed.

Key words: Trauma, Psychological Aspects

DEFINITION OF DISASTER

Researchers in this field have often avoided explicit and systematic attention to the question of defining disaster (Quarantelli, 1982a). It has commonly been accepted that "a disaster is perhaps easier to recognize than it is to define" (Barkun, 1974). However, an implicit conception of the phenomenon is essential for research and policy-making. Many attempts have been made to define or conceptualize the term disaster, the intention being to

* Correspondence: Mahmoud Mirzamani, Baqyiatallah Hospital, Mollasadra Ave., Vanak Sq. Tehran, 1435944, I. R. Iran. E-mail: Mirzamani2003@yahoo.co.uk

summarize what social and behavioural scientists presuppose and mean when they use the term disaster.

Quarantelli (1986) distinguished seven usages of the term. The first three concern disasters understood as physical events, such as earthquakes, fires, floods and explosions. Increasing emphasis is placed on the physical effects of these events and their magnitude. This increasing emphasis captures the fact that only those earthquakes, for example, with major physical effects would be likely to be called disasters. The remaining categories identified by Quarantelli (1986) may be summarized as follows:

1. Disaster as a social disruption resulting from an event with physical impacts. In this approach, a physical impact is a disaster if the magnitude of the impact, as indicated by property damage and casualties, is believed to be high enough to result in disruption of social life.
2. Disaster as a social construction of reality in perceived crisis situations which may or may not involve physical impacts. In this conception of disaster, there must also be a socially constructed perception of a crisis situation, that is, a situation that necessitates unexpected collective action because it involves high priority values. According to this view, actual physical impact is not the crucial element.
3. Disaster as a political definition of certain crisis situations. Disasters are not only social constructions but also political phenomena (e.g., Brown and Goldin, 1973; Dombrowsky, 1981; Westgate and O'Keefe, 1976). Thus, whether crisis situations are defined as disasters depend upon political decisions in the broad sense of the term. Such political decisions reflect the interest of the society or power holders in a society or community.
4. Disaster as an imbalance in the demand-capability ratio in a crisis situation. Disaster typically requires nonroutine and emergent collective behaviour. High priority values are threatened and there is a perceived urgent need to act. However the available capabilities are not enough to meet the demands of the disaster (Quarantelli, 1986).

While the definition of a "disaster" varies with the source, there is general agreement in opinions that a disaster is an event that has the following properties; it involves the destruction of property, injury, and/or loss of life; it has an identifiable beginning and end; adversely affects a relatively large group of people; is "public" and shared by members of more than one family; is out of the range of ordinary experience; and, psychologically, is traumatic enough to induce distress in almost anyone, regardless of pre-morbid function or earlier experiences (Saylor, 1993).

Barton (1969) defined disaster as a collective stress experience in which large numbers of people fail to have their usual needs met by the social system.

Acute and chronic psychopathology in survivors of disasters, including post traumatic stress disorder (PTSD), other anxiety disorders and depression, are well-documented for adults, children, and adolescents (Raphael, 1986; Sinclair, 1993; Yule et al. 1990; Yule & Udwin, 1991; Yule & Williams, 1990). The risk of a stress response in family members as well as in the survivor is acknowledged in the standard diagnostic criteria for PTSD, specifically in the definition of traumatic experience. DSM-IV has: "exposure to an extreme traumatic stress or direct personal experience of an event that involves actual or serious injury, threat to one's physical integrity, witnessing an event involving injury, death, or threat to the physical integrity of another person, or *learning about an unexpected or violent death or serious harm, or threat of such experienced by a family member or other close associate*, or learning that one's child has a life-threatening disease (American Psychiatric Association, 1994 p.424; italics added).

EFFECTS ON SURVIVORS

Acute and chronic psychological stress reactions of survivors of disasters, especially Posttraumatic Stress Disorder (PTSD) are well-documented for adults, children and adolescents (Yule, Udwin, & Murdoch, 1990; Yule & Williams, 1990; Yule & Udwin, 1991; Sinclair, 1993; Davis & Siegel, 2000).

This section and the following one focus on the primary and secondary victims of a disaster: the survivors and their relatives.

Child victims of disaster may be persons directly exposed to the trauma, or indirectly exposed by observation of family members, classmates, or neighbours suffering the direct assault. Increased media coverage of major disasters raises the possibility of children even more removed from the situation being upset by a trauma. The degree of exposure and the extent of loss may be key factors in the psychological impact of a disaster on a child and his/her family (Saylor, 1993).

The so-called disaster syndrome occurs either during the impact or immediately afterwards. The person typically appears dazed, stunned, apathetic, and passive. He or she may sit or stand immobile or may wander aimlessly, seemingly unaware of surroundings and the presence and needs of others. A number of other maladaptive behaviours have been reported in conjunction with some disasters. These behaviours may be classified as panic. They include acute confusional states or even reactive psychoses, dissociative states, fruitless activity, hysterical reactions, and behaviour that is out of touch with reality (Raphael, 1986).

Other psychophysiological reactions noted include headaches, breathing difficulties, tremors, palpitations, sweating, malaise, dizziness, and exhaustion (Raphael, 1986).

Psychosomatic or psychophysiological reactions in the post-disaster period, which have been commonly described in adults, also seem frequent in children. Children's reactions reflect many of the features and patterns found in adults but are often more direct and less disguised (Raphael, 1986).

Children who are abused, lose loved ones to accidents, survive individual house fires, and/or personally witness a murder are prime candidates for post traumatic stress disorder (PTSD) (Saylor, 1993).

Recently a growing recognition of the existence of Post-traumatic stress disorder in children has emerged (Jones and Ribbe, 1991; Saylor, 1993; Yule, 1993; Yule and Williams, 1990). There is a growing literature on the subject of Post-traumatic stress disorder in children. The literature consistently points to children's vulnerability to the development of Post-traumatic stress disorder after severe trauma. In a review by Yule and Williams (1990) it is concluded that when children suffer an extreme trauma, they do indeed react similarly to adults, and show problems very similar to adult PTSD (Yule and Williams, 1990).

Yule (1992) evaluated 334 children who survived the sinking of the cruise ship, Jupiter. These children were compared with a control group matched for sex and age. Survivors reported more fears, particularly of stimuli related to the trauma than the controls. Overall, their scores on the Impact of Events Scale were as high as those reported by adults in other disasters. Follow-up studies a year after the accident have demonstrated that nearly half the children of this study meet the DSM-III-R criteria for PTSD (Yule, 1992).

Martini , Ryan, Nakayama et al.(1990) used the revised version of the PTSD Reaction Index to evaluate five children who were injured when a speedboat crashed into spectators watching the Pittsburgh Regatta. The researchers also used this instrument to interview the parents about their traumatized children. Three of the children met DSM-III-R criteria for PTSD as confirmed by either self-report or parental report (Martini, Ryan, Nakayama et al., 1990).

DEFINITION OF POST-TRAUMATIC STRESS DISORDER

Within the diagnostic literature, Post-Traumatic Stress Disorder (PTSD) has been defined by: (a) the experience of a traumatic event; (b) persistent re-experiencing of the traumatic event; (c) persistent avoidance of stimuli associated with the trauma and numbing of general responsiveness; (d) persistent symptoms of increased arousal; (e) more than one month duration of the disturbance; (f) significant distress or impairment in social, occupational, or other impairment areas of functioning (American Psychiatric Association, 1994).

In DSM-IV the essential feature of Post-Traumatic Stress Disorder includes the development of characteristic symptoms following exposure to an extreme traumatic stressor involving direct personal experience of an event that involves actual or serious injury, threat to one's physical integrity, witnessing an event that involves death or injury, a threat to the physical integrity of another person, or learning about unexpected or violent death or serious harm, threat of death or injury experienced by a family member or other close associate, or learning that one's child has a life-threatening disease (American Psychiatric Association, 1994).

Yule and Gold (1993) write:

> "Post Traumatic Stress Disorder is defined by World Health Organization and the American Psychiatric Association as a reaction that may follow an event that is outside the range of usual human experience and would be very distressing to almost anyone. There are three main groups of symptoms or reactions:
>
> 1. The traumatic event is persistently re-experienced in thoughts, dreams or flashbacks where the individual thinks it is all happening again.
> 2. There is persistent avoidance of stimuli associated with the trauma, or there is numbing of general responsiveness.
> 3. There are signs of increased physiological arousal.
>
> These reactions can be seen in people of all ages".

Post-traumatic stress disorder currently refers to a person who has reacted with intense fear, helplessness, or horror to a major (or minor) trauma by developing (1) intrusive thoughts and the re-experiencing symptoms; (2) avoidance responses to evidence of the trauma and generalized psychological numbing and isolation; and (3) widespread physiologic arousal (Tomb, 1994).

CLASSIFICATION

There are two well known classification systems used in the psychiatric assessment of survivors of trauma. The first, the International Classification of Diseases prepared by the World Health Organization (WHO), is currently in its tenth edition, (ICD-10). Whilst the ICD-10 is accepted in the United States as a general standard, the American Psychiatric Association's (APA) Diagnostic and Statistical Manual of Mental Disorders is widely used. This is currently in its fourth edition (DSM-IV). Recognition of the psychological effects of trauma within ICD and DSM classification systems is relatively recent. The classification of Post-traumatic stress disorder in each system will be discussed in the next two sections.

THE CLASSIFICATION OF ICD-10

The Classification of Mental and Behavioural Disorders (ICD-10, 1992) classified Post-traumatic Stress Disorder under reaction to sever stress, and adjustment disorders. Major difference between the APA and ICD-10 is that, ICD-10 considers symptoms of emotional numbing as not necessary for diagnosis of disorder, but rather, as a frequent accompaniment to disorder.

THE CLASSIFICATION OF DIAGNOSTIC AND STATISTICAL MANUAL OF MENTAL DISORDERS

The original Diagnostic and Statistical Manual (DSM-I; 1952) contained the diagnosis "gross stress reaction". Although being characterised by an individual's exposure to extreme emotional and physical stress, it was thought to diminish rather rapidly unless maintained by premorbid personality traits. DSM-II (American Psychiatric Association, 1968) deleted the category of "gross stress reaction", mentioning trauma related stress only in the context of "adult adjustment reactions". It was in the DSM-III (American Psychiatric Association, 1980) that the term of Post-traumatic Stress Disorder first appeared.

The classification of Post-traumatic Stress Disorder (PTSD) in DSM-III (American Psychiatric Association, 1980) and DSM-III-R represents a curious hybrid. These manuals were avowedly written on the basis of a symptomatic classification of mental disorders, because of the opinion that insufficient information was available regarding their etiology or even pathogenesis. Post-traumatic stress disorder is currently classified among the anxiety disorders presumably because it is accompanied by the concomitants of anxiety (e.g., insomnia, exaggerated startle response, and difficulty concentrating) (Pitman, 1993).

Although DSM-III-R (1987) continued the approach initiated with DSM-III (1980) several important modifications were made to the stressor criteria (Brett, Spitzer, Williams, 1988). First, in an effort to refine the phenomenological criteria to better reflect anxiety-related symptoms, DSM-III-R notes that stressors in Post-traumatic stress disorder are "usually experienced with intense fear, terror, and helplessness". Second, in addition to direct experience of the stressor, DSM-III-R includes visual (witnessing an even) and verbal (hearing about an event) mediation. Finally, DSM-III-R provides an example of qualifying events within the criteria set, as well as nonqualifying events within the accompanying text, separating these events along quantitative and qualitative dimensions. Thus DSM-III-R also acknowledges (without operationalizing) the importance of subjective perception whilst continuing to frame Post-traumatic stress disorder as a stressor driven anxiety disorder (March, 1993).

In anticipation of DSM-IV, arguments have been presented for reformulating the stressor criterion either by abolishing them altogether or defining them as an event shocking the individual (Solomon and Canino, 1990). Advocates of the latter suggest that the stressor criterion be reformulated in terms of generic features common to the environmental event shaping Post-traumatic stress disorder phenomenology.

THE SYMPTOMS OF POST-TRAUMATIC STRESS DISORDER

An understanding of the diagnostic criteria for Post-traumatic stress disorder is crucial for a thorough assessment of the disorder. To this effect a substantial proportion of the literature is concerned directly or indirectly with the symptomatic picture of patients with Post-traumatic stress disorder. In order to be diagnosed as having Post-traumatic stress disorder, the individual must have experienced an event outside the range of typical human experience, and this experience must be one which would be considered distressing to almost anyone (Saylor, 1993).

By now a wide range of emotional responses to disasters has been described in several studies. General fears, anxieties, and tensions are frequently mentioned as common emotional responses to a disaster (e.g., Bates, Fogelman, Partenton, et al., 1963; Blaufarb and Lavine, 1972; Bolin, 1982; Milne, 1977; Richard, 1974; Taylor, Zucher, and Key, 1970). Such emotional responses have been reported across a range of disaster types, including tornadoes (Taylor, 1977), earthquakes (Greenson and Mintz, 1972), nuclear plant accidents (Houts, Miller, Tokuhata, and Ham, 1980a), hailstorms (Leivesley, 1977), cyclones (Parker, 1975), hurricanes (Bates et al., 1963), train accidents (Raphael, 1977) and floods (Ollendick and Hoffman, 1982).

Situational and deeper depression are reported as other relatively common emotional responses to impact and loss (e.g., Taylor, Ross, and Quarantelli, 1976). Severe or prolonged disasters appear to be linked to the more severe depressive reactions (e.g., Hocking, 1965; Knaus, 1975; Leivesley, 1977).

Also, in several studies grief reactions have been reported amongst disaster survivors (Gleser, Green, and Winget, 1981; Green, 1982). They are often associated with the deaths of primary group members (e.g., Perry and Lindell,, 1978), but may occur in response to the loss of home and property (Bolin, 1982). Guilt is a particularly prevalent emotional response in disasters that claim a large number of lives (Lifton and Olson, 1976; Raphael, 1977; Titchener and Kapp, 1976). Disasters with high death tolls may also leave survivors with a "death imprint" (Lifton and Olson, 1976); this is described by Erikson (1976, P. 296) as remembrances of the disaster associated with "death, dying and massive destruction."

Classic symptom patterns in Post-traumatic stress disorder consist of intrusive thoughts about the traumatic experience and psychological efforts to avoid reminders or cues related to the trauma. Intrusive thoughts may be observed in the waking state in the form of "flashbacks," or intensively vivid reenactment experiences in which the original traumatic fear and psychological distress is also reactivated. In addition, intrusion patterns may occur during the sleeping state in the form of thematically related nightmares. Avoidance patterns may be observed when trauma victims show discomfort followed by shifting attention away from reminders of their traumatic experiences. Successful efforts to avoid painful reminders by eliminating risk of exposure to them may be learned through negative reinforcement. These patterns of intrusion and avoidance are commonly seen in the natural temporary experience of acute grief following the death of a loved one. However, in the case of Post-traumatic stress disorder the process by which grief and other overwhelming emotions are eventually resolved through natural coping seems to have been arrested (Foy, 1992).

Finch and Daugherty (1993) discussed having lived through the disaster, the individual must exhibit one of the following symptoms, which are related to reliving the trauma; (1) intrusive thoughts and recurrent distressing memories of the event, which may be manifested in children as repetitive play enacting the themes of the trauma; (2) recurrent dreams about the event which are distressing; (3) sudden feeling or action as if the trauma was occurring again; and (4) intense distress at exposure to events that represent or resemble aspects of the trauma. These symptoms vary from those which are known only to the individual to those that may be obvious to those around the person (distress at exposure) (Finch and Daugherty, 1993).

Yule and Gold (1993) discussed reactions that can be seen in individuals of all ages but they concentrate on children and adolescents: (1) Re-experiencing the trauma: people may have vivid visual thoughts about the trauma that intrude at any time during the day. Such intrusions thoughts can be very distressing. In children and adolescents, re-experiencing the trauma may appear as intrusive thoughts of which, most, are repetitive thoughts about the disaster. (2) Avoiding thinking about the experience: people try to avoid thinking about the trauma or avoid dealing with the emotions. Adolescents in particular seem to find it hard to think about the future. In children there is not so much evidence of difficulty in sustaining emotional relationships or in having loving feelings. However children often show a lack of interest in hobbies they previously enjoyed and many do not want to talk about their feelings with their parents, although at some point, survivors feel a great need to talk over their experiences with peers. Children and adolescent survivors often feel guilty that they are alive when others have died. Also, they often feel guilty that they might have done more to help others during the accident. (3) Heightened anxiety and arousal: survivors have major difficulties in getting off to sleep and may wake frequently during the night. They have difficulties with concentration, memory and new learning. In children and adolescents, heightened anxiety and arousal may be shown as: lack of concentration, sleep disturbance, separation difficulties, memory problems, heightened alertness to dangers, fear, irritability, depression, bereavement reactions, anxiety and panic (Yule and Gold, 1993).

The DSM-II criteria for Post-traumatic stress disorder includes: firstly, the reexperiencing of the event through intrusive memories, nightmares, and flashbacks; Secondly, inhibitory processes such as the numbing of affect. Interpersonal isolation and withdrawal; thirdly, memory impairment, and difficulty concentrating; and fourthly, hyper alertness or exaggerated startle response. Additionally, the DSM-III criteria indicate that patients with Post-traumatic stress disorder are psychophysiologically hyper aroused, and that they show an intensification of symptoms following exposure to events associated with the trauma.

Avoidance of trauma-related cues may come to characterize the lifestyles of survivors who are unable to overcome their immediate trauma crisis reactions. Feared stimuli eliciting escape or avoidance responses may not be limited to the physical environment. Strong negative emotions, such as rage, grief, and intense anxiety or panic, may elicit patterns of responding very similar to the individual's original trauma reactions (or-enactment); they may thereby establish escape or avoidant behaviours in a much wider range of situations (Foy, 1992).

There is some evidence that avoidance of painful material is a central mechanism in Post-traumatic stress disorder. For example, Malloy, Fairbank, and Keane, (1983) found that the best predictor of the diagnosis of post-traumatic stress disorder in Vietnam veterans was the strong tendency of veterans with Post-traumatic stress disorder to terminate the viewing of simulated reenactments of combat material. Thus, while the essential features of Post-traumatic stress disorder remain the same in the DSM-III and DSM-III-R, there are several important differences. The most important change is an increased emphasis on avoidance in the DSM-III-R. This cluster of symptoms has been associated with the numbing of general responsiveness symptoms. The criteria for avoidance are listed under section C. They include:

1. Efforts to avoid thoughts or feeling associated with trauma.
2. Effects to avoid activities or situations that arouse recollections of the trauma.
3. Inability to recall an important aspect of the trauma.

The set of symptoms that is the most difficult to properly assess is the cluster of behaviours associated with avoidance. In Post-traumatic stress disorder, there must be at least three of the following avoidance symptoms; (1) attempts to avoid thoughts or feelings about the trauma; (2) attempts to avoid activities or situations that result in recollections of the trauma; (3) an inability to recall important aspects of the trauma; (4) a decreased interest in activities or in children, the loss of recently acquired developmental skills; (5) a feeling disconnected from others; (6) a restricted range of affect; and (7) a sense of a foreshortened future. These avoidance symptoms would make it very difficult for the person to respond positively when asked about the trauma. For example, a child might deny having symptoms associated with the trauma as a way of avoiding thinking about it. It could be argued that this type of avoidance makes the accurate assessment of Post-traumatic stress disorder in children impossible (Finch and Daugherty, 1993).

The final set of symptoms associated with Post-traumatic stress disorder refer to increased arousal. Two of the following symptoms must be present; (1) difficulty sleeping; (2) irritability or outbursts of anger; (3) problems in concentrating; (4) hypervigilance; (5) an exaggerated startle response; and (6) physiological reaction to exposure to events associated with or symbolizing an aspect of the trauma. Again, these symptoms may not be obvious to those around the person, and in addition, some of the symptoms are frequently associated with other disorders (e.g., irritability is associated with depression) (Finch and Daugherty, 1993). Of course as formulated in DSM-III-R, Post-traumatic stress disorder must be present for at least 1 month for the diagnosis to be made.

Of course symptom patterns in Post-traumatic stress disorder include physiological, cognitive and behavioural manifestations. Autonomic arousal upon presentation of trauma-related cues is consistently found among approximately two-thirds of PTSD-positive combat veterans (e.g., Blanchard, Kolb, Gerardi, Ryan, & Pallmayer, 1986). Although other trauma populations have not yet been assessed for physiological reactivity in laboratory analogue situations, hypervigilance, exaggerated startle responses, and panic symptoms are frequently reported by these survivors. Thus, it seems reasonable to expect that physiological arousal to traumatic cues may represent an important feature in these cases as well (Foy, 1992).

To diagnose post-traumatic stress disorder, DSM-III, and particularly DSM-III-R, demanded that there be a severe stressor "outside the range of usual human experience". DSM-IV has shifted from a primary emphasis on the severity of the stressor to a mixture of exposure to a traumatic stressor coupled with a patient's reaction to it (Tomb, 1994).

Cognitive distortions indicative of "shattered" life assumptions are also frequently observed (Janoff-Bulman, 1985). Critical assumptions about personal invulnerability, equatability and fairness of life, and personal self-worth may shift radically after traumatic victimization. Extreme self-blame, inability to trust others, and a constant fear for personal safety may develop to the extent that survivors are rarely free of the need to monitor their interpersonal and physical environments constantly for signs of danger (Foy, 1992).

PTSD in Children

It is clear from review that studies of PTSD in children and adolescents are rapidly progressing (Yule, 1993). It appears that natural and human-caused disasters take a substantial psychological toll on children. It is also evident, however, that not all children who are exposed to disasters display maladaptive responses (Compas and Epping, 1993).

Within recent years a growing recognition of the existence of Post-traumatic stress disorder in children has emerged (Jones and Ribbe, 1991; Saylor, 1993; Yule and Williams, 1990; Yule, 1993). There is a growing literature on the subject of Post-traumatic stress disorder in children. The literature consistently points to children's vulnerability to the development of Post-traumatic stress disorder after severe trauma. Few reports of occurrence of post-traumatic stress disorder in children bellow the age of 18 have been obtained. Frederick (1985); McFarlane, Policansky, and Irwin (1987); Pynoos et al. (1987); and Yule and Williams (1988) have reported that acute, chronic, or delayed symptoms of Post-traumatic stress disorder have been observed in children who experienced disaster, child molestation, or physical abuse.

Frederick (1985) evaluated 150 children (50 victims of the disaster, 50 victims of physical abuse, and 50 victims of child molestation) for Post-traumatic stress disorder, using the Reaction Index. Across all the cases, 77% of the children were diagnosed as having Post-traumatic stress disorder. In addition, Frederick (1985) stated that among 300 cases of child molestation, if the child was above the age of 6 Post-traumatic stress disorder was always in evidence. Also, Kinjie (1986) found that 20 (50%) of 40 Cambodian children refugees had Post-traumatic stress disorder four years after leaving Cambodia.

Children react to life threatening stressors with various forms of distress. Anxiety, depression, fears and bereavement reactions as well as post-traumatic stress disorder may occur. The form of PTSD varies according to age of the child (Yule and Gold, 1993). Yule (1992) evaluated 334 children who survived the sinking of the cruise ship, Jupiter. These children compared to a control group matched for sex and age. Child survivors reported more fears, particularly of stimuli related to the trauma. Overall, their score on the Impact of Events

Scale was as high as those reported by adults in other disasters. Significantly higher scores on depression and anxiety were also shown.

Most research on Post-traumatic stress disorder as based on the criteria in DSM-III and DSM-III-R concerns adults rather than children. Only recently have psychopathologists systematically studied the effects of traumatic stressors on children (Eth and Pynoos, 1985; Lyons, 1987; Malmquist, 1986; McNally, 1991; Pynoos, 1990; Sugar, 1989; Terr, 1985).

Malmquist (1986) reported that all (100%) of 16 children who witnessed either parental homicide or attempted familicide met DSM-III criteria for Post-traumatic stress disorder. Also Arryo and Eth (1985), found that one-third of 30 children traumatized by Central American warfare, were diagnosed with Post-traumatic stress disorder according to DSM-III criteria.

Martini, Ryan, Nakayama et al. (1990) used the revised version of the Post-traumatic stress disorder Reaction Index to evaluate five children who were injured when a speedboat crashed into spectators watching the Pittsburgh Regatta. The researchers also used this instrument to interview the parents about their traumatized children. Three of the children met DSM-III-R criteria for Post-traumatic stress disorder as confirmed by either self-report or parental report (Martini et al., 1990). McLeer et al. (1988) in a study assessing Post-traumatic stress disorder in children who have been recently sexually abused showed positive diagnostic rates of approximately 50% (McLeer, Deblinger, Atkins, Foa, & Ralphe, 1988).

Now, it is reasonably well established that the severity of the disaster in children, as in adults, is related to the overall level of subsequent morbidity (Yule, 1993).

There are some differences between post-traumatic stress disorder in adult and post-traumatic stress disorder in children. Seven significant differences between Post-traumatic stress disorder in children and adults are stated by Terr (1979, 1985). They are as follows:

1. Children over the ages of 3 or 4 do not become partly or fully amnesic. They do not employ the denial of reality. They do not employ massive repression.
2. Children, as opposed to adults, do not exhibit psychic numbing.
3. "Children do not experience sudden, unexpected visual flashback that interrupt their behaviour or concentration. Children do consciously choose to think about their ordeals" but they do not experience what Horowitz (1976) conceives of as alternating pattern of intrusion and massive denial. (p.52)
4. Children's school performance generally suffers only a few months after the trauma, in contrast to the long-term work problems of many adults.
5. Post-traumatic play and reenactment of the trauma happen much more frequently with children.
6. "Time skew is more common and more dramatically expressed in children." (p.53)
7. Children often demonstrate a striking foreshortening of their view of the future.

While there is considerable accord with the findings of Terr, some investigators do not agree with the conclusion that children do not have intrusive imagery. For example, Malmquist (1986) studied 16 children who had witnessed a parental murder or an attempted familicide. He found that the children did have intrusive thoughts. While he did not state that they were visual flashbacks, in response to the Impact of Events Scale (Horowitz, 1986), 88% of the children stated that images popped into their mind. He did find that psychic numbing was not present. In fact, the children tended to be hyperalert and agitated. On the other hand, the children actively avoided thinking or talking about the trauma. In addition Terr (1985) described the propensity for traumatized children to see ghosts of family members of friends who died as a result of the traumatic event. Terr reported that they "see" or "feel" the loved one. She reported that ghosts were only experienced in cases where a traumatic death occurred.

Frederick (1985) listed the following common signs to alert parents and clinicians to the possibilities of Post-traumatic stress disorder after periods of crisis:

1. Sleep disturbances that continue for more that several days, wherein actual dreams of the trauma may or may not appear.
2. Separation anxiety or clinging behaviour, such as a reluctance to return to school.
3. Phobias about distressing stimululi (e.g., a school building, TV scene or person) that remind the victim of the traumatic event.
4. Conduct disturbances, including problems that occur at home or school, which serve as responses to anxiety or frustration.
5. Doubts about the self, including comments about body confusion, self-worth, and desire for withdrawal.

The response of the parents appears to be an important mediating variable in the child's ability to cope with trauma. Nir (1985), who studied post-traumatic stress disorder in children with cancer, stated that parental coping response can also become a significant source of stress for children with cancer. Nir (1985) also pointed out that adaptive parental coping response can reduce stress for the child.

Effects on Relatives

All that we have considered as destructive to the individual through horrific trauma is equally destructive to the individual's family. When individual family members are traumatized, ramifications are felt in the entire family (Sinclair, 1993).

Much of the research attention given to the psychological problems that follow exposure to trauma was generated by the interest in the adjustment difficulties of returning Vietnam veterans. In the mild-70's it became clear that many of these veterans had serious combat-related psychological difficulties. While much of the early work focused on delineating the individual's symptom presentation, other observers called attention to the potential marital and family problems associated with the veteran's traumatization (Carroll, Foy, Cannon, and Zwier, 1991).

Dudasik (1980) describes four types of victim: "event victims" who are those who suffer hardships directly attributable to the disaster; "contact victims" who are those affected in some way by the consequences of the disaster; "peripheral victims" who are those affected by reason of their close ties with the disaster area; and finally, "entry victims" who are affected as a result of their contact with the disaster area during the aftermath, for example, rescue and recovery personnel.

More useful is the six category system designed by Taylor and Frazer (1981 and 1990). Again, the general approach adopted is to separate groups according to their proximity to the emotional epicentre of the traumatic event. Thus, "primary" victims are those who directly experienced the disaster, whereas "sixth level" victims are those who might, but for chance, have been primary victims, for example those oil rig workers who were not part of the shift that was on the Piper Alpha platform when the disaster occurred. They escaped direct involvement but nevertheless they still suffered. "Secondary" victims covers the relatives and friends of primary victims, and "third-level" victims are the equivalent of Dudasik's "entry" victims, essentially those involved in the rescue and recovery, though there is some overlap between this and the next level. The "fourth-level" of victims is the community involved in the disaster, though this category also includes those who come forward to help in the recovery operation. Those in the "fifth-level" are not directly involved, but may nevertheless find themselves upset or distressed apparently as a result of the disaster (Newburn, 1993).

It should be considered who is likely to be affected by particular types or forms of disaster and, consequently, what sort of recovery operation needs to be put in hand, and what services need to be offered or set up. It is important to help guard against the possibility of ignoring or underestimating the potential effects on some apparently distanced social groups (Newburn, 1993).

Although researchers have tended to focus on the emergency services, there is now growing recognition of the potential effects of disaster on those who are tasked with providing support for or with counselling the "primary" victims (Johnston, 1990, cited in Newburn, 1993).

It is perhaps not surprising, given the catalogue of practical, psychological and emotional problems facing those affected by disaster, that considerable strain is often placed upon relationships. Family and personal relationships in particular frequently came under stress after the disaster. There are many that have been quite radically changed and some that simply have not survived. For the bereaved in particular this can represent a "double loss" (Newburn, 1993).

It is not only those directly involved in disasters who need support, but also their relatives. Just as professional carers require supervision and support, so too do non-professionals. They are victims in their own right (Newburn, 1993).

Natural and man-made disasters have been noted to have a number of effects on family relationships. First, in the period immediately after the disaster, families have been noted to be closer and more in need of mutual reassurance (Silber, Perry, and Bloch, 1958), and contact with immediate relatives increases (Drabek and Key, 1976). Second, the psychiatric morbidity that has been precipitated by the disaster has an impact on the relationships of those affected. In particular, post-traumatic stress disorder (PTSD), which is predictably common after such adversity, is associated with estrangement in relationships and with irritability (DSM-IV, American Psychiatric Association, 1994; Figley and Sprenkle, 1978). Post-traumatic stress disorder in an individual is, therefore, disruptive for all family members (McFarlane, 1987).

While the incidence, features, and course of PTSD have received considerable research attention, few controlled investigations of the PTSD's effect on family system have appeared in the professional literature. Carroll, Rueger, Foy, and Donahoe, (1985) examined the marital adjustment of Vietnam veterans with post-traumatic stress disorder as compared to that of combat veterans without post-traumatic stress disorder and non-combat-exposed Vietnam-era veterans. They found that the combat veterans with post-traumatic stress disorder reported significantly more marital problems than the comparison groups in the following areas: self-disclosure and expressiveness, hostility and aggression toward their partners, and global marital adjustment. Complementing these findings, Rueger (1983) examined a subgroup of the wives of the veterans included in the Carroll et al. (1985) study. Although the sample was small, the data showed a clear trend for the partners of veterans with combat-related post-traumatic stress disorder to be less communicative, more expressive of anger, and more fearful of their partner than the partners of the comparison group. Results from these two studies combine to present a picture of marital and family life marked by minimal communication, considerable overt hostility, and fear of partner aggression (Carroll et al., 1991). Carroll et al. (1991) reviewed the empirical literature on the clinical significant problems found within families containing a member with post-traumatic stress disorder. Their review suggests the potential for clinically significant sequelae within the trauma victim's family system (Carroll et al., 1991). While the studies reviewed by Carroll et al. (1991) serve as an example of the attention given to marital and family factors in the early clinical literature on traumatized Vietnam veterans, the findings and observations are limited by methodological considerations (Carroll et al., 1991).

However, well-controlled and designed research on trauma-related psychopathology is relatively recent, especially as it relates to the DSM-IV diagnostic formulation of post-traumatic stress disorder. Even more recent is the emerging research on the familial effects of PTSD (Carroll et al., 1991).

The effects of disaster on families are many, and the intricacies of family dynamics may be thrown into relief by the stress produced by the impact and aftermath and the need for different coping patterns. It may be that some family members are allowed certain roles during and after the disaster and others are not. Such patterns often have a function. For example, the person allowed to be afraid during impact may carry the fear for the family (Raphael, 1986).

The person who becomes anxious, cautious, and preparatory in response to warning may, by doing so, allow the rest of the family their feeling of invulnerability. The member who is shocked and distressed after the impact may be the one who is allocated the role of receiving care, thus allowing the rest of the family to maintain its sense of strength and coping. Conflict of roles may create difficulties, as, for instance, in cases when the person who is supposed to be brave is afraid, and the one who is supposed to be sick is well. Similarly, children who take over adult roles during and after the disaster may be vulnerable. It is also difficult for others, especially those fulfilling adult roles, to have needs for regression and care met (Raphael, 1986).

The impact of the distress of some members on the functioning of others may have considerable implications for family dynamics and stability. The distress of parents is likely to be a source of upset for children (McFarlane et al., 1985, cited in Raphael, 1986) as is the disturbance of children for parents (Bolin, 1982; Milne, 1977). Parents are likely to be overprotective, and children testing. Between husbands and wives, marital harmony and intimacy may be threatened, because of a need to avoid the topic of the disaster, or because of psychic numbing and other reactions or disturbances that have resulted. Self-medication, alcohol, and acting out are likely to be further detrimental to family functioning. Stresses of dislocation and relocation, especially the disruption of normal family life and the impairment of networks (Bolin, 1982; Erikson, 1976), are likely to further mitigate against the recovery of individual members and the family as a unit (Raphael, 1986).

Apart from the victim, these are individuals who are very close to the survivor, in particular, close family members and intimates. By virtue of their relationship with the victim, their lives are also altered by the overwhelming life event (Janoff-Bulman, 1992).

Those who are very close to trauma victims are not wholly immune to the discomfort and blaming that so often define people's reactions to victims of misfortune. Nevertheless, their intimate association with the survivor suggests that they are not simply responding to another's misfortune, but suffer themselves. Some victimizations, such as fires and natural disasters, often directly involve other family members as victims. Yet even when the traumatic event does not directly involve close loved ones, these family members are apt to experience "vicarious" effects. We are extremely distressed when catastrophe strikes someone we love, our emotional attachment leads us to feel for and along with the loved one. Our own inner world is shaken as well. Overwhelming life events affect not simply individuals, but the families and intimates of these individuals as well (Janoff-Bulman, 1992).

In one study forty Cambodian high school students who survived four years under the Pol Pot regime (1975-1979) and six Cambodian students who escaped their homeland prior to Pol Pot, were studied by Sack, Angell, Kinzie, and Rath, (1986). Findings of this study have shown that many of their family members exhibited similar post traumatic stress and depression symptoms.

The longitudinal impact of a natural disaster on the patterns of interaction in families has been examined by McFarlane (1987). In this study, a group of 183 disaster-affected families were contrasted with 497 families who had not been exposed to the disaster. The finding of this study suggests that the children's reaction to the disaster may have a significant impact on the family (McFarlane, 1987).

Some investigators have looked at the impact of a psychiatrically sick member on other members of the family. Fadden, Bebbington and Kuipers (1991), in a review article about the impact of functional psychiatric illness on the patient's family, mentioned that the patients often affect the caring relative's social and leisure activities. Some other investigators looked at the problems in families of Vietnam veterans with post traumatic stress disorder. For example, Jordan, Marmar, and Fairbank, (1992) conducted interviews with a nationally representative sample of 1200 male Vietnam veterans and the spouses or co-resident partners of 376 of these veterans.

The veteran interview contained questions to determine the presence of post traumatic stress disorder and items tapping family and marital adjustment, parenting problems, and violence. The spouse or partner interview assessed the spouse or partner's view of these items, as well as his or her view of their own mental health, drug, and alcohol and behavioral problems of school-aged children living at home. Findings of this study show that, compared with families of male veterans without current post-traumatic stress disorder, families of male veterans with current post traumatic stress disorder showed marked elevated levels of severe and diffuse problems in marital and family adjustment, in parenting skills, and violent behaviour. A lot of studies show the traumatic experience of being involved in combat during any war or military action frequently yields psychological consequences for survivors and their families (Scaturo and Hayman, 1992; Williams, 1987).

PTSD IN CHILDREN AND ITS EFFECTS ON THEIR PARENT

The relationship between children's symptoms and parental symptoms has received some attention (Parker, Watts and Allsopp, 1995), and, a few studies directly assessed the effects of PTSD in children on their parents. 37 mothers of survivors participated in a study were recruited in the course of a follow-up study of survivors, the methodology and results of which have been published elsewhere (Bolton, O'Ryan, Udwin, Boyle, & Yule, 2000; Mirzamani, & Bolton, 2002 & 2003; Yule et al., 2000). Women whose children had been involved in the disaster were found to have suffered a greater number of incidents of psychological distress in the period since the disaster than the women who had suffered no major negative life event but fewer incidents of psychological distress than the widows (Mirzamani, & Bolton, 2003). Also, women whose children were involved in the disaster presented PTSD symptoms. This effect was greater in the subgroup whose children had developed traumatic stress disorder following the disaster (Mirzamani, & Bolton, 2002).

The roof blew off a Swindon Primary School, in 1991. One child died. There were 29 other children in this class in which a child was killed. Parker, Watts and Allsopp (1995) investigated PTSD symptoms in 19 of the classmates both at post-event and at 2 years follow-up. They also investigated whether parents recall PTSD symptoms of their own and whether parental factors (e.g. symptoms of PTSD or overall psychiatric morbidity as measured by the GHQ) are associated with the development or resolve of symptoms in their children. In their study they asked each parent to complete the "Impact of Events Questionnaire" (IOE) for their feelings shortly after the event. They were also asked to complete the 28 item scaled version of the General Health Questionnaire (GHQ). The parents' GHQ scores were similar to a random sample of GP attenders. Thus, no correlations were found between the parents' score (either on GHQ or recalled IOE) and their own children's score. Two years after the disaster parents' general mental health as measured by the GHQ seems unaffected. They concluded that, their study gathered information about post-traumatic reactions of parents and children following a disaster which only affected the children directly. Of course, firm conclusion seems hard to draw from this study, because sample size is small (n =19) and a relatively low take up rate of 67% (19 from 29) (Parker, Watts and Allsopp, 1995).

However, while the incidence, features, and course of PTSD have received considerable research attention, there have been few controlled investigations of the effects on the family system, such as the effects on parents of a child being involved in a disaster. In a study of Cambodian high school students who survived four years under the Pol Pot regime (1975-1979) compared with Cambodian students who escaped their homeland prior to Pol Pot, family members were also assessed (Sack, Angell, Kinzie, & Rath, 1986). Many of the family members exhibited post traumatic stress and affective symptoms. More than three-quarters of all the parents had lived in Cambodia under Pol Pot's rule. Parents were inquired regarding the level of stress they were experiencing. The results indicated that more than half of the respondents had the following symptoms: trouble sleeping, trouble concentrating, anxiety, fatigue, irritability, and sadness or depression.

ASSOCIATED SYMPTOMATOLOGY

Although it is known that high levels of stress can negatively influence human performance across a broad range of cognitive and social behaviour (Cohen, 1980). There is a noticeable increase in somatized symptoms and disorders following severe psychological trauma (Escobar, Canino, Rubio Stipec et al., 1992), particularly in the early stages of the development of PTSD (Madakasira and O'Brien, 1987). Some of these seemingly physical symptoms, such as chronic fatigue and physical weakness, may be part of the presentation for many years (Tomb, 1994).

The clinical phenomenology presented by individuals who suffer from PTSD has been broadened to include the recognition of the extensive comorbidity associated with this disorder. Post-traumatic stress disorder may exist on its own, or it may be accompanied by other psychiatric diagnoses. March (1990) notes that the diagnosis of post-traumatic stress disorder is often accompanied by other psychiatric diagnoses. In fact, the overlap of many of its symptoms with those of more common psychiatric disorders may be one of the factors that has delayed the acceptance of PTSD as a separate entity has been. The vast majority of those with all but the most minor forms of PTSD are likely to suffer at some time from another anxiety disorder, such as generalized anxiety disorder or panic disorder; a major depression or chronic dysthymia; or a substance-use disorder, most commonly alcohol abuse (Kluznik, Speed, VanValKenburg, et al., 1986; Engdahl, Speed, Eberly, et al., 1991). Other symptoms that have associated with PTSD, but at lesser frequency, are phobias, personality disorder, and somatoform disorders. The considerable overlap between PTSD and the number of other disorders with which it frequently shares symptoms is likely to remain a continuing source of diagnostic confusion and debate, particularly because several of these conditions, including PTSD, often follow a waxing and waning course (Tomb, 1994).

McFall, Murburg, Ko, and Veith (1990), found the comorbid diagnoses for PTSD in their sample were major depression (40%), dysthymia (30%), generalized anxiety disorder (20%), social phobia (20%), obsessive-compulsive disorder (10%), bipolar disorder, depressed (10%), and adjustment disorder (10%).

DSM-III-R recognises depression and anxiety as associated features of the disorder. Further, DSM-IV recognises Panic Disorder, Agoraphobia, Obsessive-Compulsive, Social Phobia, Major Depressive, Somatization, and Substance-Related as associated features of the disorder.

SUBTYPES OF POST-TRAUMATIC STRESS DISORDER

DSM-III describes three forms of PTSD; (A) acute (the onset of symptoms within six months from the event and a duration of less than six months); (B) chronic (a duration of symptoms for six months or more); and (c) delayed (the onset of symptoms at least six months after the trauma). These forms of PTSD reflect the clinical experience that there seems to be no time constraints on the development of PTSD, often taking the form of an immediate reaction, or appearing after weeks, months, or after a period of prolonged incubation, perhaps lasting years.

Also, after extensive discussion, the delayed-onset form of PTSD, DSM-IV still requires an onset of symptoms at least 6 months after the trauma. However, there are some differences between DSM-III and DSM-IV in these specifiers. Acute should be used when the duration of the symptoms of post-traumatic stress disorder is less than 3 months. When the symptoms last 3 months or longer, chronic should be used. Delayed onset, indicates that at least 6 months have passed between the traumatic event and the inset of the symptoms (DSM-IV).

EPIDEMIOLOGY OF POST-TRAUMATIC STRESS DISORDER

Determining epidemiology of Post-traumatic stress disorder in both clinical and community populations has been impeded by methodological limitations of early studies. They have often failed to make adequate distinctions between those subjects who had been exposed to the trauma and the remaining subjects who were unexposed (Foy, 1992). However, epidemiological studies are important in order for society to establish effective public policy to provide the clinical services required to treat disorders.

Thus, disorder rates were established without regard to trauma exposure status. However, more recent studies have begun to report trauma exposure rates in the study population as a primary variable of interest, in addition to actual Post-traumatic stress disorder rates among trauma-exposed individuals (e.g., Breslau, Davis, and Andreski, 1991). Thus, prevalence rates for "ecopathology" (environmental adversity through traumatic life events) are now being distinguished from psychopathology rates determined from the proportion of positively diagnosed cases in exposed populations. There is a complex relationship between traumatic ecopathology and increased risk for psychopathology (PTSD cases) (Foy, 1992).

There is no doubt that a severe trauma, such as extensive torture (Kinzie, 1993; Van der Ploeg and Klein, 1989), violent rape (Kilpatrick, Saunders, AmickMcMullan et al., 1989) and combat (Kulka, Schlenger, Fairbank, Hough, Jordon, Marmar and Weiss, 1990) will produce PTSD in a high percentage of individuals, particularly during the months following the trauma. Much has been learned in recent years about the epidemiology of Post-traumatic stress disorder, with all studies indicating it to be a problem of substantial magnitude in the general population. At least for combat-related Post-traumatic stress disorder, the etiological linkage between trauma exposure and a predictable pattern of psychological distress is well established (Foy, 1992). A number of epidemiological risk factors have been identified, strongly suggesting the importance of genetic influence, early adverse experiences in childhood, personality factors, and physical harm (Davidson and Foa, 1993).

The exact prevalence rate of post-traumatic stress disorder varies from study to study. However, prevalence rates of post-traumatic stress disorder in populations with high combat exposure, in both community and clinical samples, have been reported in the range of 18-54%; this provides an estimate of the relative risk associated with high exposure. Studies of at-risk individuals (e.g., combat veterans, victims of volcanic eruptions or criminal violence) have yielded prevalence rates ranging from 3% to 58% (APA, 1994).

For example, data presented from the National Vietnam Veterans Readjustment Study (NVVRS) (by Kulka et al., 1990), indicated 15% percent of all male and 8.5 percent of all women Vietnam veterans to be suffering from PTSD. The NVVRS analysis of the lifetime prevalence of PTSD shows that over one-third of male Vietnam veterans and over one-fourth of women serving in Vietnam had the full-blown disorder at some time during their lives.

Further, Goldstein and colleagues (1987) found a current prevalence of 50% and Kluznik and colleagues (1986) a current prevalence of 47% in former World War II prisoners of war (POWs) approximately 40 years after combat duty and prison camp confinement.

A clinical sample of Vietnam combat veterans receiving services in Los Angeles-area Veterans Administer Medical Centres, were found to have current PTSD-positive diagnostic rates often exceeding 50% (Foy et al., 1987). Consistently higher rates are also reported by others. Solomon (1987) found that 56% of 3,553 Israeli soldiers who had had acute combat stress reaction during the 1982 Lebanon war showed Post-traumatic stress disorder at 2 year follow-up, and that 18% of 236 combat soldiers who had not had combat stress reaction also showed Post-traumatic stress disorder at the 2-year follow-up point. In a study by Rowan, Rodriguez, Gallers, and Foy (1990) investigating a clinical sample of adult survivors of childhood sexual assault, a Post-traumatic stress disorder rate of 65% was obtained.

To underscore the heavy individual and societal cost of Post-traumatic stress disorder, we may refer to epidemiological data that finds a 19% risk of suicide attempts in individuals who, for the most part, had neither received treatment nor were aware of their Post-traumatic stress disorder (Davidson and Foa, 1993).

Kluznik and colleagues (1986) in a study of 188 ex-POWs from World War II, found a lifetime Post-traumatic stress disorder prevalence of 66.4% and a current prevalence of 47.3% (Kluznik et al., 1986).

62 ex-POWs from World War II, were included in a study by Speed and colleagues (1989). In this study they found that 50% of subjects (N=62) had had Post-traumatic stress disorder during the first year after release.

In their study of 442 ex-POWs from World War II, Zeiss and Dickkman (1989) found a current Post-traumatic stress disorder rate of 55.7%.

On the other hand, Kinston and Rosser (1974) suggest that only 10 percent of disaster victims may develop acute problems that require intervention.

Other studies have examined the prevalence of PTSD in the general population. Community-based studies reveal a lifetime prevalence for Post-traumatic Stress Disorder ranging from 1% to 14%, with the variability related to methods of ascertainment and the population sampled (American Psychiatric Association, 1994). For example, McFarlane (1986a) found that 14% of a community sample of disaster survivors (i.e. Brushfire fighters, whose duration of traumatic stress averaged approximately 16 hours) showed Post-traumatic stress disorder at 29 months follow-up.

Further, in a community sample of 391 adult females, of whom 295 had been victimized by some type of crime, Kilpatrick, Saunders, Veronen, Best, and Von (1987) found that the lifetime rate of Post-traumatic stress disorder postcrime was 27.8% with a current prevalence of 7.5%. This was with an average time elapse, since the criminal assault, of 15 years (Blank, 1993). Jordan, Schlenger, Hough, Kulka, Weiss, Fairbank, and Marmar (1991) in a national epidemiology study, found that within a sample of veterans in community settings a lifetime Post-traumatic stress disorder prevalence rate of 30%, with 15.2% of subjects showing a current positive diagnosis was indicated (Jordan et al., 1991).

Anyway, as mentioned before, it is estimated that 4 out of 10 Americans have experienced major trauma, and the disorder may be present in 9% of the population in the united states (Breslau et al., 1991).

Studies of at-risk individuals (e.g., combat veterans, victims of volcanic eruptions or criminal violence) have yielded prevalence rates ranging from 3% to 58% (American Psychiatric Association, 1994 - DSM-IV).

Also, some studies have been conducted for PTSD in children. The results indicate a high percentage of prevalence of PTSD in children who are involved in a disaster. For example, Malmquist (1986) found that 100% of 16 children who witnessed either parental homicide or attempted familicide met DSM-III criteria for post-traumatic stress disorder. Further, A rate of PTSD of 50% has been reported, in children who have been recently sexually abused (McLeer et al., 1988) and in massively traumatized Cambodian refugee children (Kinjie, 1986). Also, follow-up studies a year after the accident show that nearly 50% the children met the DSM-III-R criteria for PTSD (Yule, 1992).

As the results of the above mentioned studies demonstrate, the incidence of PTSD has not been conclusively determined. The epidemiology of PTSD is likely to remain poorly defined for some time to come, not only because the disorder is still evolving phenomenologically, but also because there are several difficulties in studying this group of patients. May be, for example, this is because of the difficulty in obtaining data on all survivors of any event. Also, the other factors that affect the incidence of PTSD have not yet been clearly identified. In the case of PTSD, there is the absence of agreement on reliable and valid measurement instruments for diagnosis (Joseph, 1991). Moreover, psychometric measures are still evolving, and it may be necessary to create different instrument to assess PTSD caused by different types of trauma. In addition, the cut off point for PTSD remains troublesome, particularly because PTSDlike symptoms are common in the community (Tomb, 1994).

Measurement of PTSD (Psychometric and Psychodiagnostic Testing of PTSD)

Since 1980, when Post-traumatic stress disorder (PTSD) was officially recognized as a unique diagnostic entity and included in the Diagnostic and Statistical Manual III (American Psychiatric Association, 1980), a large body of research has been done in the assessment of this disorder. Now, in 1996, to further diagnostic certainty, patients suspected of manifesting Post-traumatic stress disorder may be administered various psychological assessment, including structured clinical interviews, questionnaires, and psychophysiological procedures (Green, 1991; Resnick, Kilpatrick and Lipovsky, 1991; Sutker, Uddo-Crane and Allain, 1991). Traditional batteries of tests can provide information overlooked or missed during the structured interview and mental status examination. Of course, use of multiple instruments provides converging evidence that increases confidence in diagnostic decision making and treatment planning (Keane, Wolfe and Taylor, 1987). ....

This section will explain three methods of collecting diagnostic information: A) Clinical interview, B) Questionnaires or inventories, and C) Psychophysiological techniques.

Clinical Interview

The foundation of the Post-traumatic stress disorder assessment is the clinical interview. Interview could be relatively unstructured or could be highly structured, with standardized questions that inquire about specific diagnostic criteria. For diagnostic decision making in clinical research on Post-traumatic stress disorder it has become standard practice to use structured interviews. Also, the use of structured diagnostic interviews to assess current and lifetime diagnoses of comorbid psychiatric disorders is recommended. Structured interviews allow investigators to specify accurately how diagnoses were made and whether the diagnoses are reliable and valid. They can also be valuable in clinical work in that they allow the clinician to inquire systematically about specific Post-traumatic stress disorder symptoms and comorbid syndrome (Litz and Weathers, 1994). In the following section, there are some structured interviews that can be valuable in the assessment of trauma victims.

Clinical Administered Post-traumatic stress disorder Scale: the Clinical Administered Post-traumatic stress disorder Scale (CAPS; Blake, Weather et al., 1990) is a structured interview for Post-traumatic stress disorder, that was designed for use by clinicians. This interview is developed at the National Centre for Post-traumatic stress disorder. The CAPS yields dichotomous and continuous scores. The CAPS consists of thirty items that assess DSM-III-R symptoms of Post-traumatic stress disorder, symptoms associated with Post-traumatic stress disorder (e.g., survivor guilt), and overall symptom severity, degree of improvement and impairments in social functioning. Two versions of the CAPS are available : CAPS-1 and CAPS-2; CAPS-1 is a current and lifetime diagnostic version, CAPS-2 is a weekly symptom-rating version.

The Structured Clinical Interview of Diagnostic and Statistical Manual of Mental Disorder-III-Revised (DSM-III-R) (SCID): The SCID is a structured diagnostic interview used to assess Axis I and II disorder in the DSM-III-R. It consists of separate modules for each diagnostic category. The PTSD module of the SCID consists of probe questions for each of the seventeen PTSD symptoms in DSM-III-R, plus sensitive and clear questions on survivor guilt and guilt over acts of omission or commission. The PTSD module of SCID appears to be clinically sensitive and reliable and has been widely used in PTSD research (Litz and Weathers, 1994). For example, 47 adult survivors (aged 20-51) of childhood sexual abuse were assessed to examine the relationship between the level of childhood sexual abuse and exposure and the subsequent of development of post-traumatic stress disorder (by Rowan et al., 1994). Subjects were administered standardized measures of PTSD including the SCID. On the SCID, 69% of the survivors met full DSM-III-R criteria for PTSD. Significant correlations were found between several overall exposure measures and PTSD diagnostic status and the intensity of PTSD symptomatology. Similar relationships were identified between the duration and frequency of the abuse, the age of onset, and the use of force (Rowan, Foy, Rodriguez, and Ryan, 1994). In another study by Solomon, Benbenishty, Neria, Abramowitz et al. (1993) examined psychometric properties of the revised post-traumatic stress disorder (PTSD) Inventory and the extent of agreement between it and the Structured Clinical Interview (SCID) and the Impact of Events Scale (IES). In this study the sample included 147 soldiers from the 1973 Yom Kippur War who were treated for combat stress reaction. They were either former prisoners of war (POWs), or were matched with POWs on personal and military background. They found 84% agreement between the PTSD Inventory and SCID in the past and 85% in the present, indicating a high convergent validity (Solomon et al., 1993).

However, a significant limitation of the SCID is that it can yield only dichotomous present/absent information about PTSD (Litz and Weathers, 1994).

Post-traumatic stress disorder interview: the Post-traumatic stress disorder interview (PTSD-I; Watson, Juba, Manifold, Kucala, and Anderson 1991) yields both a dichotomous and a continuous score (Litz and Weathers, 1994). Watson et al. (1991) reported strong test-retest reliability (.95) and internal consistency.

Structured interview for Post-traumatic stress disorder (SI-PTSD): the Structured Interview for Post-traumatic stress disorder (SI-PTSD; Davidson-, Smith and Kudler, 1989) is a useful structured clinical interview for Post-traumatic stress disorder assessment (Litz and Weathers, 1994).

The Diagnostic Interview Schedule: the Diagnostic Interview Schedule (DIS) is a highly structured interview designed for use by nonclinicians and has much less recommended.

Questionnaires and Inventories

The assessment of trauma victims can be enhanced greatly through the use of standardized instruments and methods such as questionnaires. There are several questionnaires in this field that have been developed and psychometrically evaluated: such as Minnesota Multiphasic Personality Inventory (MMPI), Symptom Check List-90 (SCL-90; Derogatis, 1977) and MMPI-2 (Butcher, Dahlstrom, Graham, Tellegen, and Kaemmer, 1989). These type of measures of Post-traumatic stress disorder are easy to administer and score, and they are useful to screen for the presence of Post-traumatic stress disorder. In this section, related literature will be reviewed and some questionnaires explained.

Impact of Event Scale (IES): the Impact of Event Scale (IES; Horowitz, Wilner & Alvarez, 1979) is a fifteen-item questionnaire measuring intrusion (7 items) and avoidance (8 items) in a traumatized person. It yields an overall score, and two subscale scores: (A) intrusive thoughts, images, ideas, and feeling, and (B) avoidance of reminders and situations associated with the event. The Impact of Events Scale (IES) is the most widely used instrument for assessment of Post-traumatic stress disorder, particularly in the UK (Litz and Weathers, 1994). The Impact of Event Scale is a self-report measure that can be anchored to any specific life events and taps: (1) intrusively experienced ideas, images, feelings and dreams, and (2) the avoidance of ideas, feelings, or situations. Horowitz et al., (1979) found that the intrusion and avoidance subscales had good internal consistency (.78 for intrusion, .82 for avoidance) and test-retest reliability (.89 for intrusion, .79 for avoidance). They found a moderate correlation (.42) between the intrusion and avoidance subscales. A strong relationship between a DSM-III PTSD inventory and the IES has been demonstrated with Israeli combat veterans (Weisenberg, Solomon, Schwarzwald, and Milkulincer, 1987).

Two studies (Zilberg, Weiss and Horowitz, 1982; Schwarzwald, Solomon, Weisenberg and Mikulincer, 1987) reported intrusion and avoidance factors with bereaved outpatients and Israeli soldiers respectively.

Minnesota Multiphasic Personality Inventory: More diagnostically reliable data can be collected from the Minnesota Multiphasic Personality Inventory (MMPI). A post-traumatic stress disorder patient often manifests a characteristic pattern. Much research has been directed towards developing a Post-traumatic stress disorder sub-scale of the Minnesota Multiphasic Personality Inventory (MMPI) (e.g., Fairbank, Keane and Malloy, 1983; Keane, Malloy, and Fairbank, 1984; Penk, Robinwitz, Patterson, Dolan, and Atkins, 1981). Studies which have employed the MMPI to assess the adjustment of patients with Post-traumatic stress disorder have consistently shown elevated scores on a number of clinical scales (Penk et al., 1981; Fairbank et al., 1983). In Keane, Malloy, and Fairbank's (1984) study, they tried to develop empirically based criteria for the use of the MMPI in order to aid assessment and diagnosis of combat-related post-traumatic stress disorder. In this study 200 male Vietnam combat veterans who were assigned to a post-traumatic stress disorder group (n=100) or a non-PTSD group (n=100) were administered the MMPI. Standard clinical profiles demonstrated that Post-traumatic stress disorder group had overall higher mean elevations, and discriminant function analysis correctly classified 74% of subjects in each group. A special Post-traumatic stress disorder subscale was developed and cross-validated that improved diagnostic hit rates to 82% of subjects. In this study, a consistent MMPI-8-2 pattern was noted in the Post-traumatic stress disorder group. The F scale was also consistently, and significantly, elevated. In addition, significantly higher scores were noted on all clinical scales except Mf, and a significantly lower score on K. The decision rule developed included cutoff scores at: F=66T, Sc(8)=76T D(2)=78T. Subjects with all three scores above the cutoff levels were classified as having Post-traumatic stress disorder. This decision rule led to the correct identification of 74% of the patients with Post-traumatic stress disorder (Keane- et al., 1984). Also, in a study by Foy- et al. (1984), 43 Vietnam veterans seeking psychological services at a Vietnam veterans medical centre, were assigned to positive and negative groups of post-traumatic stress disorder based on the DSM-III. Groups were compared on profiles from the MMPI and a psychological problem checklist. Results of this study showed that the Minnesota Multiphasic Personality Inventory (MMPI) had moderate ability to correctly classify subjects on the basis of Post-traumatic stress disorder diagnosis (Foy et al., 1984).

Post-traumatic stress disorder subscale of the MMPI: Keane, Malloy, and Fairbank (1984) also developed a special subscale for combat-related Post-traumatic stress disorder. The hit rate of this scale was over 80%. They note that items included on the scale tended to relate directly to the major Post-traumatic stress disorder criteria in the DSM-III-R. In sum, Keane, Malloy, and Fairbank (1984) note that the MMPI could reliably discriminate the Post-traumatic stress disorder group from veterans with affective disorders, anxiety disorders, personality disorders, and psychotic disorders. Hyer, O'Leary, Saucer, Blount, and Boudewyns, (1986), found that inpatient veterans with Post-traumatic stress disorder also had elevated 8-2 (Sc-D) patterns on their MMPI. They also indicated that the MMPI-PTSD subscale could accurately differentiate veterans with Post-traumatic stress disorder from other inpatient combat and non-combat veterans without Post-traumatic stress disorder. However, the hit rate was somewhat lower at 69%.

Since the original work of Keane et al. (1984) much research has developed to evaluate the validity, and examine the profiles of the Post-traumatic stress disorder sub-scale of the MMPI (e.g., Blanchard, Wittrock, Lawrence, and Gerardi, 1988; Hyer, et al., 1986; Hyer, Woods, Harrison, Boudewyns, et al., 1989; Keane, Wolfe, and Taylor, 1987; McCaffrey, Bellamy, and Roxanne, 1989; Mirzamani, 1991; Munley, Bains, and Bloem, 1993; Munley, Bains, Frazee, and Schwartz, 1994; Neal, Busuttil, Rollins, Herepath, et al., 1994; Query, Megran, and McDonald, 1986; Talbert, Albrecht, Albrecht, Boudewyns, et al., 1994; Watson, Kucala, and Manifold, 1986;). Fairbank et al. (1983) indicated that the MMPI could adequately discriminate Vietnam combat veterans with Post-traumatic stress disorder from two other control groups of veterans.

Using a short form (71-item) of the Persian form of the MMPI, Mirzamani (1991) examined applicability of the F and K scales of MMPI in a group of war Post-traumatic stress disorder patients. The sample of this study was composed of four groups: A) 32 out-patient soldiers with Post-traumatic stress disorder. B) 32 soldiers without any psychiatric visit at all. C) 32 non-military neurotic matched person. D) control group including 32 non-military person without any psychiatric visit at all. Significant differences were found between subgroupings. The group of Post-traumatic stress disorder patients were significantly high in the F scale and the standard clinical profiles demonstrated that the Post-traumatic stress disorder group (A) had overall higher mean elevations in most of the clinical scales, and a significantly low mean in L scale. Findings of this study indicated Post-traumatic stress disorder soldiers showed overreporting of their problems (Mirzamani, 1991).

The main criticism is that the MMPI was designed long before PTSD was defined by the APA, and new items were included. Also most of these studies are however, with combat veterans rather than victims of civilian trauma.

MMPI-2: The MMPI-2 (Butcher et al., 1989) has also been shown to be useful in the assessment of Post-traumatic stress disorder (Litz, Penk, Walsh, Hyer, Blake, Marx, Keane, and Bitman, 1991; Lyons & Kleane, 1992). MMPI-2 has been used in several studies, for example, Litz et al. (1991) administered both the original Minnesota Multiphasic Personality Inventory (MMPI) and Minnesota Multiphasic Personality Inventory (MMPI-2) to a sample including 29 persons with post-traumatic stress disorder, 37 mixed veteran psychiatric inpatients, 64 mixed veteran inpatient substance abusers, and 32 nonveteran normals. Findings show highly significant correlations between MMPI and MMPI-2 basic scales for the PTSD sample. The MMPI-2 effectively identified PTSD subjects from the other groups. Results also showed a high degree of association between the MMPI and MMPI-2 in regard to PK scores, although minor differences were found in PK raw scores between the 2 tests (Litz et al. 1991).

Ward (1994), in a study regarding MMPI-2 assessment of positive attributes, concluded that, the T-score table for the MMPI-2 provides no values lower than 30. Use of these tables with measures of positive psychological attributes in clinical samples can produce T-score distributions that are markedly truncated at the low end. Data were from 39 men with post-traumatic stress disorder and 127 men entering a program for addiction. Data were presented to show that the statistical characteristics of several MMPI-2 scales are affected (Ward, 1994). Albrecht et al. (1994), replicated a study by Litz et al. (1991) on the comparability of the MMPI and the MMPI-2 in post-traumatic stress disorder assessment. 47 male Vietnam veterans with combat-related post-traumatic stress disorder were administered the MMPI and MMPI-2. Pairwise comparisons were performed on the clinical scales, Harris Lingoes subscales, and scales relevant to the assessment of PTSD. Although results showed a high degree of congruence between tests, differences in the tests' evaluations of the post-traumatic stress disorder and F scales may influence interpretation and treatment (Albrecht, 1994).

Mississippi Scale for Combat-Related Post-traumatic stress disorder (Mississippi Scale): the Mississippi Scale (Keane, Caddel and Taylor, 1988) is a 35-item scale designed to measure combat-related Post-traumatic stress disorder. The items of this scale were selected from an initial pool of 200 items that reflected DSM-III criteria, and additional items were included to assess substance abuse, depression, and suicidality. Keane, Caddel and Taylor

(1988) reported excellent internal consistency (.94) and test-retest reliability (.97 over a one-week interval).

The Symptom Check List-90 (SCL-90): the SCL-90 (Derogatis, 1977) is a ninety-item self-report inventory that measures current levels of psychopathology on nine symptoms dimensions: Somatization, obsessive-compulsive, interpersonal sensitivity, depression, anxiety, hostility, phobic anxiety, paranoid ideation, and psychoticism. In a preliminary study the SCL-90 has been shown to assist in the assessment of Post-traumatic stress disorder (Saunders, Mandoki, Kilpatrick, 1990). A twenty-eight-item Post-traumatic stress disorder scale from the SCL-90 was derived and reported to have adequate sensitivity (.75) and specificity (.90).

Psychophysiological Methods

Psychophysiological assessment methods have been used primarily by researchers in combat-related Post-traumatic stress disorder (e.g. Blanchard et al., 1982). For example, McFall et al. (1990) tested the hypothesis that combat veterans with post-traumatic stress disorder will experience sympathetic system activation in response to war-related laboratory stimuli. In this research, the experimental stressors consisted of two 10-min motion pictures depicting noncombat-related and combat-related situations, respectively. Circulating levels of norepinephrine and epinephrine were measured in arterialized forearm venous plasma. Heart rate and Blood pressure were measured using an automated ultrasonic detector. Circulating plasma catecholamines, vital signs, and affect ratings were measured in 10 Vietnam veterans with PTSD and 11 control subjects, during and after viewing combat and noncombat stress films. PTSD subjects responded more strongly than control group to the combat film. They calculated difference from baseline scores for dependent variables and subjected to analyses for each experimental period. In this study PTSD subjects reported significantly greater subjective emotional arousal than did controls on the affect ratings measure.

Factors Affecting the Course of PTSD: Pre-Disaster

As research has abundantly clear no stressor produces PTSD in everyone (Perry, Difede, Musngi, et al., 1992; Smith, North, McCool, et al., 1990). On the other hand, different individuals show different reaction to the same disaster. Therefore, it is important to know who is most likely to be affected. Yule and Gold (1993) list pointers to identifying the most vulnerable:

> "People whose lives were at greatest risk are most likely to suffer emotional consequences.
> Those who witness death and carnage.
> Children who come from less stable family relationships.
> Children who are less able intellectually.
> There is a higher proportion of problems among girls than among boys."

It seems there must be something else that affect the impact of disaster. May be it relates to some factors prior to the disaster (e.g., Socio-demographic factors, Attributional style, Premorbid history).

Socio-Demographic Factors

Several of the studies reported on Post-traumatic stress disorder rates separated by gender. The finding were mixed. In most studies there are no obvious sex differences, with men and women being equally affected (Raphael, 1986). Similarly, Smith and North (1988) and Madakasira and O'Brien (1987) reported no difference between genders in the rates of Post-traumatic stress disorder following a jet crash and a tornado, respectively. On the other hand, Women have been shown to be at slightly greater risk in some studies (Abrahams, Price, Whitlock, and Williams, 1976; Bennet, 1970), at least in terms of psychological morbidity. Steinglass and Gerrity's study (1990) of a West Virginia flood showed higher rates of Post-traumatic stress disorder and Post-traumatic stress disorder symptoms for women (8 of 11 cases of Post-traumatic stress disorder at 4 months were women). Higher rates for women have been found in a number of epidemiological studies (Breslau et al., 1991; Davidson, Hughes, Blazer et al., 1991; Helzer, Robin and McEvoy, 1987) and are consistent with other Epidemiologic Catchment Area (ECA) data for anxiety and depression (Myers, Weissman, Tischler et al., 1984). Wilkinson (1983) showed more frequent symptoms of sleep disturbance and difficulty concentrating in women than in men, and Buffalo Creek follow-up study (Green, Lindy, Grace et al., 1990b) showed higher Post-traumatic stress disorder rates for women than men at both 2 years (52% versus 32%) and 14 years after event (31% versus 23%). As mentioned before, there is a higher proportion of problems among girls than among boys (Yule and Gold, 1993).

Factors influencing the recovery of families in the fullest sense have been studied extensively by Bolin (1982). Examining responses to a tornado disaster, Bolin concluded that a number of factors influenced recovery. In Bolin's study (1982), family recovery seemed to be affected by bereavement, material losses, and extended stresses. Larger families were more vulnerable to stress, and the older and better educated seemed less vulnerable. Support networks helped mitigate these stresses. Higher income also seemed to make things easier for affected families. This is hardly surprising, for such families usually have many more resources to call upon in the face of crisis.

Bolin concluded that economic recovery had the largest causal effect on emotional recovery. But this finding may have been particularly relevant to a disaster such as the one he studied, where life loss and injury were not substantial, where death encounter and bereavement were not great, and where housing, shelter, and daily life issues predominated. Bolin's diagram may, in fact, represent more the path of family recovery from relocation stressors than from the range of disaster traumas.

There is a trend toward the finding that girls report more psychopathology following a disaster than boys (Yule, 1993).

As mentioned by Bolin (1982), education has been shown to have some positive effects, with the more highly educated having less morbidity, but the effect of this variable is not a great one (Raphael, 1986). Socioeconomic status may contribute, as those of lower status are often less able to bear the assaults and consequences, especially economic, of the disaster.

And there is much evidence that people with poor socioeconomic resources in underdeveloped countries may be greatly at risk from disaster and its consequences. In such circumstances the individual may be more likely to succumb to death or other destructive disaster stressors than someone who is protected by better warning systems, stronger buildings, and effective medical follow-up. Family status has been suggested to have some influence. For example, bigger families are seen as slightly more at risk, and first-born or elder children may carry a disproportionate vulnerability (Raphael, 1986). The family response may be heavily influenced by social and cultural variables, such as resignation to fate or perception of control of the world as being external to the self. Some family structures may be more vulnerable, such as those with single (especially female) parents (Raphael, 1986). Marital status has been shown clearly to correlate with disaster morbidity, in that "married previously divorced" are particularly at risk, as, to a lesser degree, are "married previously widowed," although this variable has not been so defined by other studies. Occupational status has not been shown to directly correlate, except in as much as higher and professional status may afford some degree of protection, although loss of work status post-disaster, as in the case of refugees, may add stress. Employment seems to contribute, for the unemployed seem at greater risk of important. Religion may influence the person's way of coping: it has been suggested to correlate with how people protect themselves, with those who are more fundamentalist tending to leave things to fate and thus suffering more damage, injury, and stress. This observation has not been substantiated, however. Different cultural and ethnic background factors may be influential as well, and there is a great need for studies to investigate this (Raphael, 1986).

Storm-related anxiety, sleep disturbance, and bad dreams tended to persist for those who had intense exposure to the tornado, particularly if friends, neighbours, or family were injured or killed, or if there had been little warning and greater shock effect (Raphael, 1986).

The elderly are often seen as being particularly vulnerable. It has been suggested that they are more attached to places and slower to move from them in response to warning or that they may find recovery more difficult, especially if they have lost the home and possessions of a lifetime. In conclusion, then, the old may be slow to accept the realities of disaster threat and may be injured or killed as a consequence. Bolin (1982) concluded that, contrary to expectations, the elderly seemed, for the most part, less severely affected (Bolin, 1982). Concerning the age, Bromet, Parkinson, Shulberg, Dunn and Gondek (1982a) showed that within two months or so of Three Mile Island mothers of young children were at greater risk for developing episodes of anxiety and depression, especially if they perceived the incident as a source of danger. A number developed new cases of these disorders, as evaluated by diagnostic interview (The Schedule for Affective Disorders and Schizophrenia - SADS; Endicott and Spitzer, 1978).

The evidence on the specificity of fears fairly clearly indicates that children do suffer direct effects from disaster. Unfortunately, little is written about treating child survivors from major disasters (Yule, 1993). However, Yule (1993) has discussed what work needs to be done for them.

Attributional Style

What is "outside the range of usual experience" for one person may not be extraordinary for another. Certain experiences that are prominently associated with Post-traumatic stress disorder (i.e., rape and childhood sexual abuse) are unfortunately too prevalent to be considered unusual, despite the fact that such stressors encompass the "generic" stressor dimensions described below. Furthermore, it is difficult to imagine how chronic exposure to low-level threat can be quantitatively reconciled with more severe events of shorter duration. As has been pointed out, long-term exposure may have different effects than single-trial learning (Kiser, Ackerman, Brown, et al., 1988).

Perhaps the point of agreement in this area is that the perception of a stressor as stressful is nearly as essential in its ability to generate symptoms in some individuals as its raw stressfulness. A thorough understanding of this principle, however, is yet to be achieved (March, 1993).

Echoing the quantitative and qualitative descriptors of PTSD-inducing events, the most salient empirically documented aspects of subjective perception involve the perception of life threat, perceived potential for physical violence, the experience of extreme fear, and the attribution of personal helplessness. Implicit in this picture is the assumption that the impact of the event on the individual determines whether or not the event is traumatic (i.e., whether an event becomes a stressor). This is a crucial distinction because, even under horrendous circumstances, most individuals do not develop Post-traumatic stress disorder (March, 1990). Clinical evidence suggests that relatively low objective magnitude may rarely induce Post-traumatic stress disorder, given sufficient vulnerability in the exposed individual.

On the other hand, stressful life events also elicit dysfunctional thinking in persons who are vulnerable to depression. Miranda's (1992) findings support the cognitive theory of depression which predicts that dysfunctional thinking is latent for persons who are vulnerable to depression and is elicited by stressful life events.

Premorbid History

Different people show widely different reactions to exposure to the same traumatic life event. It is important to know who is most likely to be affected by disaster. Some studies have found evidence for the existence of predispositions and vulnerabilities as pretrauma risk factors. Pretrauma risk factors include: familial psychiatric illness (e.g. family history of psychiatric disorder and family history of anxiety; Breslau et al., 1991); childhood trauma (e.g., sexual assault, abused as child; Davidson et al., 1991; Herman, 1992); previous psychiatric problem (e.g., conduct disorder; Helzer et al., 1987; Breslau et al., 1991); genetics (True, Rice, Eisen et al., 1993); personality style such as neuroticism (McFarlane, 1990); personality disorders (e.g., antisocial and narcissistic; Wilson and Krauss, 1982) early separation from parents, low education, extraversion, use of drugs and alcohol (Breslau et al., 1991); parental financial problem (Kulka et al., 1990); previous psychiatric disorder, adverse life events prior to trauma, postdisaster life events (McFarlane, 1989); Physical/somatic history (Litz and Weathers, 1994); poor self confidence at age 15 (Card, 1987).

Although DSM-III acknowledges exposure to trauma as a major aetiological agent in the onset of disaster, it also recognises that previous psychological disturbance may lead to vulnerability to emotional dysfunction following disaster. But this is difficult to determine because of the problem in obtaining a predisaster measure of psychopathology. However, there is some evidence suggesting that previous disturbance may play a role. For example, Atkeson, Calhoun, Resick, and Ellis (1982) found that if women who had been raped, had a previous history of anxiety attacks and obsessive-compulsive behaviours they were more likely to be depressed at 8 and 12 months following the event than those with no such previous history. A history of physical problems, depression, and suicidal behaviour were also predictive of depression levels four months following. Also, Frank, Turner, Stewart, Jacob, and West (1981) found that women with a history of depression and suicidal behaviour to be more depressed and anxious following a rape than those with no such previous history.

Similarly, Helzer et al. (1987) in a study on PTSD in the general population (discussed above) found that behavioural problems before the age of 15 predicted the development of PTSD among adults exposed to physical attack, or combat in Vietnam.

There is much evidence that prior psychopathology may serve to exacerbate symptomatology following disaster. Rabinowitz, Margalit, Mark, Solomon, et al. (1990) in a study including Soldiers with severe post-traumatic stress disorder (PTSD) did not respond favourably to the front echelon treatment units were treated in a rear echelon treatment canter. Subjects in this study were given individual clinical interviews, and their combat potential scores were measured to tap premorbid factors. Analysis of findings of this study indicated that subjects with Post-traumatic stress disorder treated in the rear unit tended to be at the lower end of the military combat potential level (Rabinowitz et al., 1990).

More prevalence of PTSD has been reported for survivors of childhood sexual assault. For example, Rowan et al. (1990) in a study including a clinical sample of adult survivors of childhood sexual assault, reported a Post-traumatic stress disorder rate of 65% (Rowan et al., 1990). Whereas, as mentioned before, the prevalence rates of post-traumatic stress disorder in populations with high combat exposure, in both community and clinical samples, have been reported in range of not more than 14-56%.

McFarlane (1988) investigated the onset of post-traumatic stress disorders using a longitudinal research design. In this research the sample was composed of a group of firefighters who had an intense exposure to a bushfire disaster. Similarly, Davidson et al. (1985), showed that a majority (60%) of chronic post-traumatic stress disorder sufferers had a family history of psychopathology, as well as having had at least one other psychiatric diagnosis in their lifetime (McFarlane, 1988).

In some studies, some background experiential and family factors are of interest. It has been suggested that even wartime experience may help, perhaps through a process of "stress inoculation," which makes the individual more confident, less aroused, and gives greater mastery. Past psychiatric history has been suggested to increase vulnerability in a number of studies. It may do so to some degree but has not emerged as a powerful variable, and patients have often improved in the face of disaster or managed well overall. Family history of psychiatric disorder has been investigated in the Romanian earthquake study (Predescu and Niga-Udangiu, 1979), where positive family history was found to be less likely among those whose disorder was caused by the disaster, but others see it as contributing to vulnerability (Raphael, 1986).

In recent years, with studies have indicated the epidemiology of Post-traumatic stress disorder to be a problem of substantial magnitude in the general population. A number of epidemiological risk factors have been identified, strongly suggesting the importance of genetic influence, early adverse experiences in childhood, personality factors, and physical harm (Davidson and Foa, 1993).

There is much evidence suggesting that stressful life events are associated with the onset and maintenance of psychiatric symptomatology (Brown and Harris, 1978). Following this, it is hypothesised that stressful life events prior to the disaster may be related to earlier onset and longer duration of symptoms. Further, many life changes may occur in the period after the disaster (Raphael, 1986). McFarlane in his study of survivors of the Australian bushfire found that individuals with PTSD had more adverse life events before and after the trauma. However, the question remains as to whether or not life events impact on core PTSD symptoms or only those related disturbances such as depression.

FACTORS AFFECTING THE COURSE OF PTSD: WITHIN DISASTER

Several impact related variables have been shown to affect outcome following disaster. The severity, duration, and proximity of an individual's exposure to the traumatic event are the most important factors affecting the likelihood of developing post-traumatic stress disorder. This disorder can develop in individuals even without any predisposing conditions, particularly if the stressor is especially extreme (American Psychiatric Association, 1994).

The results of a review by Blank (1993) indicate that the types of events producing Post-traumatic stress disorder are very different in a multiple of ways, including duration, complexity, content qualities, and kinds and amounts of associated losses. Blank also suggests that longer and more complex traumatic stress experiences may tend to produce more severe or longer-lasting Post-traumatic stress disorder (but not in everyone).

Disaster stressors seem to be a critical variable in risk, as has been discussed earlier. The more intense the disaster experience, the greater the confrontation with death, mutilation, destruction, loss, and dislocation, the greater the likely effects on psychological functioning and mental health. Whether specific disasters lead to greater risk of mental problems is not really clear, but certainly high levels have been found in association with many of the "man-made" disasters that are extremely destructive, such as Buffalo Creek. Being injured in a disaster seems to add to the stress, but there have not been any adequate systematic studies to evaluate this effect (Raphael, 1986).

Also, death and injury have been found to exert an influence in the area of PTSD. For example, Solkoff, Gray and Keill (1986) found that the stressor variable accounting for most of the variance in PTSD symptoms in survivors of Vietnam was exposure to death and injury. They found that PTSD patients had experienced more intense combat and had been involved with more death and killing than non PTSD veterans. PTSD patients were found to perceive themselves as having been closer to personal death and the death of others. They also reported more personal involvement in killing, more friends killed, and that they were more likely to have observed their death. Moreover, PTSD patients were in combat for a longer time and frequently sustained more injuries. In another study, Lund, Foy, Sipprelle and Strachan (1984) found that the severity of war experiences reported strongly predicted intensity of PTSD symptoms.

Also, some studies have reported that special assignment and exposure to grotesque death were more predictive of persistent symptoms. Foy, Resnick, Sipprelle, and Carroll (1987) found that being wounded, involvement in the death of noncombatants, and exposure to atrocities are critical elements in the development of PTSD in combat veterans. The findings with combat veterans are largely congruent with findings from civilian studies where some of the same elements, for example violent loss, injury, and exposure to the grotesque, have been identified as associated with increased symptoms (Raphael, 1986).

Factors Affecting the Course of Post-traumatic Stress Disorder: Post Disaster

Increasing attention is being turned to those factors that may mediate between disaster and subsequent outcome (Joseph, Andrews, Williams, and Yule, 1992). There is some evidence that family history, children experiences, personality variables, and preexisting mental disorders may influence the development of post-traumatic stress disorder (American Psychiatric Association, 1994).

The stressor the patient endures remains the most important risk factor in the development of Post-traumatic stress disorder. The intrinsic vulnerability of the patient and the treatment received by the patient after the traumatic event are also important risk factors (Tomb, 1994). Social support as a post-disaster factor needs some attention, and literature review.

Social Support

Lin, Simeone, Ensel, and Kuo, (1979) defined social support as support accessible to an individual through social ties to other individuals, groups, and the larger community (Lin et al., 1979).

The benefits of social support are well-documented. The results of numerous prospective studies have shown that such support, typically measured in terms of reported social ties and help received, is positively related to mental health and negatively related to physical illness and mortality from all causes. In studies of various crises, social support has consistently been associated with better adjustment, including decreased distress following job loss, increased rehabilitation success among the physically disabled, recovery from illness, and emotional adjustment among the bereaved (Janoff-Bulman, 1992).

The positive impact of social support is also very evident in studies of trauma victims. For example, Joseph, Brewin, Yule, and Williams, (1993) assessed crisis support over an 18-months period with survivors of the "Jupiter" cruise ship disaster. It was found that higher crisis support in the immediate aftermath was found to predict less post-traumatic symptomatology at a later period.

Burgess and Holmstrom (1974) in a study of trauma victims concluded that social support is strongly associated with recovery from rape trauma.

There are considerable empirical evidences of the positive role of social support among victims of life-threatening diseases. Studies of cancer patients, for example, suggest that the amount of social support at time of diagnosis is positively associated with psychological well-being up to two years later, and even with the patients' length of life (Janoff-Bulman, 1992).

The results of many prospective studies have shown that social support is negatively related to psychiatric symptoms (Janoff-Bulman, 1992; Lin et al., 1979; Tennant and Andrews, 1978). For example, Lin et al. (1979) examined the effects of social support and stressful life events on illness (psychiatric symptoms). They collect data from a representative sample of the China-American adult population in Washington, D.C. The result of data analysis of this study shows that, stressful life events are positively related to the incidence of psychiatric symptoms, and social support is significantly and negatively related to psychiatric symptoms (Lin et al., 1979).

The cultural avoidance of tragedy and misfortune is echoed in the interpersonal avoidance of victims. People often choose not to notice, or to avoid victims. In addition to the lack of social support and validation that this rejection involves, there is also an odd juxtaposition that often becomes painfully obvious to survivors who have experienced a traumatic life event: life for others typically goes on as usual (Janoff-Bulman, 1992). There are, of course, cultural differences in the responses of social support systems. In cultures with strong kinship systems, extended kin function as a primary giver of both emotional and material aid in promoting family recovery (Bolton and Bolin, 1983). In less kinship-oriented societies, support networks have been shown to provide important affective aid and support in mitigating the effects of disaster trauma (Bolin, 1976; Drabek and Key, 1984). After large-scale major disasters, the stress-ameliorating effects of social support may be enhanced by the emergence of a "therapeutic community" (Huerta and Horton, 1978; Rosenberg, Fine, and Robinson, 1980); as a consequence, there may be little or no demand for mental health services (Wettenhall, 1979)

Also Brugha (1995) concluded that the available crisis support from friends, was of critical importance for the hospitalised women without partners and the non-recovered had far less support. However, Brugha mentioned that, it is, noteworthy that when the age of subjects and the chronicity of depression are taken into account, the association between recovery status at discharge/baseline and the patients' satisfaction with available support resources was reduced considerably (Brugha, 1995).

In the aftermath of traumatic life events, all of these resources- whether emotional, material, instrumental, or informational- are apt to contribute positively to the survivor's psychological adjustment. Yet simply concluding that all are helpful does not provide any understanding of the special role of social support after victimization, for the responses of other people, particularly close family members and friends, plays a vital role in survivors' efforts to reconstruct their inner world (Janoff-Bulman, 1992).

In a recent comprehensive review of empirical studies, Sheldon Cohen and Wills (1985) found that interpersonal support protects people from the potentially adverse effects of stressful events (referred to as the " buffering model of social support"), and integration in a social network has beneficial effects on people even in the absence of stressful events ("main-effect model").

In Bolin's study (1982, mentioned before), support networks helped mitigate stresses.

Relatives' Role

Ollendick and Hoffman (1982) showed symptom frequency in children to be correlated with the mother's reaction to stress (Ollendick and Hoffman, 1982). McFarlane (1987a) found the mother's response to an Australian bush fire was a better predictor of Post-traumatic symptoms in the child that the child's direct exposure to trauma (McFarlane, 1987a).

PSYCHOLOGICAL SEQUELAE OF NEGATIVE LIFE EVENTS

Introduction

Much research has been concerned with the relationship between stressful life events and psychological symptomatology. One of the main, consistent findings has been that adverse life-events increase risk for psychological difficulties such as stress, anxiety and depression (Brown, Bifulco and Harris, 1987; Brown and Harris, 1978; Miller, Ingham, Kreitman, Curtess and Sashidharan, 1987; Parkes, 1970; Paykel, 1983) and anxiety (Brown and Harris, 1978; Jacobs, Hansen, Kasl, Ostfeld, Berkman and Kim, 1990; Goodyer, Kolvin and Gatzanis, 1985; Sable, 1989).

This body of research is essential background for the present project and relevant points will be reviewed in this chapter.

STRESSFUL LIFE EVENTS AND MENTAL HEALTH

Definition and Types of Life Event

Goodyer (1990) defined a life event as:

> "A life event may be defined as a social experience with a definable onset and circumscribed course, the effects of which can be judged to have a psychological impact on an individual".

There may be different types of life events which can have varying effects on individuals, depending on whether or not they adversely affect the persons' coping capacity or inflict psychological injury. Major events have been studied in order to investigate the hypothesis that they make a substantial contribution to the onset of psychopathology (e.g., Holmes and Rahe, 1967). This does not imply that other sources of social experience are not potentially important factors in the onset of psychopathology. Classes of adverse social experience occur, which fall outside the definition of a major life event, but still exert important adverse effects on mental health. Other major events may occur as wanted and desirable experiences (such as social and educational achievements). On the other hand, life events can be classified according to their degree of undesirabity (Goodyer, 1990). They can also be classified with regard to the time (recent or chronic), the number of events and the personal appraisal of the world.

Recent Stressful Life Events

Social adversity may be recent but cause ongoing difficulties. These can affect everyday life and increase the risk of psychiatric disorder. For example, children who experience difficulties with friendships over weeks or months will not be able to describe a circumscribed onset and ending to such experiences (Goodyer, Wright and Altham, 1989; Rutter, 1985).

Chronic Stressful Life Events

Recent ongoing difficulties must be discriminated from chronic difficulties. There is considerable evidence that chronic social and family adversity exerts a significant effect on the risk of psychopathology in children and adolescents (Quinton and Rutter, 1988; Rutter, 1983, 1987, 1990; Shaw and Emery, 1988).

Daily Difficulties

There are sources of social adversity other than ongoing difficulties or chronic life events. Minor daily difficulties have tended to be overlooked as a potential causal factor in the psychopathology of children, adolescents and adults (Edwards and Cooper, 1988; Lazarus, 1984; Patterson, 1983).

Future Events

Some individuals may become distressed or develop a psychiatric disorder as a consequence of their psychological appraisal of the world (Lazarus & Folkman, 1984).

Life events can be classified in ways other than by their degree of undesirability or in terms of time, number and personal appraisal of the world. For example, life events may be classified according to their general social characteristics (such as family, marital, illness, or accident) and as to whether or not they constitute permanent separations (termed exit events) or additional entrance events to the child's social field (Goodyer, 1990).

In addition, there may be different types of stressor events that can have different psychological effects on individuals. In the field of traumatic stress studies, trauma is commonly defined by the nature of the stressors that impact on the individual (Wilson, 1994). For example, Terr (1991) defined two types of stressor events. Type I stressors are unanticipated single events outside the range of usual daily stress. Type II stressors are continuing or repetitive in nature. Both types are traumatic and can lead to Post-traumatic stress disorder (Terr, 1991).

The next three sections will provide a literature overview of the effects of stressful life events on mental health.

The Issue of Independence

While it has been shown that negative life-events can be a causal factor in the generation of a psychological disorder it is important to recognize that psychological factors can actively affect life events. A simple example would be that a person becoming depressed may cease working at college, fail exams and have to leave. This result would count as a negative life event but would be in the first instance a result of depression rather than a cause, though it may then of course become a cause of the depression worsening or maintaining. Therefore some researchers have attempted to distinguish between life-events which result from psychopathology and those which are independent from psychopathology and which can therefore be regarded as causes. This distinction requires interview methodology and cannot be drawn from questionnaire instruments. Some researchers have been interested in the ways events motivate individuals. Such studies involve investigating the change in people's behaviour as a consequence of life events, independent of any contribution to psychopathology events may make (Goodyer, 1990). The role of life events as motivational agents of behaviour is an important area of stress research (Edwards & Cooper, 1988; Fisher & Reason, 1988).

Life Events and Depression

It has long been recognized that clinical depression can be provoked by happenings in the environment, as indicated by the widespread use in psychiatry of the term "reactive" depression (Brown and Harris, 1989). Life events as a cause for depression have long been suspected on theoretical grounds (Cadoret, Winokur, Dorzab, and Baker, 1972). The literature reviewed tends to suggest that between 68 to 87 percent of bereaved adults manifest some Symptomatologies during the first few months after the death of a "significant other" (in most studies, the " significant other is a spouse). Depressed mood, dysphoria, sleeplessness, and appetite disturbances are the reactions most commonly reported among adults (Ball, 1976-77; Bornstein, Clayton, Halikas, et al., 1973; Clayton, Desmarais and Winokur, 1968; Maddison and Walker, 1967; Parkes, 1964a; Parkes, 1970; Richards and McCallum, 1979; Sanders, 1980-81; Vachon, Rogers, Lyall, et al., 1982). Such reactions tend to subside during the first few months after the death or first year of bereavement; however, somewhere between 16 to 28 percent of the bereaved appear to remain symptomatic or to become more symptomatic 12 months or more after the death of a significant other (e.g., Bornstein et al., 1973; Carey, 1979-80; Clayton and Darvish, 1979; Maddison and Viola, 1968; Parkes and Brown, 1972; Sanders, 1980-81; Vachon et al., 1982; Zisook et al., 1982). Depression is reportedly the most frequent long-term disturbance; however, persistent symptoms of ill health (Maddison and Viola, 1968; Parkes, 1970), unresolved grief (Singh and Raphael, 1981), poor adjustment (Parkes, 1970; Sanders, 1980-81), suicidal ideation (Blanchard et al., 1976), increased alcohol consumption (Maddison and Viola, 1968), and increased sedative use (Parkes, 1964a) have also been reported. Mortality is an added risk. The death rate among bereaved individuals exceeds that in the general population and reportedly remains elevated for widowers several years after the loss (Helsing and Szklo, 1981; Rees and Lutkins, 1967).

During the 29 years since the original work of Holmes and Rahe (Holmes and Rahe, 1967) research into stressful life events has developed. Research in the general population must be an important part of any such effort. So far, such research has largely been carried out with women. For example, two groups of women form the core of Brown's and Harris' research (1978)-114 psychiatric in-and out-patients living in Camberwell and two separate random samples, totalling 458 women living in the same community. The main patient group had recently contacted a psychiatrist either as in-patients (73) or out-patients (41). All were between eighteen and sixty-five and resident in Camberwell. In-patients were selected from admissions to hospital. Admissions were regularly screened to identify possible subjects and a research psychiatrist interviewed them with the systematic clinical interview (Present State Examination or PSE). Comparison groups, consisting of two surveys of women living in Camberwell, were carried out, the first in 1969/71 of 220 and the second in 1974/75 of 238 women, giving in all a sample of 458 women. The women, like the patients, were aged between eighteen and sixty-five. A somewhat shortened version of the same psychiatric interview (the PSE) was used and the date of any onset in the twelve months before interview was established for anyone considered to have experienced a psychiatric disorder in the past year. A relative was not interviewed. There is a large and apparently causal link between life-events and depression. At least half the depressed women in this study had a recent life-event of etiological importance. This is an explanation that still assumes that there is a causal link. Severe events are relatively rare, forming only 16 per cent of the events occurring to normal women living in Camberwell, but they are almost four times more common among patients. There is evidence that multiple events do increase risk of breakdown. In the above mentioned study: of those who had a severe event, 21 per cent of depressed women had three or more sever events compared with 8 per cent of normal women (Brown and Harris, 1978). There have been some population-based studies of men, and these suggest that the etiological ideas developed from the study of women are also applicable to them (Bolton and Oatley, 1987; Bebbington, Hurry, Tennant and Sturt, 1981).

A review, by FinlayJones (1981), showed that life events are a cause of depression. Studies which may have been regarded as refuting a causal link between life events and depression are analysed in detail and their conclusions are challenged. It was concluded that the hypothesis that severely unpleasant life events, particularly events involving loss, are a cause of depression has not been refuted. The evidence is that life events, or more specifically some quality of life events such as the degree of loss involved, are one of the causes of depression (FinlayJones, 1981).

The frequency of depressive syndromes have been assessed during the first 13 months after the death of a spouse (by Zisook and Shuchter, 1991). The result showed depressive episodes are common after the death of a spouse. In this study, the rate of depressive episodes among the widows and widowers at each time point was considerably higher than the 4% rate found in the comparison group or the 2% 6-months prevalence rate for major depression found in the National Institute of Mental Health Epidemiologic Catchment Area study, which used the National Institute of Mental Health Diagnostic Interview Schedule and DSM-III-R for diagnosis, (Zisook and Shuchter, 1991). Clinicians should maintain a high index of suspicion for the possibility of depression, particularly in young widows and widowers who have a past history of depression or who experience a full depressive syndrome soon after death of a spouse. Carey (1979-80), on the other hand, found widows more depressed and less well adjusted than widowers.

Harlow et al., (1991) described the natural history of changes in depressive symptomatology after widowhood, using the Centre for Epidemiologic Studies Depression Scale. They studied elderly married women who completed a baseline interview; 139 women who were subsequently widowed, and a subset of 409 still-married women, selected as control, were reinterviewed at 1, 6, 12, 18, and 24 months after bereavement. Widows were more depressed than their married controls and their baseline at every interview,(Harlow et al., 1991).

Brown and Harris (1978) found that over 60% of their subjects diagnosed as clinical depressed had experienced at least one provoking agent before depression onset, compared with 20% of "normals" in a comparable thirty eight week period. They concluded that severe events, usually involving a major loss, bring about clinical depression among women in the general population. The evidence for such a causal effect is good, if the methodological procedures employed are borne in mind (Brown and Harris, 1978). Based on the conclusion reached by this literature and Brown and Harris' study, there is considerable evidence that stressful events and depression are causally related.

Of course, cumulative distress and life change scores depended on the number of experienced events (Tennant and Andrews, 1978).

Life Events and Anxiety

In the main study of Brown and Harris (1978) life-changes and anxiety both have small associations with subsequent illness (.07 and .15 respectively): but the correlation between anxiety and life-events themselves is a relatively high (.32). There are several possible interpretations. It is possible that life-events have several causal significances and that anxiety is merely an intervening variable linking life-events to illness. However life-events may be equally irrelevant. A high life-change score may simply be the result of anxiety (Brown and Harris, 1978). The first two components of the Brown and Harris' (1978) model were; the 'dependent' variable, i.e. the onset of depression and the 'independent variable, i.e. factors capable of producing a depressive disorder which were called the latter provoking agents and include life-events occurring at a particular point in time (Brown and Harris, 1978).

Using a conceptual framework of attachment, an interview study of 81 women whose spouses had died indicated that anxiety and fear are prevalent throughout the first three years of bereavement (Sable, 1989).

In a survey of a representative sample by Jacobs et al. (1990), more than forty percent of bereaved participants reported at least one type of anxiety disorder at some time during the first year of bereavement. In this study, the sample was reasonably representative of the community from which it was drawn. The sample composed of a subgroup (N=48) assessed six months after bereavement and another subgroup (N=54) assessed twelve months after bereavement. A 15 to 20-minute systematic telephone interview was structured and precoded to include questions on sociodemographic information to confirm the widow's or widower's age and marital relationship to the deceased spouse. The core of the interview was two sections on depressive disorder and anxiety disorders from the Structured Clinical Interview for DSM-III (SCID, Spitzer, Williams and Gibbon, 1985). Additionally, the interview included the 20-item Centre for Epidemiologic Studies-Depression Scale (CES-D, Comstock, Helsing, 1976), the 10-item Psychiatric Epidemiology Research Interview (PERI) anxiety scale (Dohrenwend, Shrout, Egri et al. 1980), and the Texas Inventory of Grief (TIG, Faschingbauer, DeVaul, and Zisook, 1977), a 7-item assessment of the intensity of grief. A large overlap of anxiety disorders with depression was observed in this study, which indicates the estimated rates of anxiety disorder are not independent of major depression in most cases and raises questions about whether the anxiety disorders of bereavement are concomitant, or residual with respect to major depression (Jacobs et al., 1990).

Also, anger is one of the strongest emotions amongst both the bereaved and the survivors after the disaster (Newburn, 1993). There is, and for many there remains, a burning sense of anger and injustice. Anger is, of course, closely associated with grief (Parkes, 1975) and was very clearly evident amongst those who were bereaved (Newburn, 1993).

Life Events and Psychiatric Illness

Since its publication in 1967 Holmes' and Rahe's Social Readjustment Rating Scale (SRRS) has generated an extensive body of research as well as a considerable amount of criticism (e.g. Brown, 1974). The research on this scale has been generalized by its proponents to conclude that "The greater the magnitude of life crisis, the greater the probability that the life crisis would be associated with disease onset and the greater the probability that the population at risk would experience disease (Dohrenwend, Krasnoff, Askenasy, and Dohrenwend, 1978).

There is considerable evidence that a relationship exists between life stress and psychological difficulties. Rahe (1968) found a relationship between life stress and major and minor health changes, and Wyler, Masuda, and Holmes (1971) have shown that life change is related to seriousness of chronic illness.

A number of studies have reported a relationship between stressful life events or life crises and psychiatric status. Several studies have documented unusually high numbers of stressful events prior to the onset of psychiatric disorder or prior to entering treatment for such disorders (Brown and Birley, 1968; Brown and Goldin, 1973; Cooper and Sylph, 1973; Paykel, 1974). Community studies have indicated that those who report more life events tend to report more psychiatric symptoms (Dohrenwend, 1973b; Myers, Lindenthal, and Pepper, 1971). Data collected at two time points (spaced two years apart) by Myers, Lindenthal, Pepper, and Ostrander, (1972), show that an increase in life events is related to a worsening of psychiatric symptoms, while a decrease is associated with improvement in symptoms. It appears, then that changes in psychiatric symptomatology over time are associated with the occurrence of life events (Mueller, Edwards, and Yarvis, 1977).

In a longitudinal study of the population of a community mental health centre Catchment area, Myers et al. (1971), found a significant relationship between scores of psychiatric impairment in the community, and the occurrence of life events in the year pervious to their interview. In this study, there was a very strong association between the number of events experienced and the individual's mental status: the greater the number of events reported by respondents, the greater the proportional difference between the percentage of unimpaired and the percentage of very impaired who experienced that number of events (Myers et al., 1971).

Concerning schizophrenia and life-events, in 1960 a pilot study showed that life-events were particularly common in the three weeks immediately before the onset of a schizophrenic attack (Brown and Harris, 1978). In the main study of Brown and Harris (1978) this was confirmed: 60 per cent of the schizophrenic patients had at least one event in the three-week period before onset (Brown and Harris, 1978).

In a longitudinal study about life events and mental status Myers et al. (1972) published a preliminary report on relationships between changes in life events and changes in psychiatric symptomatology in a community sample of 720 adults in New Haven. Information was gathered for each respondent on the following dimensions: (1) basic demographic variables; (2) physical health status; (3) mental health status (as measured by items which have been found to discriminate between psychiatrically sick and healthy populations); (4) social and instrumental health and social agency facilities; and (5) help-seeking behavior and use of community health and social agency facilities; (6) life crises that occurred during the past year. In this study, the important research question was whether or not there is a relationship between changes in scores and changes in the occurrence of life events. As shown in this research there is such a relationship: the greater the number of changes in life events the it is more likely that the mental status of the individual will have changed substantially. More specifically, a net increase in life events is associated with a worsening of symptomatology and a decrease in improvement. They undertook multiple regression analyses, correlation analyses, and contingency controls. The results of all three analyses were similar and in no way negated their basic finding; the greater the change in events, the greater the change in mental status (Myers et al., 1972).

Studies of patients with fatal illness have led some investigators to consider the effects of a very significant life change, death of a spouse, for example, on the subsequent health of the survivor of the marriage. Madison and Viola (1968), as well as Parkes (1964a, 1970), have found that widows and widowers develop significantly more illness during the six months to one year immediately following the death of their spouse than do matched control groups (Rahe and Arthur, 1978).

There is, then, a body of research which indicates that life events are associated with a wide range of disorders and distress (Dohrenwend, 1978)

The Effects of Life Events on Children and Adolescents

It is also well known that adverse life-events increase risk for psychological difficulties such as stress, anxiety and depression in school age children. A study was conducted in Newcastle-upon-Tyne to investigate whether qualitative measures of life events would improve our understanding of the potential causal effects of recent undesirable events in the lives of school age children (Goodyer, et al., 1985). The results showed that the inclusion of qualitative measures of life events improved the strength of association between recent events and psychiatric disorder. Thus, moderate to severely undesirable life events occurring in the 12 months before the onset of disorder were significantly associated with psychiatric disorder, and occurred in about 60% of new onset cases.

Data suggest that negative life events have some effects on children and adolescents. For example, young children experience dysphoria and anxiety after the death of a parent. They also exhibit exaggerated separation responses and an increase in withdrawal, aggressive behaviour, disorders in eating and toileting, and school adjustment problems (Johnson, 1982; Raphael, 1982). In adolescents, grief reactions appear to be similar to those experienced by adults (Van Eerdewegh, Bieri, Parrilla and Clayton, 1982; Balk, 1983).

Instrument of Negative Life Events

Decisions about the likely impact of life events were essentially quantitative and derived from self-report life event checklists. Firstly, the number of events experienced over a given period of time (generally the preceding 3-12 months from the day of interview) can be counted (Goodyer, 1990). The second measurement issue is to determine which events are a cause rather than a consequence of psychiatric disorder or illness-related behaviours (Brown & Harris, 1978; Paykel, 1983).

The stress caused by life events has been computed in a number of different ways. For example, some investigators having constructed inventories of life events, had them scaled for importance by normal populations, and then applied this life event scaling to the events experienced by various patient groups. Homles and Rahe (1967) constructed a 43-item inventory and had it scaled for the degree of "life change" caused by the events, whereas Paykel, Prusoff, and Uhlenhuth (1971) used a different concept and had their 61-item inventory scaled for amount of "distress and upset" caused by each event. Other investigators, for example, Brown et al. (1973) ascertained the degree of stress by having independent raters assess each event experienced by the individual patient for the "severity of threat" to that patient.

Life events were first subjected to systematic operationalization by Holems and Rahe (Holems and Rahe, 1967). In their study, Holmles and Rahe (1967), a sample of 394 subjects completed the Social Readjustment Rating Questionnaire (SRRQ). They asked subjects to rate a series of life events as to their relative degrees of necessary readjustment. They used a method of assessing life events according to "weights". The "weights" are obtained to characterize each class of event. The weights are derived from averaging the scores of a number of judges who were asked to assess the disruption caused by such events, in relation to a standard maximum score provided by an event such as "loss of spouse". In the commonly used Schedule of Recent Experiences (SRE), where 100 is the standard provided for death of a spouse, marriage is given a score of 50, any birth of a child is simply given a score of 39 with regard to the readjustment required by the event; dismissal from work is given a somewhat higher score of 47; and minor violation of law is given a score of 11 (Homles and Rahe, 1967). The more a person is subjected to "heavyweight" life events, the greater the chance of their developing, at a later stage, some form of behavioural disturbance. The list was intended for self-reporting (Oei, 1988).

During the years since the original work of Holmes and Rahe (1967), research into stressful life events on human subjects has tended towards the development of longer and more complex inventories (e.g., Brugha, Bebbington, Tennant, and Hurry, 1985; Brugha and Conroy, 1985; Brugha and Cragg, 1990; Cochrane and Robertson, 1973; Paykel et al., 1971; Sarason, Johnson, and Siegel, 1978; Tennant and Andrews, 1976; Tennant and Andrews, 1977). Tennant and Andrews (1976) constructed a comprehensive life event inventory suitable for questionnaire or interviewer administration. To aid constructing this inventory, sixty-seven life event items were derived from the 61 items used by Paykel et al. (1971) and the forty three items of Holmes and Rahe (1967). These items were selected so that the widest possible range of human experience could be included in an inventory of manageable size. Relatively uncommon events were only included if they were obviously major stressors and relatively minor events were included only if likely to occur relatively frequently. As a result of this study, the original wording of many items was changed to aid understanding in the Australian setting. This inventory and the scaling are suitable for use an Australian urban population.

Brown and Harris (1989), based on earlier work with schizophrenic patients (Brown and Birley, 1968), developed the Bedford College Life Events and Difficulties Schedule (LEDS) interview. They decided to define events in terms of their likelihood of producing strong emotion of any kind. The interviewers are provided with a comprehensive list of incidents that would be likely, for most people, to be followed by negative or positive emotion. Events are largely restricted to those involving the subject and close ties (i.e., spouse; parent; sibling; child; a close friend). Their list of incidents contained 40 events which fell into eight groups, in every instance involving change in an activity, role, person, or idea (Brown and Harris, 1989). The eight groups of their list of events are as follows:

1. "Changes in a role for the subject, such as changing a job and losing or gaining an opposite-sex friend for the unmarried.
2. Major changes in a role for close ties or household members, such as a husband's staying off work because of a strike.
3. Major changes in subject's health, including hospital admissions and development of an illness expected to be serious.
4. Major changes in health for close ties or household members.
5. Residence changes or any marked change in amount of contact with close ties or household members.
6. Forecasts of change, such as being told about being rehoused.
7. Fulfilments or disappointments of a valued goal, such as being offered a house to rent at a reasonable price.
8. Other dramatic events involving either the subject (e.g., witnessing a serious accident or being stopped by the police while driving) or a close tie (e.g., learning of a brother's arrest)."

The interviewers are given explicit instructions that emphasize the importance of accurate recording of all that has happened in the given period, (Brown and Harris, 1989).

Of course, a certain level of accuracy and interrater reliability is essential for any research instrument. This is usually tested by the comparison of the independent reports of two informants (typically the respondent and a household member), test-retest studies (e.g., Jenkins, Hurst, and Rose, 1979) and record checks based on written records (e.g., Belloc, 1954). Results with using the Bedford College Life Events and Difficulties Schedule (LEDS) have shown satisfactory levels of agreement between patients and relatives. For example, there was a 79% agreement between depressed patients and their relatives, and a 81% agreement between schizophrenic patients and their relatives (Brown and Harris, 1989).

To develop a list of threatening experiences, Brugha et al. (1985), obtained recent life events from 310 individuals from the general population and 74 psychiatric out-patients with affective disorders. In this survey, recent life events were identified through the methods of Brown and Harris (1978). Where possible, each event was also recorded under the rubric of the 67-item life events inventory of Tennant and Andrews (1977). It was found that 82.5% of all events collected were covered by the inventory, and 12 of the 67 event categories accounted for 77% of life events with an aetiologically significant rating of marked or moderate long-term threat. Where practical and economic constraints oblige researchers to choose the inventory method, a brief list of event categories, such as the present list of threatening experiences, is recommended in preference to longer lists. Use of this short inventory, rather than an existing longer inventory, will not reduce the degree of association between life events and depression or other psychiatric disorders. Although specific events may be more salient to particular disorders (Brugha et al., 1985).

In a study of 50 psychiatric patients and informants, by Brugha and Cragg (1990), the questionnaire version of the List of Threatening Experiences (LTE; Brugha et al., 1985) was shown to have high test-retest reliability and good agreement with informant information. Using the Bedford College Life Events and Difficulties Scales (LEDS) method developed by Brown and Harris (1978), concurrent validity, based on the criterion of independently rated adversity derived from a semistructured life events interview, showed both high specificity and sensitivity. The questionnaire form of the List of Threatening Experiences (LTE-Q) is particularly recommended for use in psychiatric, psychological and social studies in which other intervening variables such as social support, coping, and cognitive variables are of interest, and resources do not allow for the use of extensive interview measures of stress (Brugha and Cragg, 1990).

By virtue of the List of Threatening Experiences' brevity, it overcomes difficulties of clinical application. Also, this brief list of 12 major categories of life events could overcome some of the earlier problems of longer inventories, which listed more than 60 event categories (or a subset of 25 or more particular types of events). The List of Threatening Experiences omitted common events that were unlikely to be of aetiological importance (for example, promotion at work or a minor financial problem). The discriminating power of this new classification over previous ones was soon supported by the results of a study of neurotic and endogenous depression by Brugha and Conroy (1985) (Brugha and Cragg, 1990).

In the present study, an adapted form of the description of 12 prescribed life event categories (Brugha et al., 1985) is used. This is in oppose to the subset of undesirable life events, because extended lists of life event categories is counter-productive, and the events added are unlikely to have aetiological importance (Brugha et al., 1985).

Demographic Factors and Life Events

Several studies including widows show that younger widows are at higher risk for psychiatric disorders than older ones (Ball, 1976-77; Carey, 1979-80; Maddison and Viola, 1968; Maddison and Walker, 1967; Parkes, 1964b; Vachon et al., 1982). In addition, Carey (1979-80) found widows more depressed and less well adjusted than widowers.

This literature review lend considerable support to a causal hypothesis between stressful events and psychological symptomatology. It would be expected, then, that traumatic events will also have a causal impact. However, this is not to define in advance the nature of that impact.

Post-Traumatic Stress Disorder

The explosion of scientific research and clinical understanding of all aspects of human traumatization during the last 15 years is well covered in a large number of books (e.g., Davidson, and Foa, 1993; Foy, 1992; Janoff-Bulman, 1985; Janoff-Bulman, 1992; Peterson, Prout, and Schwarz, 1991; Raphael, 1986; Saylor, 1993; Sinclair, 1993; Wilson, 1994; Wilson and Raphael, 1992). There is at least one journal exclusively devoted to the study of psychological trauma being published: the Journal of Traumatic Stress. Some of the critical developments that have occurred during the last 15 years follow; the epidemiology of PTSD, post-traumatic stress disorder in children, and affects of trauma on both soma and psyche. During these past 15 years at least two journals have sprung up that are devoted to the subject of childhood trauma, i. e. Child Abuse and Neglect and Developmental Psychopathology. During this time, psychiatry has come to realize that vast numbers of psychiatric patients have trauma histories. For example, Herman, Perry and van der Kolk (1989) and van der Kolk, Perry and Herman (1991) have demonstrated that borderline personality disorder and a variety of aggressive behaviours against self and other are usually associated with childhood histories of trauma. This finding now has been replicated repeatedly. The understanding of the relationships between certain psychological problems and trauma allows for a deeper appreciation of how these patients came to feel and behave the way they do (Van der Kolk et al., 1994).

As mentioned the clinical descriptions from a traumatized adult from second world war tend to be as fresh as those of today. Modern technology and advances in the neurosciences and in psychopharmacology have allowed contemporary trauma work to gain a deeper understanding and to provide effective interventions. Large amounts of data on how animals respond to extreme stress has began to be applied to the study of humans, (e.g., Van der Kolk et al., 1985, Van der Kolk et al., 1994).

The following sections provide a useful framework for understanding certain aspects of PTSD.

Background

This section concerns the time dimension or natural history of post-traumatic stress disorder, as reflected in published literature. Post-traumatic stress disorder (PTSD) has came of age and was introduced into the diagnostic system in 1980 with the advent of the third edition of the Diagnostic and Statistical Manual of Mental Disorders (DSM-III) of the American Psychiatric Association (Foy, 1992). Prior to 1980 Case-oriented literature, stretching back to early psychoanalytic writings on traumatic war neurosis in world war I veterans, provides some information about the longitudinal course (Blank, 1993). However, consistent patterns of psychological distress following such sudden traumatic experiences as natural disasters or combat horrors had been described in both professional and popular literature for many years prior to the formal DSM-III inclusion of Post-traumatic stress disorder. For example, "shell shock" and "combat fatigue" formulations denoting a presumed organic basis for trauma-related psychological symptoms, were used during the both world war I and II. Diagnoses previously used for the disorder have included "adjustment reactions" and "pathological" grief responses (Foy, 1992).

It is ironic that wars bring not only killing and wounding but also new ways of treating the wounds. The symptoms of post-traumatic stress disorder have been described since the inception of war. The Civil War brought morphine into use. Addiction to morphine became known as the "Soldier's Disease". Since that time, when morphine came to use, a major contribution has been made to the medical management of pain. World War II brought with it many advances in modern medicine, including the development and use of sulpha drugs and the advent of antibiotic medicines. On the other hand, the Korean War brought with it the development of the MASH unit, a mobile surgical hospital that has excellent use in so many types of civilian emergency situations. In addition, the Vietnam War brought an understanding of the concept of Post-traumatic stress disorder and some initial ways of treating it. In the treatment of Vietnam veterans, it was not long before it become clear that the concept, process, and treatment of Post-traumatic stress disorder applied to an overwhelming number of civilian conditions as well (Sinclair, 1993). But this is getting ahead of the story. We need to go back a few years to the war itself and to some of the events that followed it.

About the end of the Vietnam War, military psychiatrists published reports stating that the Vietnam War was a major exception to other wars that the United States had been involved in. This was so, they said, because of the greatly reduced number of psychiatric casualties. The teams of military mental health providers (and their significant use of minor tranquillizers) were credited with this reduction in psychiatric casualties. Emotionally disturbed soldiers were not shipped out of the country, they were returned to their units as soon as possible. The famous R&R (Rest and Recuperation) and the fixed length of the tour in Vietnam were designed to reduce the number of emotional and mental casualties. Toward the end of the war, and for a short period after it ended, it looked as though this system had worked. What was not known then was the fact that psychiatry did not have a category to understand the peculiar nature of the severe emotional and mental condition that the Vietnam War had generated (Sinclair, 1993).

Post-traumatic stress disorder (PTSD) has a long tradition, having been described in association with battle and masquerading under a variety of names. Many of these names highlighted certain aspects of the disorder. The first World War produced exhaustion, fatigue, and anxiety. This "shell shock" was thought to reflect profound, subtle brain damage and to have a significant psychological component in some cases, such as neurotic manifestations "combat neurosis", exhaustion "battle fatigue", and "traumatic neurosis" to refer to the singular link with a traumatic event. The American Civil War generated large numbers of soldiers with generalized weakness, and cardiac symptoms a presumed biologic condition thought to be due to physical stress and referred to variously as "soldier's heart" or "irritable heart" (Tomb, 1994). For the most part, at least historically, interest in traumatic disorders waxed around wartime and waned during peace. As an example, the first edition of Diagnostic Statistical Manual of Disorder (American Psychiatric Association, 1952), which was published after the second world war, recognized traumatic neurosis, gave it a deserved emphasis in the nomenclature, and provided two subtypes. DSM-II (American psychiatric Association, 1968), on the other hand, which was published more than 20 years after the end of world war II but before Vietnam war (1968), relegated trauma-related disorders to just one example of situational disturbances of adult life, equating it with the Ganser syndrome and resentment associated with unwanted pregnancy. Post-traumatic stress disorder (PTSD) was officially recognized as a unique diagnostic entity and codified in the third edition of Diagnostic and Statistical Manual (DSM-III; American Psychiatric Association, 1980). Now it is recognized that Post-traumatic stress disorder does not belong to wartime alone, but may also arise from a variety of traumatic events that can occur throughout the life cycle to both men and women and also children. It is estimated that 4 out of 10 Americans have experienced major trauma, and the disorder may be present in 9% of the population in the united states (Breslau, Davis, and Andreski, 1991).

References

Abrahams, M. J., Price, J., Whitlock, F. A., and Williams, G. (1976), The Brisbane Floods, January 1974: Their impact on health. *Medical Journal of Australia, 2, 936-939.*

Albrecht, N. N., Talbert, F.S., Albrecht, J.W., Boudewyns, P.A., et al. (1994). A comparison of MMPI and MMPI-2 in PTSD assessment. *Journal of Clinical Psychology, 50(4), 578-585.*

American Psychiatric Association (1994). *Diagnostic statistical manual of disorders, 4th ed.* Washington, DC: American Psychiatric Association.

Arryo, B. and Eth, S. (1985). Children traumatized by Central American Warfare. In S. Eth and R. Pynoos (Eds.), *Post-traumatic stress disorder in children.* Washington, DC: American Psychiatric Press.

Atkeson, B. M., Calhoun, K. S., Resick, P.A., and Ellis, E.M. (1982). Victims of rape: Repeated assessment of depressive symptoms. *Journal of Consulting and Clinical Psychology,* ***50,*** *96-102.*

Balk, D. (1983). Effects of sibling death on teenagers. *Journal of School Health 53(1): 14-18.*

Ball, J.F. (1976-77). Widow's grief. The impact of age and mode of death. *Omega 7(4), 307-333.*

Barton, A. H. (1969). *Communities in disaster: A Sociological analysis of collective stress situations. Doubleday, New Yourk.*

Bates, F.L., Fogelman, C.W., Partenton, V.J., et al. (1963). *The Social and Psychological Consequences of a Natural Disorder: A Longitudinal Study of Hurricane Audrey.* Disaster Study 18. Washington, D.C.: National Academy of Sciences-Natural Research Council.

Bebbington, P., Hurry, J., Tennant, C., Sturt, E., & Wing, J.K. (1981). Epidemiology of mental disorders in Camberwell. *Psychological Medicine,* 11, 561-579.

Belloc, N.B. (1954). Validation of morbidity survey data by comparison with hospital records. *Journal of the American Statistical Association, 49, 832-846.*

Bennet, G. (1970). Bristol Floods 1968: Controlled survey of effects on health of local community disaster. *British Medical Journal* ***3,*** *454-458.*

Blake, D. D., Weathers, F. W., Nagy, L. M., Kaloupek, D. G., Klauminzer, G., Charney, D., & Keane T. M. (1990) A clinician rating scale for assessing current and lifetime PTSD: the CAPS-1. *Behaviour Therapist,* 18, 187-188.

Blanchard, C.G., Blanchard, E.B. and Becker, J.V. (1976). The young Widow: Depressive symptology throughout the grief process. *Psychiatry 39, 394-399.*

Blanchard, E.B., Kolb, L., Geraldi, R., Ryan, P. and Pallmeyer, T., (1986). Cardac response to relevant stimuli as an adjunctive tool for diagnosing post-traumatic stress disorder in Vietnam veterans. *Behavior Therapy, 17, 592-606.*

Blanchard, E.B., Kolb, L.C., Pallmeyer, T.P., and Geraldi, R.J. (1982). The development of a psychophysiological assessment procedure for Post-traumatic stress disorder in Vietnam veterans. *Psychiatric Quarterly, 54, 220-229.*

Blanchard, E.B., Wittrock, D.K., Lawrence, C. and Gerardi, R.J. (1988). Cross-validation of a Minnesota Multiphasic Personality Inventory (MMPI) subscale for the assessment of combat-related post-traumatic stress disorder. *Journal of Psychopathology and Behavioral Assessment. 10(1), 33-38.*

Blank, A.S. (1993). The Longitudinal Course of Posttraumatic Stress Disorder. In M.D. Davidson, And E.B. FOA, (Eds.), *Posttraumatic Stress Disorder DSM-IV AND Beyond.* Page 3-22. American Psychiatric Press: Washington, D.C.

Blaufarb, H., and Levine, J. (1972). Crisis intervention in an earthquake. *Social Work 17(4), 16-19.*

Bolin, R.(1976). Family recovery from natural disaster: A preliminary model. *Mass Emergencies 1(4), 267-277.*

Bolin, R.C. (1982). *Long-term family recovery from disaster.* Monograph No.36. Boulder: University of Colorado, Institute of Behavioral science. (or: Boulder: Institute of Behavioral science, University of Colorado.

Bolton, D., O'Ryan, D., Udwin, O., Boyle, S., & Yule, W. (2000). The long-term psychological effects of a disaster experienced in adolescence II: general psychopathology. *Journal of Child Psychology and Psychiatry*, 41, 513-523.

Bolton , W., and Oatley, K. (1987). A longitudinal study of social support and depression in unemployment men. *Psychological Medicine, 17, 453-460.*

Bornstein, P.E., Clayton, P.J., Halikas, J.A., et al. (1973). The depression of widowhood after thirteen months. *British Journal of Psychiatry, 122, 561-566.*

Breslau, N., Davis, G.C., and Andreski, P. (1991). Traumatic events and post stress disorder in an urban population of young adults. *Archives of General Psychiatry, 48, 216-222.*

Brett, E., Spitzer, R., Williams, J. (1988). DSM-III-R criteria for posttraumatic stress disorder. *American Journal of Psychiatry, 145, 1232-1236.*

Bromet, E. J., Parkinson, D. K., Shulberg, H. C., Dunn, L. O. and Gondeck, P. C. (1982a). Mental health of residents near the Three Mile Island Reactor: A comparative study of selected groups. *Journal of Preventive Psychiatry, 1, 225-236.*

Brown, G. W. (1974). Meaning, measurement, and stress of life events. In Dohrenwend, B. S., and Dohrenwend, B. P., (Eds.), *Stressful Life Events: Their Nature and Effects, pp. 217-243.* John Wiley and Sons, New York.

Brown G.W., and Birley, J.L.T. (1968). Crises and life changes and the onset of schizophrenia. *Journal of Health and Social Behavior, 9, 203-214.*

Brown, M., and Goldin, A. (1973). Collective behaviour: A review and reinterpretation of the literature. Pacific palisades, alif.: Goodyear.

Brown, G.W. & Harris, T. (1978). *Social origins of depression: A study of psychiatric disorder in women.* London: Tavistock.

Brown, G.W. & Harris, T.O. (1989). *Life events and illness.* Unwin Hymam: London.

Brugha, T.S. (1995). *Social support and psychiatric disssorder: Research findings and guidelines for clinical practice.* Cambridge University press: Great Britain. (IMJC/Bru)

Brugha, T.S., Bebbington, P., Tennant, C., and Hurry, J., (1985). The List of Threatening Experiences: a subset of 12 life event categories with considerable long-term contextual threat. *Psychological Medicine, 15(1), 189-194.*

Brugha, T. S., & Cragg, D. (1990). The List of Threatening Experiences: the reliability and validity of a brief life events questionnaire. *Acta Psychiatr Scand,* 82. 77-81.

Burgess, A.W. and Holmstrom, L.L. (1974). *Rape: victims of crisis. Bowie, Md.: Robert J. Brady.*

Butcher, J.N., Dahlstrom, W.G., Graham, J.R., Tellegen, A. and Kaemmer, B. (1989). *Minnesota Multiphasic Personality Inventory (MMPI-2): Manual for administration and scoring.* Minneapolis: University of Minnesota Press.

Cadoret, R.J., Winokur, G., Dorzab, J. and Baker, M. (1972). Depressive disease: Life events and onset of illness. *Archive of General psychiatry, 26, 133-136.*

Card, J.J. (1987). Epidemiology of PTSD in a national cohort of Vietnam veterans. *Journal of Clinical Psychology, 43, 6-17.*

Carey, R.G. (1979-80). Problem and adjustment of the widowed during the first year. *Omega 10(2), 163-174.*

Carroll, E. M., Foy, D. W., Cannon, B.J. & Zwier, G. (1991). Assessment issues involving the families of trauma victims. *Journal of Traumatic Stress,* 4(1), 25-40.

Carroll, E. M., Rueger, D. B., Foy, D. W., and Donahoe, C.P. (1985). Vietnam combat veterans with posttraumatic stress disorder: Analysis of marital and cohabital and cohabitating adjustment. *Journal of Abnormal Psychology,* 94: 329-337.

Clayton, P.J., and Darvish, H.S. (1979). Cours of depressive symptoms following the stress of bereavement. In J.E. Barrett, et al., (Eds.), *Stress and Mental Disorder. New Your: Raven Press, pp. 121-136.*

Clayton, P.J., Desmarais, L. and Winokur, G. (1968). A study of normal bereavement. *American Journal of Psychiatry, 125(2), 168-178.*

Cochrane, R. and Robertso, A. (1972). The life events inventory: A measure of the relative severity of psycho-social stressors. *Journal of Psychosomatic Research. 17, 135-139.*

Cohen, S. (1980). Aftereffects of stress on human performance and social behaviour: A review of research and theory. *Psychological Bulletin, 88, 82-108.*

Compas, B.E. and Epping, J.E. (1993). Stress and Coping in Children and Families. In C.F. Saylor (Ed). *Children and Disasters: Issues in Clinical Child Psychology.* pp.11-28. New Yourk: Plenum.

Comstock, G. W. and Helsing, K.J. (1976). Symptoms of depression in two communities. *Psychol Med, 6, 551-563.*

Cooper, G. and Sylph, J. (1973). Life events and the onset of neurotic illness: An investigation in general practice. *Psychological Medicine, 3, 421-435.*

Davidson, J.R.T., and FOA, E.B. (1993), *Posttraumatic Stress Disorder DSM-IV and Beyond.* In M.D. Davidson, and E.B. FOA (Eds.), page ix-xiii. American Psychiatric Press: Washington, D.C.

Davidson, J.R.T., Hughes, D., Blazer, D. et al. (1991). Post traumatic stress disorder in the community: an epidemiological study. *Psychological Medicine, 21, 1-9.*

Davidson, J.R.T., Lipper, S., Kits, C. D. Et al. (1985). Platelet MAO activity in posttraumatic stress disorder. *American Journal of Psychiatry, 142, 1341-1343.*

Davis, L., & Siegel, L. J. (*2000*) Posttraumatic stress disorder in children and adolescents: a review and analysis. *Clinical Child & Family Psychology Review,* 3, 135-154.

Derogatis,L.R. (1977a). Confirmation of the dimensional structure of the SCL-90: A study in construct validation. *Journal of Clinical Psychology, 33(4), 981-989.*

Derogatis,L.R. (1977b). SCL-90: *Administration, scoring, and procedure manual-I for the R (revised) version.* Baltimore: Jons Hopkins University School of Medicine.

Dohrenwend, B.S.(1973b). Life events as stressors: A methodological inquiry. *Journal of Health and* Social Behaviour, 14, 167-175.

Dohrenwend, B.S. and Dohrenwend, B.P.(1978). Some issues in research on stressful life events. *The Journal of Nervous and Mental Disease, Vol.166, No.1, 7-15.*

Dohrenwend, B.S., Krasnoff, L., Askenasy, A.R. and Dohrenwend, B.P.(1978). Exemplification of a method for scaling life events: The PERI life events scale. *Journal of Health and Social Behaviour, Vol.19(june):205-229.*

Dohrenwend, B.S., Shrout, P.E. Egri, G. Et al. (1980). Nonspecific Psycholgical distress and other dimensions of psychopathology. *Archive of General psychiatry, **37**, 1229-1236.*

Dombrowsky, W. (1981). *Another step toward a social theory of disaster.* Preliminary Papeer No. 70. Newark, Del: Disaster Research Center, University of Delaware.

Drabek, T.E. and Key, W.H. (1976). The impact of disasters on primery groups linkages. *Mass Emergencies* 1, 89-105.

Drabek, T.E. and Key, W.H. (1984). *Conquering Disaster: Family Recovery and Long-Term Consequences.* New Yourk: Irvington Press.

Dudasik, S.W. (1980). Victimisation in natural disaster. Disasters 4, 329-338.

Edwards, J.R. And Cooper, C.L. (1988). Research in stress, coping and health: theoretical and methodological issues. *Psychological Medicine, **18**, 15-20.*

Endicott, J. and Spitzer, R.L., (1978). A diagnostic Interview: Scheduale for Affective Disorders and Schizophrenia, *Archives of General Psychiatry,* 35, 837-844.

Engdahl, B.E., Speed, N., Eberly, R.E., et al. (1991). Comorbidity of Psychiatric disorders and personality profiles of American World War II prisoners of war. *J Nerv Ment Dis, **179**, 181-187.*

Erikson, K.T. (1976). Everything in Its Path: Destruction of Community in the Buffalo Creek Flood. New York: Simon and Schuster.

Escobar, J.I., Canino, G., Rubio-Stipec, M., et al. (1992). Somatic symptoms after a natural disaster: A prospective study. *Am J Psychiatry, **149**, 965-967.*

Fadden, G., Bebbington, P. and Kuipers, L. (1987). The burden of care: The impact of functional psychiatric illness on the patient's family. *British Journal of Psychiatry, 150, 285-292.*

Fairbank, J.A., Keane, T.M., and Malloy, P.F.(1983). Some Preliminary data on the psychological characteristics of Vietnam veterans with posttraumatic stress disorders. *Journal of Consulting and Clinical Psychology. 51(6), 912-919.*

Faschingbauer, T.R., DeVaul, R. A. and Zisook, S. (1977). Development of the Texas Inventory of Grief. *Am J Psychiatry, **134**, 696-698.*

Figley, C.R., and Sprenkle, D. (1978). Delayed stress response syndrome: family therapy implications. *Journal of marriage and family counseling,* 6, 53-59.

Finch, A.J. and Timothy, K.D. (1993). Issues in the Assessment of Posttraumatic Stress Disorder in Children. In C.F. Saylor (Ed.), *Children and Disasters: Issues in Clinical Child Psychology.* pp.45. New Yourk: Plenum.

Finaly-Jones, Robert. (1981). Showing that life events are a cause of depression – a review. *Australian and New Zealand Journal of Psychiatry, 15:229-238.)*

Fisher, S. and Reason, J. (Eds) (1988). *Handbook of life stress and health.* New York: John Wiley.

Foy, D.W. (1992). *Treating PTSD: Cognitive-behavioral strategied.* Guilford Press. New York.

Foy, D.W., Resnick, H.S., Sipprelle, R.C., and Carroll, E.M. (1987). Premilitary, military, and postmilitary factors in the development of combat-related posttraumatic stress disorder. *The behaviour Therapist, **10**,* 3-9.

Foy, D.W., Sipprelle, R.C., Rueger, D.B. and Carroll, E.M. (1984). Etiology of Posttraumatic Stress Disorder in Vietnam veterans: Analysis of premilitary, military, and combat exposure influences. *Journal of Consulting and Clinical Psychology. 52(1) 79-87.*

Frank, E., Turner, S.M., Stewart, B. D., Jacob, M., and West, D. (1981). Past psychiatric symptoms and the response to sexual assault. *Comprehensive Psychiatry, 22, 479-487.*

Frederick, C.J. (1985b). Selected foci in the spectrum of post-traumatic stress disorders. In S. Murphy and J. Laube (Eds.) *Perspectives on disaster recovery.* New Yourk: Applenton-Century-Crofts.

Gleser, G. C., Green, B. L. and Winget, C. (1981). *Prolonged psychosocial effects of disaster: a study of Buffalo Creek.* New York: Academic Press.

Goldstein, G., van Kammen. W., Shelly, C., et al. (1987). Survivors of imprisonment in the Pacific Threater during World War II. *American Journal of Psychiatry, 144, 1210-1213.*

Goodyer, I. M. (1990). Annotation: recent life events and psychiatric disorder in school age children. *J. Chil Psychol. Psychiat. 31 (6), 839-848.*

Goodyer, I. M., Kolvin, I. And Gatzanis, S. (1985). Recent undesirable life events and psychiatric disorder in childhood and adolescence. *British Journal of Psychiatry, 147, 517-523.*

Green, B.L. (1982). Assessing levels of psychological impairment following disaster: Consideration of actual and methodological dimensions. *Joural of Nervous and Mental Disease 170(9), 544-552.*

Green, B.L. (1991). Evaluating the effects of disasters. Psychological Assessment: *A journal of Consulting and Clinical Psychology, 3, 538-546.*

Green, B.L., Lindy, J. D., Grace, M. C., et al. (1990b). Buffalo Creek survivors in the second decade: Stability of stress symptoms. *Am J Orthopsychiatry 60, 45-54.*

Greenson, R., and Mintz, T. (1972). California earthquake 1971: Some psychoanaytic observations. *International Journal of Psychoanalytic Psychotherapy* 1(5), 7-23.

Harlow, S. D., Goldberg, E. L. & Comstock, G. W. (1991). A longitudinal study of the prevalence of depressive symptomatology in elderly widowed and married women. *Archives of General Psychiatry,* 48, 1065-1068.

Helsing, K.J. and Szklo, M. (1981). Mortality after bereavement. *American Journal of Epidemiology. 144(1), 41-52.*

Helzer, J.E., Robins, L.N., McEvoy, L. (1987). Post-traumatic stress disorder in the general population. *N Engl J Med 317, 1630-1634.*

Herman, J.L. (1992). *Trauma and Recovery.* New York, Basic Books.

Herman, J.L., Perry, J.C. and van der Kolk, B.A. (1989). Childhood trauma in borderline personality disorder. *American Journal Psychiatriy 146,* 390-395.

Hocking, F. (1965). Human reaction to extreme environmental stress. *The Medical Journal of Australia 2(18), 247-250.*

Holmes, T.H. and Rahe, R.H. (1967). The social readjustment rating scale. *Journal of Psychosomatic Research, Vol. 11, pp.213-218.*

Horowitz, M.J. (1976). *Stress response syndromes.* New Yourk: Jason Aronson.

Horowitz, M.J. (1986). *Stress response syndromes (2nd. ed.).* New Yourk: Jason Aronson.

Horowitz, M., Wilner, N. and Alvarzm W. (1979). Impact of Events Scale: A measure of subjective stress. *Psychosomatic Medicine* 41(3), 209-218.

Houts, P.S., Miller, R.W., Tokuhata, G., and Ham, K.S. (1980a) *Health-Related Behavioral Impact of Three Mile Island Nuclear Incident, Part I.* Report submitted to the TMI

Advisory Panel on Health Research Studies of the Pennysylvania Department of Health. Hershey, Pennsylvania: Pennsylvania State University, College of medicine.

Hyer, L., O'Leary, W., Saucer, R.T., Blount, J., and Boudewyns, P.A. (1986). Inpatient diagnosis of Postraumatic Stress Disorder. *Journal of Consulting and Clinical Psyhology.* 54(5), 698-702.

Hyer, L.A., Woods, M.M., Harrison, W.R., Boudewyns, P.A., et al. (1989). MMPI F-K index among hospitalized Vietnam veterans. *Journal of Clinical Psychology. 45(2), 250-254.*

Jacobs, S., Hansen, F., Kasl, S., Ostfeld, A., Berkman, L. and Kim, K. (1990). Anxiety disorders during acute bereavement: risk and risk factors. *Journal of Clinical Psychiatry; 51:269-274.*

Janoff-Bulman, R. J. (1985). The aftermath of victimization: Rebulding shattered assumptions. In C.R. Figley (Ed.), *Trauma and its wake, Vol. 1. The study and treatment of posttraumatic stress disorder (pp. 15-35).* New Yourk: Brunner/Mazel.

Janoff-Bulman, R.J. (1992). *Shattered assumption toward a new psychology of trauma.* New York: Free press.

Jenkins, C. D., Hurst, M. W., Rose, R. M. (1979). Life changes: Do people really remember? *Archives of General Psychiatry, 36, 379-384.*

Johnson, P. A. (1982). After a child's parent has died. *Child Psychiatry and Human Development 12(3)*: 160-169.

Jones, R.T. and Ribbe, D.P. (1991). Child, Adolescent, and adult Victims of Residential Fire. *Behaviour Modification,* 15(4), 560-580.

Jordan, B.K., Marmar, C.R. and Fairbank, J.A. (1992). Problems in families of male Vietnam Veterans with posttraumatic stress disorder. *Journal of Consulting and Clinical Psychology,* 60, 916-926.

Jordan, B.K., Schlenger, W.E., Hough, R., Kulka, R.A., Weiss, D., Fairbank, J.A. and Marmar, C. R. (1991). Lifetime and current orevalence of specific psychiatric disorders among Vietnam and controls. *Archives of General Psychiatry, 48, 207-215.*

Joseph, S. A. (1991). *Attributions and emotional processing in victims of major disaster.* Unpublished doctoral dissertation.

Joseph, S. A., Brewin, C. R., Yule, W. and Williams, R. (1993). Causal attribution and post-traumatic stress in adolescents. *Journal of Child Psychology and Psychiatry,* 34, 247-253.

Joseph, S., Andrews, B., Williams, R. and Yule, W. (1992). Crisis support and psychiatric symptomatology in adult survivors of the Jupiter cruise ship disaster. *British Journal of Clinical Psychology,* 31, 63-73.

Keane, T.M., Caddell, J.M. and Taylor, K.L. (1988). Mississippi scale for combat-related PTSD: Three studies in reliability and validity. *Journal of Consulting and Clinical Psychology,* 56, 85-90.

Keane, T.M., Malloy, P.F., and Fairbank, J.A. (1984). Empirical development of an MMPI subscale for the assessment of combat-related posttraumatic stress disorder. *Journal of Consulting and Clinical Psychology. 52(5), 888-891.*

Keane, T.M., Wolfe, J. and Taylor, K.L. (1987). Post-traumatic stress disorder: Evidence for diagnostic validity and methods of psychological assessment. *Journal of Clinical Psychology. 43(1), 32-43.*

Kilpatrick, D.G., Saunders, B.E., Amick-McMullan, A., et al. (1989). Victim and crime factors associated with the development of crime-related post-traumatic stress disorder. *Behavior Therapy, 20, 199-214.*

Kilpatric, D.G., Saunders, B.E., Veronen, L. J., Best, C. L., and Von, J. M. (1987). Criminal victimization: Lifetime prevalence, reporting to police, and psychological impact. *Crime Delin.* **33,** 479-489.

Kinjie, J.D. (1986). Severe posttraumatic stress disorder among Cambodian refugees: Symptoms, clinical course, and treatment approaches. In J.H. Shore (Ed.), *Disaster stress studies: New methods and finding (123-1140).* Washington, D.C.: American Psychiatric Press.

Kinston, W., and Rosser, R. (1974). Disaster: Effects on mental and physical state. *Journal of Psychosomatic Research* 18(6), 437-456.

Kinzie, J.D. (1993). *Posttraumaic effects and their treatment among Southeast Asian refugees.* In J.P. Wilson and B. Raphael (Eds.), International Handbook of Traumatic Stress Syndromes. New York, Plenum Press. Pp 311-319.

Kiser, L., Ackerman, B., Brown, E., et al. (1988). Post-traumatic stress disorder in young children: a reaction to purported sexual abuse. *Journal American Academy of child and Adolescent Psychiatry,* 27, 645-649.

Kluznik, J.C., Speed, N., VanValKenburg, C., et al. (1986). Forty-year follow-up of United States prisoners of war. *American Journal Psychiatry 143, 1443-1446.*

Knaus, R.L., (1975). Crisis intervention in a disaster area: The Pennsylvania flood in Wilkes-Barre. *Journal of the American Osteopathic Association 75, 297-301.*

Kuipers, L. (1991) Schizophrenia and the family. *International Review of Psychiatry,* 3, 105-117.

Kulka, R.A., Schlenger, W.E., Fairbank, J.A., Hough, R. L., Jordan, B. K., Marmar, C. R., and Weiss, D. S. (1990). *Trauma and the Vietnam War Generation.* New York: Brunner/Mazel.

Lazarus, R. S. (1984). *Stress, coping and adaption.* New York: Springer.

Leivesley, S. (1977). Toowoomba: Victims and helpers in an Australian hailstorm disaster. *Disaster 1(3), 205-216.*

Lifton, R.J., and Olson, E. (1976). The human meaning of total disaster: The Buffalo Creek experience. *Psychiatry 39(1), 1-18.*

Lin, N., Simeone, R. S., Ensel, W. M. and Kuo, W. (1979). Social support, stressful life events, and illness: A model and an empirical test. *Journal of Health and Social Behaviour,* 20, 108-119.

Litz, B.T. and Weathers, F.W. (1994). The need for an integrative theory of post-traumatic stress disorder. In M.B. Williams and J.F. Sommer Jr. (Eds.), *Handbook of Post-traumatic Therapy.* Greenwood Press. London.

Litz, B.T. Penk, W.E., Walsh, S., Hyer, L., Blake, D.D., Marx, B., Keane, T.M. and Bitman, D. (1991). Similarities and differences between Minnesota Multiphasic Personality Inventory (MMPI) and MMPI-2 applications to the assessment of post-traumatic stress disorder. *Journal of Personality Assessment 57, 238-253.*

Lund, M., Foy, D., Sipprelle, C., and Strachan, A. (1984). The combat exposure scale: A systematic assessment of trauma in the Vietnam war. *Journal of Clinical Psychology, 40, 1323-1328.*

Lyons, J.A. (1987). Posttraumatic Stress Disorder in children and adolescents: a review of the literature. *Developmental and behavioral, 8, 349-356.*

Lyons, J.A., and Keane, T.M. (1992). Keane PTSD scale: MMPI and MMPI-2 update. *Journal of Traumatic Stress, 5, 111-117.*

Madakasira, S. and O'Brien, K.F. (1987). Acute post-traumatic stress disorder in victims of a natuural disaster. *J Nerv Ment Dis 175, 286-290.*

Maddison, D., and Viola, A. (1968). The health of widows in the year following bereavement. *Journal of Psychosomatic Research 12, 297-306.*

Maddison, D., and Walker, W.L. (1967). Factors affecting the outcome of conjugal bereavement. *British Journal of Psychiatry 113, 1057-1067.*

Malloy, P.F., Fairbank, J.A., and Keane, T.M. (1983). Validation of a multi-method assessment of post-traumatic stress disorder in Vietnam veterans. *Journal of Consulting and Clinical Psychology, 51, 488-494.*

Malmquist, C.P. (1986). Children who witness parental murder: Posttraumatic aspects. *Journal of the American Academy of Child Psychiatry, 25(3), 320-325.*

March, J. S. (1990). The nosology of post-traumatic stress disorder. *Journal of Anxiety Disorder, 4, 61-82.*

March, J.S. (1993). What constitutes a stressor? The "criterion A" issue. In J.R.T. Davidson and E.B. Foa, (Eds.), *Posttraumatic Stress Disorder: DSM-IV and beyond.* Washington, DC, American Psychiatric Press. pp 37-54

Martini D.R., Ryan C., Nakayama D., et al. (1990). Psychiatric sequelae after traumatic injury: the Pittsburgh Regatta accident. *Journal American Academy of child and adolescent Psychiatry,* 29, 70-75.

McCaffrey, R.J. and Bellamy-Campbell, R., (1989). Psychometric detection of fabricated symptoms of combat-related post-traumatic stress disorder: A systematic replication. *Journal of Clinical Osychology. 45(1), 76-79.*

McFall, M.E., Murburg, M.M., Ko, G.N. and Veith, R.C. (1990). Autonomic responses to stress in Vietnam combat veterans with posttraumatics stress disorder. *Biol. Psychiatry 27, 1165-1175.*

McFarlane, A. C. (1986a). Post-traumatic morbidity of a disaster. A study of case presenting for treatment. *Journal of Nervous and Mental Disease, 174, 4-14.*

McFarlane, A. C. (1987). Family functioning and overprotection following a natural disaster: The longitudinal effects of post-traumatic morbidity. *Australian and New Zealand of Psychiatry, 21, 210-218.*

McFarlane, A.C. (1987a). Post-traumatic phenomena in a longitudinal study of children following a natural disaster. *Journal American Academy of child and adolescent Psychiatry,* 26, 764-769.

McFarlane, A.C., (1988). The aetiology of Post-traumatic stress disorders following a natural disaster. *British Journal of Psychiatry, 152, 116-121.*

McFarlane, A.C. (1989). The aetiology of post traumatic morbidity: predisposing, precipitating and perpetuating factors. *Br J Psychiatry 154, 221-228.*

McFarlane, A.C. (1990). Vulnerability to Posttraumatic stress disorder. In M.E. Wolf and A.D. Mosnaim (Eds.), *Posttraumatic Stress Disorder: Etiology, Phenomenology, and Treatment.* Washington, DC, American Psychiatric Press. pp 2-20.

McFarlane, A. C. Policansky, S. K., and Irwin, C. (1987). A longitudinal study of the psychological mortality in children due to a natural disaster. *Psychological Medicine,* 17, 727-738.

McLeer, S.V., Deblinger, E., Atkins, M.S., Foa, E.B. and Ralphe, D.L. (1988). Posttraumatic stress disorder in sexually abuse children. *Journal of the American Academy of Child and Adolescent Psychiatry, 27, 650-665.*

McNally, R. J. (1991). Assessment of PTSD in children. Psychological Assessment: *A Journal of Consulting and Clinical Psychology, 3, 531-537.*

Miller, P. McC., Ingham, J. G., Kreitman, N. B., Curtess, P. G. and Sashidharan, S. P. (1987). Life events and other factors implicated in the onset and remission of psychiatric illness in women. *Journal of Affective Disorder, 12, 73-88.*

Milne, G. (1977). Cyclone Tracy: I. Some consequences of the evacuation for adult victims. *Australian Psychologist* 12(1), 39-54.

Miranda, J. (1992). Dysfunctional thinking is activated by stressful life events. *Cognitive Therapy and Research, Vol, 16, No. 4, pp. 473-483.*

Mirzamani, S. M. (1991). *Application of the F and K scales of MMPI to a group of PTSD out-patients.* Unpublished M.Sc dissertation.

Mirzamani, S.M., and Bolton, D. (2002). PTSD Symptoms of mothers following occurrence of a disaster affecting their children. *Psychological reports, 90, 431-438.*

Mirzamani, S.M., and Bolton, D. (2003). Mothers' Psychological Adjustment following Disaster Affecting their children. *The Journal of Psychology, 137(1), 54-62.*

Mueller, D.P., Edwards, D.W. and Yarvis, R.M. (1977). Stressful life events and psychiatric symptomatology: change or undesirability? *Journal of Health and Social Behaviour, 18, 307-317.*

Munley, P.H., Bains, D.S., and Bloem, W.D. (1993). F Scale elevation and PTSD MMPI profiles. *Psychological Reports. 73(2), 363-370.*

Munley, P.H., Bains, D.S., Frazee, J. and Schwartz, L.T. (1994). Inpatient PTSD treatment: A study of pretreatment measures, treatment dropout, and therapist ratings of response to treatment. *Journal of Traumatic Stress.* 7(2), 319-325.

Myers, J.K., Lindenthal, J.J., and Pepper, M.P. (1971). Life events and psychiatric impairment. *The Journal of Nervous and Mental Disease. Vol. 152, No. 3, 149-157.*

Myers, J.K. , Lindenthal, J.J. , Pepper, M.P. and Ostrander, D.R. (1972). Life events and mental status: A longitudinal study. *Journal of Health and Social Behaviour, 13:395-406.*

Neal, L.A., Busuttil, W., Rollins, J., Herepath, R. et al. (1994). Convergent validity of measures of post-traumatic stress disorder in a mixed military and civilian population. *Journal of Traumatic Stress.* 7(3), 447-455.

Newburn, T. (1993). *Disaster and after: Social work in the aftermath of disaster.* London: Jessica kingsley. Pp.76 pp.134

Nir, Y. (1985). Post-traumatic stress disorder in children wih cancer. In S. Eth and R. Pynoos (Eds.), *Post-traumatic stress disorder in children.* Washington, D.C.: American Psychiatric Press.

Oei, T.I. (1988). Method and technique of life events research in depression and anxiety. *Comprehensive psychiatry, 29(6), (November/December) 566-574.*

Ollendick, D.G., and Hoffman, Sister M. (1982). Assessment of psychological reaction in disaster victims. *Journal of Community Psychology 10(2), 157-169.*

Ollendick, T. H., Yule, W. and Ollier, K. (1991). Fears in British children and their relationship to manifest anxiety and depression. *J chil Psychol mPsychiat, 32, 321-331.*

Parkes, C.M. (1964a). Effects of bereavement on physical and mental health- A study of the medical records of widows. *British Medical Journal 2 274-279.*

Parkes, C.M. (1970). The first year of bereavement: A longitudinal study of the reaction of London widows to the death of their husbands. *Psychiatry 33(4), 444-467.*

Parkes , C.M. and Brown, R.J.(1972). Health after bereavement. Controlled study of young Boston widows and widowers. *Psychosomatic Medicine 34(5), 449-461.*

Paykel, E. (1983). Methodological aspects of life events research. *Journal of Psychosomatic Research, 27, 341-352.*

Paykel, E.S. (1974). Life stress and psychiatric disorder: Applications of the clinical approach. Pp. Dohrenwend (eds.), *Stressful Life Events:* Their Nature and Effects. New York: Wiley.

Paykel, E.S., Prusoff, B.A. and Uhlenhuth, E.H. (1971). Scaling of life events. *Archives of General Psychiatry 25, 340-347.*

Parker,G. (1975). Psychological disturbance in Darwin evacuees following Cyclone Tracy. *The Medical Journal of Australia 1(21), 650-652.*

Parker, J. Watts, H. and Allsopp, M. R. (1995). Post-traumatic stress symptoms in children and parents following a school-based fatality. Child: *care, health and development,* 21(3), 183-189.

Penk, W.E., Robinwitz, R., Pattenson, E.T., Dolan, M.P., and Atkins, H.G. (1981). Adjustment differences among male substance abusers varying in degree of combat experiences in Vietnam. *Journal of Consulting and Clinical Psychology, 49, 426-437.*

Perry, R.W., and Lindell, M.K. (1978). The psychological consequences of natural disaster: A review of research on American communities. *Mass Emergencies 3, 105-115.*

Perry, S., Difede, J., Musngi, G., et al. (1992). Predictors of posttraumatic stress disorder after burn injury. *Am J Psychiatry, 149, 931-935.*

Peterson, K.C., Prout, M.F. and Schwarz, R.A. (1991). *Pos-Traumatic Stress Disorder: A Clinician's Guide.* London: Plenum Press.

Pitman, R.K. (1993). Biological Finding in Posttraumatic Stress Disorder: Implications for DSM-IV Classification. In M.D. Davidson and E.B. Foa (Eds.), *Posttraumatic Stress Disorder DSM-IV AND Beyond.* Page 173-189. American Psychiatric Press: Washington, D.C.

Predescu, V., and Niga-Udangiu, S., (1979). Postseismic reactions, observations on a group of patients displaying psychic disorders determined by March 4, 1977 earthquake in Romanian. *Romanian Journal of Neurology and Psychiatry, 17, 179-188.*

Pynoos, R.S., Frederick, C., Nader, K., Arroyo, W., Steinberg, A., Eth, S., Nunez, F., and Fairbanks, L. (1987). Life threat and post-traumatic stress in school-age children. *Archives of General Psychiatry, 44, 1057-1063.*

Quarantelli, E.L (1982a). What is disaster: An agent specific or an all disaster spectrum approach to socio-behavioural aspects of earthquake. In: Jones, B. G., and Tomazevic, M., eds. Social and economic aspects of earthquakes. Ithaca, N. Y.: program in regional studies, Conrnell University, pp. 453-478.

Quarantelli, E.L. (1986). What is disaster? The need for clarification in definition and conceptualization in research. In Sowder, B.J. and Lystad, M. (eds): *Disaster and Mental Health. National institute of Menal Health. Washington, DC. American Psychiatric Press. Pp. 49-82.*

Query, W.T., Megran, J. and McDonald, G. (1986). Applying Posttraumatic Stress Disorder MMPI subscale to World War II POW veterans. *Journal of Clinical Psychology. 42(2), 315-317.*

Quinton, D. and Rutter, M. (1988). *Parenting breakdown: making and breaking of inter-generational cycles.* Epping, U.K.: Gower Press.

Rabinowitz, S., Margalit, C., Mark, M., Solomon, Z. et al. (1990). Debate reawakened: Premorbid factors for soldiers with refractory posttraumatic stress disorder. *Psychological Reports: Dec 67, 1363-1366.*

Rahe, R. H. (1968). *Life-change measurement as a predictor of illness.* Proceedings of the Royal Society of Medicine, 61, 1124-1126.

Rahe, R.H. and Arthur, R. J.(1978). Life-change and illness studies: Past history and future directions. *Journal of Human Stress, 4(1), 3-15.*

Ranga-Rama-Krishan, K., France, R.D., Pelton, S., McCann, U.D., Davodson, J. and Urban, B.J. (1985). Chronic pain and depression: I. Classification of depression in chronic low back pain patients. Pain, 22(3), 279-287.

Raphael, B. (1977). The Granville train disaster: Psychological needs and their management. *The Medical Journal of Australia 1(9), 303-305.*

Raphael, B. (1982). The young child and the death of a parent. In: Parkes, C.M. and Stevenson-Hinds, J., eds. *The place of Attachment in Human Behavior.* New York: Basic Books, pp. 131-150.

Raphael, B. (1986). *When disaster strikes: A handbook for the caring professions.* London: Hutchinson.

Rees, W.D., and Lutkins, S.G. (1967). Mortality of bereavement. *Medical Journal 4, 13-16.*

Resnick, H.S., Kilpatrick, D.G. and Lipovsky, J.A. (1991). Assessment of rape-related post-traumatic stress disorder: Stressor and symptom dimensions. *Psychological Assessment: A Journal of Consulting and Clinical Psychology, **3**, 561-572.*

Richards, J.G., and McCallum, J. (1979). Bereavement in the elderly. *The New Zealand Medical Journal 89(632), 201-204.*

Rowan, A.C., Rodriguez, N., Gallers, J., and Foy, D.W. (1990). *Sexual abuse exposure factors in the development of PTSD in adult survivors of childhood assault.* Paper presented at the convention of the International Society for Traumatic Stress Studies, New Orleans.

Rueger, D.B. (1983). *Posttraumatic Stress Disorder of Female Partner's Relationship Perception.* Paper presented at the annual meeting of the American Psychological Association Anaheim, California.

Rutter, M. (1983). Stress, coping and development. Some issues and some questions. In N. Gramezy and M. Rutter (Eds). *Stress, coping and development.* New York: McGraw-Hill.

Rutter, M. (1985). Family and school influences. Meanings, mechanisms and implications. In A. R. Nichol (Ed.). *Longitudinal studies in child psychology and psychiatry.* New York: John Wiley.

Rutter, M. (1987). Resilience in the face of adversity: protective factors and resistance to psychiatric disorder. *British Journal of Psychiatry, 147, 598-611.*

Rutter, M. (1990). Psychiatric disorder in parents as a risk factor for children. *Journal of the American Academy of Child and Adolescent Osychiatry,*

Sack, W. H., Angell, R. H., Kinzie, J. D., & Rath, B. (1986). The psychiatric effects of massive trauma on Cambodian children: II. The family, the home, and the school. *Journal of the American Academy of Child Psychiatry,* 25, 377-383.

Sanders, C.M. (1980-81). Comparison of younger and older spouses in bereavement outcome. *Omega 11(3), 217-232.*

Sarason, I. G., Johnson, J. H., & Siegel, J. M. (1978). Assessing the impact of life changes: Development of the Life Experiences Survey. *Journal of Consulting and Clinical Psychology*. 46, 932-946.

Saunders, B.E., Mandoki, K.A., and Kilpatrick, D.G. (1990). Development of a crime-related post-traumatic stress disorder scale within the Symptom Checklist-90 Revised. *Journal of Traumatic Stress, 3, 439-448.*

Saylor, C.F. (1993). Children and Disasters: Clinical and Research Issues. In C.F. Saylor (Eds.), *Children and Disasters: Issues in Clinical Child Psychology*. pp.2. New Yourk: Plenum.

Scaturo, D.J. and Hayman, P.M. (1992). The impact of combat trauma across the family life cycle: Clinical considerations. *Journal of Traumatic Stress,* 5, 273-288.

Schwarzwald, J., Solomon, Z., Weisenberg, M., and Mikulincer, M. (1987). Validation of the impact of event scale for psychological sequelae of combat.

Shaw, D. and Emery, R. (1988). Chronic family adversity and school age children's adjustment. *Journal of the American Academy of Child and Adolescent Psychiatry, 2, 200-206.*

Silber, E., Perry, S.E. and Bloch, D.A. (1958). Patterns of parent-child interaction in a disaster, *Psychiatry,* 21, 159-167.

Sinclair, N. D. (1993). *Horrific Traumata: A pastoral Response to the Post-Traumatic Stress Disorder.* New York: Haworth Pastoral Press.

Singh, B., and Raphael, B. (1981).Postdisaster morbidity of the bereaved. A possible role for preventive psychiatry? *Journal of Nervous and Mental Disease 169(4), 203-212.*

Smith, E.M., North, C. S. (1988). *Aftermath of a disaster: psychological response to the Indianapolis Ramada jet crash.* Quik Response Research Report #23. Boulder, CO, Natural Hazards Research and Applications Information Center.

Smith, E.M., North, C.S., McCool, R.E., et al. (1990). Acute Postdisaster psychiatric disorders: Identification of persons at risk. *Am J Psychoatry 147, 202-206.*

Solkoff, N., Gray, P., and Keill, S. (1986). Which Vietnam veterans develop posttraumatic stress disorders? *Journal of Clinical Psychology, 42, 687-698.*

Solomon, S., Canino, G. (1990). Appropriateness of the DSM-II-R criteria for post-traumatic stress disorder. *Compr Psychiatry, 32, 227-237.*

Solomon, Z. (1987). Combat-related PTSD among Israeli soldiers. *Bull menninger Clin, 51, 80-95.*

Solomon, Z., Benbenishty, R., Neria, Y., Abramowitz, M., et al. (1993). Assessment of PTSD: Validation of the revised PTSD Inventory. *Israel Journal of Psychiatry and Related Sciences, 30(2), 110-115.*

Spitzer, R.L., Williams, B. W., Gibbon, M. (1985). *Structured Clinical Interview for DSM-III.* New York, NY: Biometrics Research Department, New York State Psychiatric Institute.

Steinglass, P. and Gerrity, E. (1990). Natural disasters and post-traumatic stress disorder: Short-term versus long-term recovery in two disaster-affected communities. *Journal of Applied Social Psychology, 20, 1746-1765.*

Sugar, M. (1989). Children in disaster: an overview. *Child Psychiatry Hum. Dev. 19, 163-179.*

Sutker, P.B., Uddo-Crane, M. and Allain, A.N. (1991). Clinical and research assessment of post-traumatic stress disorder: A conceptual overview. *Psychological Assessment: A Journal of Consulting and Clinical Psychology, 3, 520-530.*

Talbert, F.S., Albrecht, N.N., Albrecht, J.W., Boudewyns, P.A. et al. (1994). MMPI profiles in PTSD as a function of comorbidity. *Journal of Clinical Psychology. 50(4), 529-537.*

Taylor, A.J.W. and Frazer, A.G. (1981). *Psychological sequelae of operation overdue following the DC10 aircrash in Antarctica.* Victoria University: Wellington publications in psychology No. 27.

Taylor, A.J.W. and Frazer, A.G. (1990). The field of disaster and disaster stress. *British Journal of Guidance and counseling.* 19, 1-7.

Taylor, J.B., Zucher, L.A. and Key, W.H. (1970). *A community Research to Disaster. Seattle, Washington:* University of Washington Press.

Taylor, V.A. (1977). Good news about disasters. *Psychology Today 11(5), 93-94.*

Taylor, V.A., Ross, G.A. and Quarantelli, E.L. (1976). *Delivery of Mental Health Services in Disasters: The Xenia Tornado and Some Implications.* Book and Monograph Series, No. 11. Netwark: Disaster Research Centre, University of Delware.

Tennant, C. and Andrews, G. (1976). A scale to measure the cause of life events. *Australian and New Zealand Journal of Psychiatry. 10, 27-32.*

Tennant, C. and Andrews, G. (1977). A scale to measure the cause of life events. *Australian and New Zealand Journal of Psychiatry. 11, 163-167.*

Tennant, C. and Andrews, G. (1978). The pathogenic quality of life event stress in neurotic impairment. *Archive of General Psychiatry,* 35, 859-863.

Terr, L.C. (1979). Children of Chowchilla: A study of psychic trauma. *Psychoanalytic Study of the Child, 34, 547-623.*

Terr, L.C. (1985). Psychic trauma in children and adolescents. Psychiatr. Clin. North. *Am. 8, 815-835.*

Terr, L.C. (1991). Children traumas: An outline and overview. *American Journal of Psychiatry, 148(1), 10-20.*

Tomb, D.A. (1994). The phenomenology of post-traumatic stress disorder. *Psychiatric Clinics of North America; 17(2), 237-250.*

True, W.R., Rice, J., Eisen, S.A., et al. (1993). A twin study of genetic and environmental contributions to liability for posttraumatic stress symptoms. *Archive of General psychiatry, 50, 257-264.*

Vachon, M.L.S., Rogers, J., Lyall, W.A., et al. (1982). Predictors and correlates of adaptation to conjugal bereavement. *American Journal of Psychiatry 139(8), 998-1002.*

Van der Kolk, B.A., Greenberg, M.S., Boyd, H., et al. (1985). Inescapable shock, neurotransmitters, and addiction to trauma: Towards a psychobiology of post-traumatic stress. *Bio Psychiatry; 20, 314-325.*

Van der Kolk, B.A., Herron, N. and Hostetler, A. (1994). The history of trauma in psychiatry. *Psychiatric Clinics of North America; 17(3), 589-600.*

Van der Kolk, B.A., Perry,J.C. and Herron, N. (1991). Childhood origins of self-destructive behavior. *Am J Psychiatry; 148, 16671-1671.*

Van der Ploeg, H. M. and Klein, W. C. (1989). Being held hostage in the Netherlands: a study of long-term aftereffects. *Journal of Traumatic Stress, 2(2), 153-169.*

Van Eerdewegh, M.M., Bieri, M.D., Parrilla, R.H. and Clayton, P.J. (1982). The bereaved child. *British Journal of Psychiatry, 140, 23-29*

Ward, L.C. (1994). MMPI-2 assessment of positive attributes: A methodological note. *Journal of Personality Assessment, 6(3), 559-561.*

Watson, C.G., Kucala, T., and Manifold, V. (1986). A cross-validation of the Keane and Penk MMPI scales as measures of post-traumatic stress disorder. *Journal of Clinical Psychology. 42(5), 727-732.*

Watson, C.G., Juba, M.P., Manifold, V., Kucala, T. and Anderson, P.E.D. (1991). The PTSD Interview: Rationale , description, reliability, and concurrent validity of a DSM-III-based technique. *Journal of Clinical Psychology, 47, 179-188.*

Weisenberg, M., Solomon, Z., Schwarzwald, J. and Milkulincer, M. (1987). Assessing the severity of posttraumatic stress disorder: Relation between dichotomous and continuous measures. *Journal of Consulting and Clinical Psychology, 55, 432-434.*

Westgate, K., and O'Keefe, P. (1976). *Some definitions of disaster.* Bradford, England: Disaster Research Unit, University of Bradford.

Wettenhall, R.L. (1979). Organisation and disaster: The 1967 bushfires in Southern Tasmania. In R.L. Heathcote and B.G. Thorn (Eds.), *Natural Hazards in Australia.* Canberra, Australia: Academy of Science, pp.431-435.

Williams, T., editor. (1987). *A handbook for clinicians.* Cincinnati, Ohio: Disabled American veterans.

Wilson, J.P. (1994). The need for an integrative theory of post-traumatic stress disorder. In M.B. Williams and J.F. Sommer Jr. (eds.), *Handbook of Post-traumatic Therapy.* Greenwood Press. London.

Wilson, J.P. and Krauss, C.E. (1982). Predicting post-traumatic stress disorder among Vietnam veterans. In W.E. Kelley (Ed.), *Post-traumatic Stress Disorder and the War Veteran Patient.* New York, Bnuurer/Mazel. Pp 102-147.

Wilson, J.P. and Raphael, B. (1992). *International Handbook of Posstraumatic Stress.* New York, Plenum Press.

Wyler, A.R., Masuda, M. and Holmes, T.H. (1971). Magnitude of life events and seriousness of illness. *Psychosomatic Medicine, 33, 115-122.*

Yule, W. (1992). Post-traumatic stress reactions in child survivors of shipping disasters: the sinking of the "Jupiter". *Journal of Psychosomatics,* 57, 200-205.

Yule, W. (1993). Technology-Related Disasters. In C.F. Saylor (ed.), *Children and Disasters: Issues in Clinical Child Psychology, pp.105-121. New Yourk: Plenum.*

Yule, W., and Williams, R.M.(1990). Post-traumatic stress reactions in children. *Journal of Traumatic stress, 3, 279-295.*

Yule, W., Bolton, D., Udwin, O., Boyle, S., O'Ryan, D., & Nurrish, J. (*2000*) The long-term psychological effects of a disaster experienced in adolescence: I. The incidence and course of PTSD. *Journal of Child Psychology and Psychiatry,* 41, 503-511.

Yule, W., & Gold, A. (1993) Wise before the event: planning with schools to help child survivors of catastrophes. In G. Forrest (Ed.), Trauma and crisis management. Paper presented at the ACPP day meeting, 24 February 1993. No. 8, pp. 26-34.

Yule, W. and Williams, R. M. (1988). *Post-traumatic stress reactions in children.* Paper presented at the meeting of the First European Conference on Traumatic Stress Research, Lincoln, England.

Yule, W. & Williams, R. M. (1990). Post-traumatic stress reactions in children. *Journal of Traumatic Stress,* 3, 279-295.

Yule, W., Udwin, O. & Murdoch, K. (1990). The "Jupiter" sinking: Effects on children's fears, depression and anxiety. *Journal of Child Psychology and Psychiatry,* 31, 1051-1061.

Yule, W., & Udwin, O. (1991). Screening child survivors for post-traumatic stress disorders: Experiences from the "Jupiter" sinking. *British Journal of Clinical Psychology,* 30, 131-138.

Zeiss, R. and Dickkman, H. (1989). PTSD 40 years later: incidence and person-situation correlates in former POWs. *J. Clin. Psychol. 45, 80-87.*

Zilberg, N.J., Weiss, D. S., and Horowitz, M. J. (1982). Impact of Event Scale: A cross-validation study and some empirical evidence supporting a conceptual model of stress response syndromes. *Journal of Consulting and Clinical Psychology, 50, 407-414.*

Zisook, S., Devaul, R.A. and Click, M.A. (1982). Measuring symptoms of grief and bereavement. *American Journal of Psychiatry. 139(12), 1590-1593.*

Zisook, S. & Shuchter, S. R. (1991). Depression through the first year after the death of a spouse. *American Journal of Psychiatry,* 148, 1346-1352.

In: Posttraumatic Stress Disorder: New Research ISBN 1-60021-078-3
Editor: Guida D. Kume, pp.81-114

Chapter 3

PSYCHOLOGICAL ASPECTS OF TRAUMA

Medha Mohta, Anup Mohta and A. K. Sethi
University College of Medical Sciences and associated Guru Tegh Bahadur Hospital, Delhi, India.

ABSTRACT

Trauma management requires a multidisciplinary approach. This includes treatment of physical injuries involving different organ systems. At the same time, it is essential to prevent and treat the behavioral and psychological sequelae of trauma. These problems not only affect patients but also their family members and the caregivers.

The causes of psychological disturbances in trauma patients may include pain, sudden and unexpected events, various life-saving procedures and interventions, trauma ward and ICU environment, sleep and sensory deprivation, medications, fear of loss of body function or death, damage to CNS or underlying medical diseases. Helplessness, humiliation, threat to body image and mental symptoms are some problems specifically concerning these patients. The patients react to these stressors by various defense mechanisms like conservation withdrawal, regression, anger, denial, anxiety, depression or grief reaction. Some of the patients develop delirium or more severe problems like acute stress disorder or post-traumatic stress disorder. A number of scales have been used for assessment of post-traumatic psychological symptoms. Various physical, pharmacological and psychological interventions to prevent or manage such problems have been described. Problems and management of specific patient groups e.g. patients with burns, spinal cord injury, traumatic brain injury and amputation are also highlighted.

The experience of having a seriously injured relative in hospital is a source of intense psychological stress for family members. They demonstrate symptoms of denial, fear, helplessness, confusion, depression and sometimes even post-traumatic stress disorder. Two way communications between clinical staff and families, hope for survival, support and reassurance from the personnel, proper counseling of relatives and some organizational changes have been found to be helpful.

The healthcare professionals involved in the care of trauma patients are also under threat of developing psychological problems. Stressful working environment especially in the critical care units; repeated exposure to very sick, disfigured or dying patients; need to communicate with patients' relatives and face their emotional reactions are some of the factors which trigger emotional and psychological reactions in the caregivers.

In conclusion, knowledge of psychological problems along with their prevention and management in patients, families and caregivers is an important aspect of trauma care.

INTRODUCTION

Present day trauma management essentially involves a multidisciplinary approach. Apart from management of the physical effects of the trauma on various body systems, its psychosocial sequelae on the patients require preventive and therapeutic measures. Physicians strive hard to treat the trauma victims from the time they enter the emergency room till they are discharged so that they are left with minimal physical disability but the psychological and behavioural effects of trauma are often overlooked leading to high incidence of long term psychiatric morbidity [1-7]. In order to return the patient to normal functioning, understanding these problems and providing psychological care is an important requisite besides management of physical injuries.

Relatives of the trauma patients who are involved in their care also face a lot of stress and consequent psychological trauma.

Constant exposure to trauma patients in the emergency room, operating theatre or intensive care unit exposes the medical personnel to a stressful environment. They witness severe morbidity and mortality in the trauma victims and at the same time have to attend to the relatives and friends of the patients. These exacting situations predispose the caregivers to development of psychological problems that can be prevented and managed by suitable interventions.

This article aims to discuss various psychological problems faced by trauma patients, their relatives and caregivers. Various aspects of their preventive and therapeutic management are also discussed.

CAUSES OF PSYCHOLOGICAL PROBLEMS IN PATIENTS

Most of the injuries are associated with some kind of psychological stress. A mentally healthy patient can successfully overcome these stressors but the nature and mode of injury, extent of trauma as well as the current life circumstances of the patient modify this response. [8].

Sudden and Unexpected Nature of Events

Apart from the accident itself, transportation to the hospital, emergency room procedures, surgical procedures and/or transfer to the intensive care unit (ICU) are sudden, unexpected, unfamiliar and frightening events that occur at a time when the patient's abilities to comprehend and adapt have been severely compromised [9]. The patients have no knowledge about the graveness of their injuries, various painful or complicated procedures to be performed and the duration of their hospitalization.

It is necessary for the emergency room team to expose the body of the trauma victims to fully assess the injuries sustained. The patients usually require procedures like peripheral and central venous cannulation, catheterisation, and nasogatric tube insertion. They may also need to undergo radiological and haematological investigations. In critically ill patients, tracheal intubation and ventilatory support become necessary. Various surgical procedures with or without anaesthesia may also be required.

Pain

Pain associated with trauma has severe impact on the patient's reactions to injury and even attitude towards life. Pain symptom complex characterized by anxiety, depression, loneliness, hostility and sleep disturbances is likely to develop when acute pain is inadequately treated [10]. Each of these factors can exacerbate the perception of pain. Inadequate pain relief in a medical facility also induces feelings of disappointment in the patients.

Pain plays an important role in development of psychological regression amongst trauma victims. The person feels helpless and is in a dependent position. Sometimes a patient may consciously identify pain as a symbol of illness and harbinger of death. [11].

ICU Environment

Many trauma victims need management in ICU for their physical disability. Both admission and discharge from ICU can lead to development of psychological reactions in these patients.

ICU admission places the patients in strange and frightening surroundings for which they have no frame of reference [12,13]. All their personal belongings including clothes are taken away. They are exposed to various stress producing unfamiliar sounds and unpleasant odours. Numerous monitoring and life saving devices restrict movements. Patients who have been intubated or subjected to tracheostomy are unable to verbally communicate with caregivers and the family. The inability to express one's thoughts verbally to ICU staff or to convey feelings to loved ones leads to severe emotional distress. The tendency of staff to talk about, but not to, the patients increases their anxiety. Patients become totally dependent on others for personal needs and lose control over their environment and well-being. Proximity to other critically ill patients and being witness to cardiac arrest or death leads to severe stress.

Self-contained nature and secluded environment of ICU can result in sensory deprivation. The person is exposed to very little outside stimulation with minimal body movement, constant temperature, continuous monotonous sounds of monitoring and life sustaining equipments and inability of caregivers to provide personal attention. Patients usually become disoriented to time and place. On the other hand, constant lighting, unpleasant or loud noise of various equipments and overcrowding with invasion of personal space can lead to sensory overload [14].

Severe sleep deprivation is a commonly observed phenomenon amongst trauma patients admitted to ICU [15]. The bright lights that are switched on all the time lead to loss of natural circadian rhythm of a day-night cycle. Constant monitoring and need to perform certain procedures also disturb sleep of the patients. Other factors that also contribute to sleep deprivation include altered routine and the strange environment, traumatic injury, pain and nightmares [16]. All these factors can lead to ICU psychosis syndrome, which is a diagnosis often applied to patients exhibiting acute agitation varying from mild confusion to advanced delirium. There is a greater tendency to develop this phenomenon in patients who have sustained severe trauma, prolonged surgical procedures and lengthy anaesthesia [13].

On the other hand, these areas of intensive and specialized care are actually perceived as secure, safe and familiar environments by some patients and family members and transfer to general ward may induce psychological reaction that is known as transfer anxiety, relocation anxiety, or translocation anxiety. [17]

Specific Problems Threatening Traumatized Patient [18]

Helplessness

An injured person has to depend on others for healing, comfort and even basic bodily needs. Separation from family members also evokes a feeling of helplessness. The intensity of this feeling is proportional to severity of the physical injury.

Humiliation

Traumatized patients have to undergo a number of hospital procedures which generate a feeling of indignity and an assault on the self-esteem e.g. bedpan, urinary catheters, rectal examination etc. If they are unconscious at the time of admission, they experience this humiliation in retrospect when they gain consciousness. In semiconscious states, removal of clothes and other interventions may be perceived as assault on the body.

Body Image

It is one's conscious and unconscious concept of the physical appearance of one's body. It contributes to the sense of identity. In a severely traumatized patient, the threat of harm to the body image is severe e.g., a female feels threatened after facial trauma.

Other Factors

Fear of loss of bodily function or death and sometimes guilt associated with events leading to trauma add to the psychological stress in the trauma victims [8]. Financial implications of trauma are also an important factor. In case the victim is the sole earning member of the family, loss of income and expenditure of the medical care contribute to the psychological problems for both the victim as well as the family. The emotional and the situational stress at the time of the accident also play an important role in determining the patient's response.[19]

A pre-existing psychiatric disorder makes the patients more prone to development of trauma related psychological disorders. A constellation of psychological or behavioural signs and symptoms can also occur in trauma patients due to direct damage to central nervous system, underlying medical disease, metabolic disturbances and medications [11]. It is necessary to rule out hypoxia, alcohol or drug intoxication, and other physiologic causes of agitation, irritability and uninhibited behaviour.

Severely traumatized patients may be in shock, unconscious or near death. The altered state of consciousness can be due to either physical or emotional causes. The period of unconsciousness is usually filled with dreams and fantasies. Schnaper conducted a very interesting study on emotional sequelae to unconsciousness following severe trauma [18]. He selected 68 patients, who had recovered consciousness and were oriented. Forty-three of them were amnesic at the time of the interview and 25 patients shared their experiences. Most of these patients felt like being prisoners or had death like experience. Sometimes they wondered if they were dead or alive. They were reassured when someone called their name or touched them. Some patients were aware of their surroundings during their unconsciousness. One patient heard the staff talking about not being able to control the bleeding and the possibility of her death.

The impact of stress may also vary according to the age and needs of the patient [20]. A young boy, who has to undergo an amputation, may be more worried about his appearance and others' reactions towards it, whereas a middle aged man with similar injuries may be more concerned about losing his job and his ability to earn.

Psychological Reactions

People cope with their environmental and endogenous anxieties by a coordinated complex system of defenses [18]. Traumatized patients also react by using various types of defense mechanisms [11]. These help to maintain psychological integrity and homeostasis of the ego. [20]

Conservation Withdrawal

A conservation withdrawal response is the initial phase of the withdrawal during acute phase of injury and is more likely to occur in severe trauma with loss of a body part or in life threatening situations [21]. It is a psychophysiological state characterized by decreased interaction with the environment, reduced energy, decreased activation of body functions and immobilization [22,23]. There may be a decrease in heart rate, blood pressure, body temperature, muscle tone and motor activity. Patients exhibiting this response become withdrawn from their environment. They do not like to communicate and sleep for most of the time. They are least interested in their families, friends, other injured persons and external events. They are preoccupied with pain and critical care procedures being performed on them. The implications and consequences of their injuries have not yet dawned upon them. This state often subsides within 1 or 2 weeks, but may persist for a longer period in severe cases.

Regression

Regression is reversion to an earlier developmental stage. Most of the traumatized patients initially become dependent on their caregivers. This gives rise to a regressed psychological state. Patients may behave in a very dependent manner even when capable of doing things for themselves. They may, at times, have unjustified demands and show inappropriate behaviour. Simultaneously they may also have guilt feelings about this childlike behaviour.

Denial

This defense mechanism can be utilized by most of the trauma patients but is more likely to be seen in patients who have suffered loss of limb. It becomes apparent only if it is possible to communicate with them. They may deny the extent of injury, loss of body part or function, or loss of property. They are not concerned about their friends or family members who were there in the accident. Even if they acknowledge the loss, they deny its psychological importance.

Denial acts as a protective mechanism in the initial phase of the injury that helps to relieve anxiety and fear associated with the possibility of pain, mutilation and death. But it can become dangerous in certain situations when it interferes with proper management of the patients. The patients may fail to assess the severity of their condition and limitations. They may refuse essential medications, necessary surgical procedure or like to leave the hospital against medical advice.

Anxiety

Any injury that is considered as dangerous by the patient and reawakens basic fears and threats encountered during early childhood development gives rise to anxiety [24,25]. The fears can be related to the strange environment, separation from the family, loss of body integrity and loss of bowel, bladder, or motor and sensory functions.

The patients do not perceive themselves as being fully intact because of their injuries. Therefore the feeling of being independent and self-sufficient is lacking. Dependence upon hospital staff, who are strangers to them, generates 'stranger anxiety'. The patients have to stay away from their family and friends. They are also anxious about their physical appearance and the reactions of their loved ones. Sometimes the injury is seen as a punishment for their previous sins that induces feelings of guilt and shame.

Depression

Any loss or threatened loss can give rise to depression. Trauma is usually associated with many such feelings and fears which may sometimes become distorted. There may be feelings of irrational guilt and self-accusation. The extent of helplessness and hopelessness may not be in proportion to the restrictions imposed by the severity of injury. The patients may have a decrease in self-esteem as well as sense of worthiness and usefulness for their families and society.

Anger

Anger is a very common problem encountered in trauma patients. On the psychological level, it is aimed at the correction of some appraised wrong [26]. The most obvious cause of anger in trauma patients is loss or threatened loss and resulting grief response. It is, in fact, a part of normal grief response. Inadequately relieved pain and the feeling of total dependence on others with no control over one's body also give rise to anger. Organic mental syndrome, head injuries, substance abuse and withdrawal and side effects of medication contribute to this behaviour.

Grief

A traumatized person often experiences a grief reaction that can be severe and prolonged. It is a natural process of mourning and intra-psychic readjustment necessary for resolution of the loss [27]. Even a threatened loss can start an anticipatory grief reaction. The process of grief is divided into five stages viz. denial, bargaining, anger, depression and acceptance [28]. Every person may not pass through all the stages. Sometimes it may not be possible to differentiate between various stages, the order of which may also differ.

Epidemiology of Psychological Problems

Psychological consequences are commonly observed in the trauma victims and these can sometimes be more severe than the injuries themselves. These may have detrimental effects on day-to-day functioning, education, employment and marital relationships [29]. Many variables like nature of injury; individual vulnerability and perception of traumatic event; time since trauma and sex of the patients affect the magnitude and nature of these problems.

In the immediate period after trauma, the victim may present with wide range of behavioural problems and psychological symptoms. Most patients have at least short periods in which they show emotional reactions like anxiety, worry or delirium [30-32]. Over the following period, various psychological problems including mood disorders, anxiety, depression, and specific post-traumatic symptoms have been noted. Mayou et al [4] found a high level of anxiety and depression (41%) in motor vehicle accident (MVA) victims whereas Sen et al [33] reported an incidence of 30% in patients with maxillofacial trauma. Mason et al [34] studied the prevalence of post-trauma psychological problems in injured males admitted in accident and emergency department and found significant anxiety in 13.8% and significant depression among 9.2% of responders by six months.

Post-traumatic stress disorder (PTSD) is a complex, chronic and severe disorder with substantial costs to the individual and to the society both in terms of psychosocial well-being and financial consequences [29]. It is characterised by persistent re-experiencing of the event, avoidance of the stimuli associated with the event and symptoms of increased arousal [35]. It has been shown to have a varying incidence in trauma patients, ranging from 5% to 50% [1,3-5,7,34,36]. According to Michaels et al [9], PTSD compromises self-reported general health outcome in injured adults independent of baseline status, Injury Severity Score or degree of physical recovery suggesting that psychological morbidity is an important part of the patients' perceived general health.

Besides developing PTSD, MVA survivors may also develop phobic anxiety about travel, both as a driver and passenger [1,3-5]. Kuch et al [37] reported a very high incidence (77%) of driving phobia in MVA victims, which was defined as avoidance of, or reduction in driving, or endurance of driving with marked subjective discomfort.

The diagnosis of acute stress disorder (ASD) was included in the fourth edition of the Diagnostic and Statistical Manual of Mental disorders (DSM-IV) [35] to cover the symptoms experienced by trauma survivors within the first month post-trauma. It covers a period from two days to one month after the injury, after which diagnosis of PTSD should be considered. The symptoms required for diagnosis of ASD include at least three dissociative symptoms along with one each of intrusive, avoidant and arousal symptoms.

Harvey and Bryant [38] reported 12.7% overall incidence of ASD in various trauma types with 12.5% for MVA survivors, 16% for assault victims, 10% for burns patients, and 12% for industrial accident survivors. An almost similar incidence was reported in other studies e.g., 19% in assault victims [39], 13% in MVA survivors [40], 14% in mildly head injured MVA survivors [41] and 19% in burn patients [42].

Ozaltin et al [7] examined the rates of and factors associated with the development of ASD and PTSD after MVAs. Forty patients hospitalized with orthopaedic injuries after MVAs and 26 patients who had orthopaedic injuries without MVA were compared. 20% of the patients in the MVA group developed ASD in the first month, 30% developed PTSD in the third month and 17% developed PTSD in the sixth month, while in the control group none of the patients developed either ASD or PTSD.

Difede et al [42] studied 83 hospitalized adult burn patients and found that patients diagnosed with ASD were at high risk for developing PTSD. Similar association between development of ASD within first month of trauma and symptoms of PTSD 6 months to 2 years after trauma has been reported in many other studies conducted in adults injured by violence and motor vehicle accidents [39,43,44]. Thus early and timely intervention can prevent development of PTSD.

Holbrook et al [45] highlighted the importance of gender on psychological outcome after major trauma. They reported a higher incidence of depression and symptoms of acute stress reactions in women than in men (42% vs. 34%). In a later follow-up [46] of the same study group, PTSD was found to be more frequent in women (39%) than in men (29%) and in younger low-income groups. Similar findings have been reported by other workers [47,48]. Stein et al [48] found women to be at significantly increased risk for PTSD following exposure to serious trauma even when sexual trauma, which predominates in women, was excluded.

Usually the severity of injury is expected to correlate with psychological response, but many workers have shown no relation between these two factors [1,34,49,50]. This finding stresses upon the need to take care of the psychological aspects even if the injuries are not very severe in nature.

ASSESSMENT OF PSYCHOLOGICAL REACTIONS

Various questionnaires and structured interviews have been developed for assessment of post-traumatic psychological symptoms. The commonly used ones are discussed below.

Impact of Event Scale (IES)

The IES is a broadly applicable self-report measure designed to assess current subjective distress for any specific life event. It was developed by Horowitz et al in 1979 [51] and is among the most frequently used instruments in traumatic stress research. The IES scale consists of 15 items, 7 of which measure intrusive symptoms, 8 tap avoidance symptoms and combined, provide a total subjective stress score. Respondents are asked to rate the items on a 4-point scale according to how often each has occurred in the past 7 days. This questionnaire has high reliability and validity as a screening instrument for PTSD.

The revised IES i.e. IES-R was developed by Weiss and Marmar in 1997 [52] to parallel the DSM-IV criteria for PTSD. IES-R was intended to tap hyperarousal cluster of symptoms. The IES-R has 22 items, 7 items having been added to the original 15-item IES. Out of these 6 items are related to hyperarousal symptoms and 1 new item has been added to intrusion cluster.

Clinician Administered PTSD Scale (CAPS) [53]

It is a structured clinical interview used to assess core and associated symptoms of PTSD. It assesses the frequency and intensity of each symptom using standard prompt questions and explicit, behaviorally-anchored rating scales. Its administration requires clinical skills, judgement and experience. Intended for use by experienced clinicians, it also can be administered by appropriately trained paraprofessionals. The CAPS provides a means to evaluate a current and/or lifetime DSM-IV diagnosis of PTSD, its overall severity and the impact of the seventeen PTSD symptoms on social and occupational functioning.

Structured Clinical Interview for DSM-IV Disorders (SCID-IV) [54]

As with CAPS, SCID-IV relies on clinical judgement and experience. It provides specific prompts and follow-up inquiries to assess presence or absence of each symptom. Although specific instructions for probe questions and guidelines for response interpretation are provided, the instrument is intended for use by clinicians and highly trained interviewers.

Post-Traumatic Diagnostic Scale (PDS) [49]

The Post-traumatic Diagnostic Scale (PDS) assessment is a 49-item self-report instrument designed to aid in the detection and diagnosis of PTSD. The structure and content of the PDS assessment mirror the DSM-IV diagnostic criteria for PTSD. The PDS assessment was developed specifically to fill the need for a brief self-report instrument that would help provide a reliable diagnosis of PTSD. In addition, the PDS assessment quantifies severity of PTSD symptoms.

Davidson Trauma Scale (DTS) [55]

Davidson Trauma Scale (DTS) is a 17-item scale measuring each DSM-IV symptom of PTSD on 5-point frequency and severity scales. The DTS shows good reliability and validity, and is particularly suited to assessing symptom severity, treatment outcome and in screening for the likely diagnosis of PTSD.

Mississippi Scale for Post-Traumatic Stress Disorder (MISS) [56, 57]

This has been used in numerous epidemiological studies of PTSD from which a cut-off score has been derived to define caseness (the presence or absence) of PTSD. The scale consists of 39 self-report items derived from the Diagnostic and Statistical Manual of Mental Disorders III-R criteria for PTSD.

Stanford Acute Stress Reaction Questionnaire (SASRQ) [58, 59]

Stanford Acute Stress Reaction Questionnaire (SASRQ) is a 30 item self-report questionnaire designed to assess symptoms of ASD following a traumatic experience. It includes subscales of dissociation, re-experiencing, avoidance and hyperarousal. Responses are recorded on a 6-point Likert type scale (from 0 = not experienced to 5 = very often experienced) to indicate the frequency with which each symptom has been experienced. Scoring is done by summing all of the relevant items for each subscale. This measure has been found to have high reliability and validity.

Interventions to Prevent Psychological Problems

Immediate and aggressive management is required to stabilize the condition of a trauma victim. However, after resuscitative and other necessary therapeutic interventions, clinician should also pay attention to the psychological aspects of management. At this stage, it is important to realize that this person may be feeling threatened and may have mobilized his defenses [60].

As an injured patient in acute pain is less likely to respond to psychotherapeutic interventions, treatment of pain is of prime importance. Besides using analgesic drugs and surgical measures, psychological intervention can be of great help [10]. One should be reassured that sincere efforts are being made to relieve the suffering. Information about medications and other interventions that are expected to alleviate pain should also be provided.

The severely traumatized patients and their families constantly perceive a fear of death. Liberal reassurance is needed as the patients cannot themselves evaluate the severity of their injuries [11].

A feeling of guilt is also a common finding in these patients. The staff should encourage them to explore the circumstances and events leading to injury, and also to share their feelings. By doing so, patients can be more objective and put events into perspective, which can be less disturbing to them [20].

An opportunity should be provided for the patient and the family to see each other as soon as possible. Visits of the relatives who are able to provide support to the patient should be encouraged. Presence of familiar faces in an otherwise alien environment helps in orientation and provides psychological support.

Kornfeld [61] suggested changes in recovery rooms and intensive care units to decrease the incidence of psychological problems in patients, which are equally applicable to trauma wards and trauma ICUs. Nursing procedures should be modified to allow the maximum number of uninterrupted sleep periods. The usual day-awake, night-asleep cycle should be maintained whenever possible. The patients should be allowed increased mobility by removing as many wires and tubes from their extremities as possible. The constant and monotonous sounds like that of an air conditioner should be minimized. There should be a large clock, calendar and outside window visible to the patients to help with orientation. Where possible, personally familiar bedside objects such as clock, radio or family photographs can be kept at the bedside. Patients, who can write, should be encouraged to write down their needs. A bell can be provided at the bedside to enable them to call the caregivers. They should be allowed to use spectacles or hearing aids if required.

Radio or television sets can provide meaningful sensory stimuli but their volume should be set as per the patients' desire in order to have a control over the noise factor. Noises that create expectations of something unpleasant or untoward such as sound of an X-ray machine rolled through the ICU or sound of the dressing cart can be particularly upsetting and cause the patients unnecessary anxiety even if the treatments expected are not for them [11].

As the trauma ward or ICU is a new place and the events unexpected and unknown for the patients, the atmosphere created by staff members should be made more supportive. They should identify themselves and explain all the procedures to the patients in simple words. Repeated explanations or instructions may, sometimes, become necessary due to deficit in recent memory. The patients also need to be told about the plan of their management and the expected duration of stay in the hospital. They can be made more comfortable by a friendly approach, calling them with respect and valuing their wishes.

Even when patients are unconscious or seem to be so, they need to be spoken to, called by name, touched and handled as gently as possible [18]. Greater caution should be exercised in bedside conversation avoiding ominous prognostic and other medical discussions. The medical personnel should remain alert to identify development of any psychiatric symptoms in order to prevent more florid forms of psychosis. Any psychological problem already existing at the time of the accident should be identified and managed appropriately. If delirium does develop, patients should be allowed more sleep or if possible, transferred out more quickly.

Once the condition of the patient has improved and critical care is no longer required, adequate explanation and reassurance should be provided before withdrawing intensive care. The patient and the relatives should be psychologically prepared for relocation from ICU in order to avoid transfer anxiety.

Trauma victims need social support to overcome their financial problems. Without this support it is very difficult for them to come to terms with their situation and try to rebuild their life [62].

Management of Defense Mechanisms [11]

Usually, in the early phase of injury, conservation withdrawal does not interfere with resuscitation after initial acute phase of trauma care. There is no advantage in forcing communication at this point as it may subside within 1-2 weeks after the injury. When there is sustained withdrawal, more vigorous treatment with psycho-stimulants, antidepressants, or psychological intervention is required.

Denial as a defense mechanism may be allowed to persist in the early stages since abrupt removal may lead to marked anxiety, severe depression or even overt psychosis. The patients should be encouraged to ask more questions and more and more information should be provided gradually. In established cases help of the psychiatrist or mental health personnel should be sought but it is essential to stress that this defense mechanism should be confronted jointly by critical care team, nursing staff and mental health team.

For management of anger, relief of acute pain is important. Organic mental syndrome with subsequent confusion and agitation should be recognized and corrected when possible.

Patients demonstrating regression need support, extra care and encouragement from the attending health care providers to gradually become more independent. It is necessary not to subject them to verbal attack or negative rewards.

The grief process takes time and cannot be hastened. The caregivers should facilitate the grief work by acknowledging the loss, allowing the person to be with the pain and providing assurance. At the same time one should monitor the danger signals like persistent thought about self-destruction, persistent mourning and prolonged depression and abuse of medications and alcohol. Psychotherapy and psycho-pharmacological support may be required at various stages.

Management of PTSD

There have been continuing developments in the management of PTSD. Although psychosocial modalities and pharmacotherapy have been studied individually, a combination of these has been found to be the most efficacious.

Psychosocial Treatment

The importance of psychosocial treatment approaches in the management of PTSD has been well established. Some commonly used approaches include cognitive-behavioural therapy, psychodynamic therapy and Eye Movement Desensitization and Reprocessing (EMDR).

Cognitive-Behavioural Therapies [63]

Exposure Based Treatment

The exposure therapy has been found to be the most effective for PTSD management. This technique uses imaginary exposure to the patient so as to recall the traumatic memories in the therapist's office or repeatedly confronting realistically safe situations, places or objects that are reminders of the trauma until they no longer elicit such strong emotions. The objective of this treatment is that the trauma should be emotionally processed to make it less painful.

Systematic Desensitization

Patients are trained in relaxation skills and then are exposed in imagination to fear producing situations. The exposures are brief, repetitive and involve only one situation at a time. Situations producing less fear are mastered initially followed gradually by those causing greater fear.

Flooding or Direct Therapeutic Exposure

This technique employs intensive exposure therapy involving imaginal or live exposures to moderate or strong fear-producing situations. In contrast to systematic desensitization, these exposures are prolonged until the anxiety and fear associated with the situation is reduced or eliminated.

Anxiety Management Approaches

These approaches are based on the assumption that trauma related stimuli usually produce conditioned emotional reactions and therefore trauma victims are required to learn to manage these responses. Stress inoculation training is the most widely used anxiety management approach for treating PTSD. It aims at increasing self-monitoring of conditioned stimuli so that coping strategies can be used to curtail anxiety responses early in the process.

Eye movement Desensitization and Reprocessing Therapy

Eye Movement Desensitization and Reprocessing (EMDR) is an integrative form of psychotherapy for PTSD that includes both exposure and cognitive components along with lateral eye movements. A primary benefit of this modality is its time efficiency, requiring as few as 3 to 5 hours of treatment [64]. Recently it has been the focus of extensive research and initial results suggest that it is efficacious in management of PTSD but larger series with longer duration of follow-up periods are required [65,66].

Psychodynamic Therapy

Psychodynamic therapy is a therapeutic approach that tries to get the patients to bring to the surface their true feelings, so that they can experience and understand them. It uses a supportive therapeutic relationship to uncover what the specific event and circumstances that follow mean to the individual and the obstacles to normal psychological processing of these events. Dynamic therapists pay particular attention to the traumatized individuals' current phase of response and the typical ways that the individuals avoid threatening information and then seek to help re-establish a sense of coherence and meaning in their lives by making links among the recent trauma, earlier developmental experiences and ways that conflicts are reenacted in the therapeutic dyad [67].

Psychological Debriefing

Psychological debriefing is a form of preventive therapy whereby the person is assisted in developing coping skills to deal with the traumatic event. Techniques like critical incident stress debriefing aim to reduce the risk of PTSD and other psychopathological sequelae of traumatic experiences. However, according to Cochrane review [68], single session individual debriefing did not reduce psychological distress nor prevent the onset of PTSD. There was also no evidence that debriefing reduced general psychological morbidity, depression or anxiety.

Hypnotherapy

Hypnotherapy allows the trauma victim to discharge repressed material and integrate the traumatic event in memory. As a number of PTSD individuals have shown high hypnotizability, hypnosis can be easily combined with other therapies used for treatment of PTSD [69]. For example, hypnotic principles can be integrated in EMDR protocol to promote ego strengthening and facilitate therapeutic change [70].

Pharmacotherapy

Pharmacotherapy has an important role to play in the management of PTSD and it facilitates initiation and progress of psychosocial treatment modalities.

Selective Serotonin Reuptake Inhibitors (SSRIs)

SSRIs should be considered as first-line treatment for PTSD [71]. These have been the most extensively studied, have demonstrated the most impressive therapeutic effects and have a relatively benign safety profile. These drugs block the pre-synaptic receptor responsible for the reuptake of serotonin into the neuron; thus increasing the availability of serotonin in the synaptic cleft. Of these, sertraline [72-74], paroxetine [75,76] and fluoxetine [77,78] have been used in the largest number of placebo controlled, double blind studies. SSRIs usually show response in 6-12 weeks after initiating treatment, but some patients continue to improve even after longer periods [79]. It is seen that relapse rates decrease if treatment is continued for 6-12 months [74,80].

Serotonin–Potentiating Non-SSRIs

If SSRIs are not tolerated or are ineffective, serotonin-potentiating non-SSRIs should be considered. They may block the reuptake of serotonin but are non-selective. Some block postsynaptic serotonergic and noradrenergic receptors or reuptake of norepinephrine. Venlafaxine [81], nefazodone [82], trazodone [83,84] and mirtazapine [85] have been evaluated for management of PTSD. Because of their promising results and relatively good safety profile, they should be considered as second-line treatment [86,87].

Monoamine oxidase inhibitors and tricyclic inhibitors

Monoamine oxidase inhibitors (MAOIs) and tricyclic antidepressants (TCAs) have also been used in these patients. Phenelzine [88] is the main MAOI studied while TCAs studied include imipramine, amitriptyline and desipramine [88-90]. A small number of double-blind, placebo-controlled studies that have evaluated these agents have shown promising but inconsistent results. MAOIs appeared superior to TCAs but patients continued to have residual symptoms. These drugs have significant adverse effects, such as cardiovascular complications, and safety issues, such as ease of overdose. Therefore, TCAs and MAOIs should be considered as third-line treatment [86,87].

Anticonvulsants

Anticonvulsants like carbamazepine, valproic acid, topiramate and gabapentin have been evaluated in PTSD in open-label studies with positive results. A small double-blind, placebo-controlled study demonstrated efficacy of lamotrigine for PTSD [91].

Benzodiazepines

Although benzodiazepines have a role in anxiety disorders, they have been found to be ineffective in management of PTSD [92]. They should be avoided or used only for short term because of depressogenic effects, and the possibility that they may promote or worsen PTSD [93].

Other agents

Buspirone, a non-benzodiazepine anxiolytic, was found to be effective in PTSD only in open-label studies [94,95]. Recently, atypical antipsychotics e.g. clozapine [96] and olanzapine [97] were as effective as monotherapy and as an augmenter to SSRIs in open-label/case studies. Propranolol may be useful for mitigating PTSD symptoms or perhaps even preventing the development of PTSD [98].

SPECIFIC PATIENT GROUPS

Most of the injuries result in psychological problems that need similar preventive and therapeutic management. But patients with traumatic brain injury, spinal cord injury, amputation and burns need a special mention because of the specific nature of their injury and loss.

Patients with Traumatic Brain Injury

Traumatic brain injury is a major health problem in young adults. Its occurrence peaks in 15-24 years old [99]. These adolescent and young adult survivors have relatively normal life expectancies and constitute a major burden on families and services [100]. In USA, traumatic brain injury results in significant morbidity and cost, as high as 37.5 billion dollars per year [101].

Brain injury gives rise to physical as well as mental impairments. Physical disability usually improves within few months, whereas mental impairments including personality change, chronic affective disturbance, intellectual and memory deterioration and impaired concentration persist for a longer period thus contributing to chronic disability and handicap [102].

Damage to frontal and temporal lobes usually results in severe personality changes [100]. Frontal lobe damage is characterised by disinhibition, euphoria, lack of tact and childishness. Irritability and increased aggressiveness can occur in temporal lobe involvement. Damage to central and basal frontal areas is accompanied by loss of spontaneity and lack of vitality.

A large percentage of patients note changes in their personality during first year following injury. These changes are the principal reasons for the family consultation as the patients face the physical disability better than emotional and behavioural changes [103].

The commonest emotional and behavioural changes described are depression, anxiety, irritability, anger, complaining, impatience and fatigue [104,105]. These problems are thought to be associated with poor social adjustment, decreased social contact, inability to return to work and decreased participation in leisure activities [106]. Many patients with severe head injury fail to return to work [107] while those who do return usually cannot take very responsible positions. This leads to reduced job satisfaction and other psychological problems. Inability to return to work further compounds other difficulties mentioned as it also decreases leisure activities and opportunity to develop social contacts. Many patients live at home and become more dependent on their family members. On the other hand, those who return to work or continue to live independently have better social interaction [108].

Social contact and meaningful friendships are considered to be critical elements of survivors' quality of life [109]. Karpman et al [110] attributed social isolation to lack of agility, lack of mobility and lack of exposure. They recommended that injured individuals should be assisted to establish and build up their social networks and also to become active with their peer groups.

High level of dependency has been demonstrated in a study of patients with severe closed head injury [111]. Almost half of these patients were not capable of taking charge of the home and over 20% required someone to look after them.

Kersel et al [112] assessed the psychological functioning of a group of 65 adults at 6 months and 1 year following severe traumatic brain injury. The prevalence of depression remained constant (24%) over time. Impatience was the most frequently reported behavioural problem at both assessments. There was a slight increase in the number of behavioural problems and level of distress reported over time but there was no obvious relationship between the prevalence of a behavioural problem and the degree of distress associated with it. However the behaviours that caused most distress changed between 6 months and 1 year post-injury, representing a change in the patients' perception of their difficulties. In this study, 70% patients lost employment, 30% returned to live with their parents and 38% suffered a breakdown of relationship. There was also a significant and ongoing decrease in social and leisure activities.

Personality and behavioural changes including loss of emotional control, irritability, reduced initiative and childishness contribute significantly to family stress and burden of care [113]. As a result, spouses have to face major life and role changes. Difficulties in interpersonal relationships and high rates of marital breakdown have also been reported in such cases [114].

Bornstein et al [115] found a positive association between the degree of neuropsychological deficit and the level of emotional disturbance following closed head injury. However, various neurological indicators of injury severity or complications demonstrated little relationship to the degree of emotional disturbance. The authors suggested that the compromise of adaptive abilities in these patients was an important factor in development of emotional disturbance. Some patients with very good pre-morbid personality had pronounced emotional disturbance in association with mild neurobehavioural deficit. Inability to function at previous levels of excellence probably resulted in great loss of self-esteem in these patients. Thus facilitating emotional adjustment may represent a more important issue than treatment of a cognitive deficit.

Interventions

The head injured patients coming to ICU have a compromised neurological status and may already be confused, delirious, disoriented and sensory deprived. All these problems are further aggravated by ICU environment and it is essential to take particular care to prevent or minimize the effects of ICU stressors on these patients. Besides interventions already described for care of trauma patients, certain issues specific to brain injured patients should be kept in mind [116]. The confused patient should be kept in a single room, if possible and many visitors should not be allowed at a time. The staff should try to reorient the patient with regards to the person, place and time to minimize confusion and fear. It is often necessary to repeat information several times to these patients because of their memory deficits.

The rehabilitation services should not only focus on physical disabilities, but adequate attention should be provided to psychological and behavioural aspects of the problem. For this, a team approach involving psychiatrists, psychologists, occupational therapists, social workers and family members is required. Time period between injury and beginning of rehabilitation is an important prognostic factor [60]. If rehabilitation starts within first 6 months, the results are usually good. If it is undertaken after 2 years, the rehabilitation potential falls drastically, as by this time the patient becomes dependent on spouse or family for financial and emotional support.

In adults with severe head injuries, intensive behaviour modification programmes have been found to be effective in management of difficult behaviour problems. However these programmes are required to continue for at least 18 months and in some cases several years [117].Cognitive retraining and psychotherapy may also be needed to achieve optimal psychological rehabilitation.

Patients with Spinal Cord Injury

Spinal cord injury is an event that abruptly changes the entire life of the patient. It often results in permanent physical and emotional disabilities and is frequently considered in the context of physical and emotional rehabilitation. The role reversal from independent to dependent usually results in emotional problems [118]. The initial reaction is depression, despair, bitterness and grief. Specific problems of the spinal cord injury patients are related to loss of bladder, bowel and sexual function along with inability to accept the disability as real and permanent [119]. The embarrassment of excretory incontinence and the partial or complete loss of sexual function is very difficult to overcome. Most of these patients retain their libido but are unable to perform the sexual act which adds to their frustration.

Kennedy and Rogers [120] examined the prevalence of anxiety and depression longitudinally in patients with spinal cord injury and illustrated the highest scores in the acute phase of injury and during the months leading up to discharge. They highlighted the requirement of interventions to prevent and treat psychological disorders during this period and stressed upon the need to ensure that appropriate psychological care is available within spinal cord injury rehabilitation settings.

Brackett et al [121] shared their experiences at Acute Spinal Cord Injury Center at Florida. They emphasized the importance of emotional care in spinal cord injured patients and recommended certain principles of management. People with spinal cord injury have dignity, value and importance. It is important to recognize and make the patients realize that their worthwhileness has not changed as a result of the injury. Staff members should communicate their respect for the patients by announcing their presence before entering the room. Eye contact should be made while talking to them. When feeding the patients, it is important for the nurse to sit beside them rather than stand and look down on them. This gives the patients a feeling of equality. Detailed explanation of various procedures with constant presence and reassurance of the treating personnel and talking about interests, hobbies and habits prior to the injury with the patients and families is found to be very useful. Whenever possible, the patients should be included in discussions about their capabilities and be informed about procedures. When a patient is receiving kinetic therapy, tears usually trickle down to ears. Wiping the face with a wet cloth, cleaning the ears with alcohol or plugging the ears with cotton can be of help. Spinal cord injury often gives rise to fear of surgery, being alone and neglected or even death. Efforts should be made to alleviate these fears by active listening, providing accurate information and reassurance. It is an art to provide information in such a way so as to keep the patients in a positive yet realistic frame of mind, without any false hopes. Issues of privacy, body image and sexuality are usually of over-riding concern. Every effort should be made to respect their modesty. One should try to assign nurses of the same sex. Patients should be properly covered and informed about it if there is loss of sensations. Questions regarding sexual relations and functioning should be dealt with honestly. The authors concluded that to maximize the potential of the patients with spinal cord injury and the quality of their life, emotional care is as important as physical care.

The abrupt loss of sensation over part of the body can lead to a situation similar to sensory deprivation syndrome. Das [122] recommended an increase in stimulation over areas of the body having sensation and increased use of other sensory modalities e.g. auditory and visual, to prevent such situation.

Curcoll [123] found relaxation techniques to have a positive influence on spinal cord injured patients as learning and practising these exercises provided the patients with an opportunity to come to terms with their new body image and the possibility of seeking more pleasing corporal sensations instead of painful ones.

Once the acute phase is over, these patients should be involved in activities and sports according to their capabilities. Paraplegics should be encouraged to be independent and make social and occupational adjustments. The situation is more difficult for quadriplegics as their sphere of normal functioning is very limited. They find it very difficult to channel their aggressive drives into productive accomplishment. Therefore a continuous effort has to be made to avoid antisocial aggressive reactions or indifference in these patients [119].

Mathew et al [124] highlighted the importance of taking the psychological, social and biological aspects into consideration while dealing with somatic complaints of spinal cord injured patients. They studied four such patients and correlated the relationship of their somatic complaints to psychological and social issues. Two patients suffered unexplained pain, another excessive spasm uncontrolled with intrathecal baclofen pump and the fourth with several pressure sores, constipation and other physical problems. The resolution of the psychosocial issues in these patients resulted in significant improvement in their somatic complaints. The authors proposed that persisting physical symptoms presenting to the clinician in a spinal injury population merit a thorough evaluation of their psychosocial components.

Patients with Amputated Limbs

Tumours and traumatic injuries are common indications for performing amputation. Though most of the psychological problems and adjustments are common in all these cases, post-traumatic amputation presents greater difficulties, as there is hardly any time for pre-operative preparation, explanation and counselling.

The loss of limb parallels the death of a loved one [125]. Initially there is often a period of disbelief, numbness, preoccupation with the loss, anger, tearfulness and insomnia [126]. This is followed by intense grief. It is a profound assault on the body image, self esteem and self respect. In addition, it results in functional loss. The patients may view themselves as 'just cripples'. There may be feelings of helplessness and hopelessness. They may become physically, emotionally and economically dependent on others. If they happen to be the earning members of family the impact may be even more severe. People often avoid such patients as they remind them of their own vulnerability and possible losses. Sometimes patients may interpret amputation as a punishment for their past sins. An additional factor promoting a strong psychological reaction in the patient is the very visible nature of the event to the patient [127]. Watching themselves become mutilated aggravates the psychological components. Sometimes the patients may present with overwhelming cosmetic concerns and pronounced aversion of gaze. They avoid looking at the injured limb during change of dressing, keep it covered in public and may even show reluctance to have medical personnel see it [127].

The effects on sexuality after amputation are physical, mechanical and psychological. Psychological issues in the sexual adjustment of the patients with an amputation include presence of depression, performance anxiety and altered body image [126].

Another major problem encountered is phantom sensation or phantom pain [128]. Phantom sensation is a non-painful sensation of the phantom limb whereas phantom pain is a painful sensation felt in the stump or phantom limb that is due to neuroma, post-operative pain, and pain felt by abnormal sensitivity. While all amputees experience phantom sensation, a majority of them (>80%) also experience phantom pain [129].

Interventions

The patients who are faced with amputation should be prepared psychologically by counselling. On the other hand the patients who have already undergone sudden unexpected amputation should be managed as crisis cases. Psycho-therapeutic interventions should be designed as per needs of the patients, considering the present and past traumatic and psychological experiences. In addition they should get support in vocational retraining, change of life style and behavioural impairments.

Liberal use of analgesic drugs along with psychological support is required for management of phantom pain and sensations. They need adequate information about these sensations. They should be reassured that this pain will gradually diminish and in the meantime adequate pain relief will be provided to them. Families should also be explained about this phenomenon so that they can also provide adequate support to the patient.

Patients with Burn Injury

Approximately 2.4 million burn injuries are reported and 75,000 burn patients hospitalized annually in United States. Burns are one of the most expensive catastrophic injuries to treat. Sustaining a burn injury is often a traumatic experience with far reaching physical, social and psychological implications [130]. With improved facilities for treatment and rehabilitation of burned patients, more and more such patients are surviving and thus the need to manage their long-term physical and psychological aspects is gaining importance.

There are certain problems that are specific to burn patients. First, the inpatient procedures associated with burn wound care e.g. skin grafting, dressings, debridement etc are extremely painful. The pain associated with these procedures may be much more than that with injury itself [131]. Second, burn injuries usually cause permanent scarring and disfigurement affecting physical appearance. When the injury occurs in a highly visible or highly valued location, the burn victim must endure the perceived and actual social stigma associated with scarring [132]. Scarring can also lead to formation of contractures resulting in deformities and dysfunction. Functional impairments include decrease in range of motion, reduced muscle force, altered sensitivity and pruritus [133]. Finally, the patients with burn wounds are kept in isolation to prevent infection. Such isolation contributes to a sense of social deprivation in the patient [134]. Moreover, family and friends frequently avoid visiting the patient because of their discomfort with the physical disfigurement caused by the burns.

In the early phases following burn injuries, patients show a variety of distressing symptoms such as delirium, depression, anxiety and pain [135]. Depression manifests as decreased appetite, inability to sleep, apathy and lack of desire to live. Also there is an increase in the intensity of pain complained. Refusal to eat and exercise to maintain strength and prevent contractures interferes with physical recovery [136].

PTSD can also complicate recovery process in hospitalized patients. Thirty to 40% patients meet all criteria for a diagnosis of ASD or PTSD [137] and 63% of patients experience some symptoms of ASD or PTSD [138]. Patients with PTSD reported higher levels of pain than patients without PTSD despite receiving similar doses of analgesic medication [137]. They were also more anxious before, during and after painful medical procedures [139]. The incidence of PTSD was found to be related to the severity of burn injury in terms of total burned surface area [138]. But according to Tedstone and Tarrier [130] patients with small burn injuries of 1 percent or less also experienced clinically significant levels of psychological difficulties post-burn.

Goodstein [140] described a reaction and recovery trajectory in burn wound survivors. According to him, during first 48 hours the patients are dissociated from their surroundings and appear calm. For next 2 to 7 days they are worried about the length of their life. Anxieties and fears manifest in next 2 to 4 weeks. They express fear of death and guilt for having survived the accident if others died. They are also concerned about their family members, lost employment and uncertain future. They often experience fear of rejection by family and friends and lowered self-esteem [141]. Weeks 5 and 6 have been labelled by Goodstein as a stage of psychological emergency when patients begin to react and respond to the changes in their body, life and relationships. The emotions begin to emerge as anger which is often displaced on the staff, friends and family. Delirium can accompany surgical procedures in severely burned patients.

Several workers have studied the psychosocial adjustment of child burn victims and have drawn contradictory conclusions [142,143]. Sawyer et al [144] examined the psychosocial impact of a burn injury at different developmental stages and concluded that adolescent burn victims show a markedly poorer psychosocial adjustment when compared with younger burned children. Visible burns, emotional distress in the mother and multiple home moves were all associated with poorer psychosocial adjustment in adolescence.

Interventions

A multidisciplinary team approach is essential to meet the holistic biopsychosocial needs of the burn patients [134].

The importance of pharmacologic interventions to minimize pain and discomfort in these patients can not be underestimated. The psychological interventions involve maintaining a supportive psychotherapeutic environment in which the patients can thrive [134]. The patients should be encouraged to express their feelings. Efforts should be made to develop their trust in the caregivers. Patients should be assisted to regain their sense of autonomy by involving them in scheduled daily activities as soon as possible. The help of a psychiatrist involving psychotherapy and use of psychotropic drugs may be required.

As physical healing takes place, role of family gains importance. The family members should be encouraged to get actively involved in the patients' recovery course. They require education about the patients' needs and psychological support to face the patients' disfigurement and emotional reactions to trauma.

Programmes aimed to help burned children need to pay more attention to adolescents [144]. The injuries to the body image at a previous time lead to extra stresses during adolescence and support systems including an emotionally untroubled home are essential to tide over this crisis.

The Dying Patient

There are certain patients in whom death becomes inevitable despite providing best possible treatment. It becomes a demanding task on the part of the treating clinician to support a patient who is confounded by the fear of being alone and in pain [11]. Adequate pain relief and sedation help to make the patient calm and comfortable. The patient's self-respect and dignity should be given due importance. The spouse, other family members or close friends may be allowed to spend time with the patient. If desired, a visit by a spiritual person or performance of a religious ceremony may be arranged. Having a loved one present at the time of death is considered to contribute to a good death. Compassionate care and soothing words from the caregivers are very effective in providing comfort to the patient as well as the relatives.

Families of Trauma Patients

Having a seriously injured relative in the trauma ward or ICU is an extremely stressful experience. As described for the patients, it is an unexpected event for the family members also, for which they are not at all prepared. In the hospital, they find themselves in a strange environment where they have no influence. They have to leave their familiar role and status. Such surroundings and their inability to predict or change the outcome give rise to feeling of helplessness.

During initial period, the family members usually have feelings of denial, fear and loss of control [13]. By using the defense mechanism of denial, the relatives try to avoid facing painful reality of the situation, especially in critically ill patients where there is always a fear of death of their loved one. This gives them some time to accept the facts and adjust to the situation.

Jamerson et al [145] labelled behaviour of family members of ICU patients as 'hovering'. This is defined as an initial sense of confusion, stress and uncertainty in the family members before seeing the patient, knowing the diagnosis and apprehending the prognosis. This experience is characterized by an altered perception of time and emotions like anxiety, shock, worry, fear, and a sense of being overwhelmed.

Tracking is the process of observing, analysing and evaluating the patient's care and status and relates to the family's satisfaction with the environment and caregivers[145]. However, it is difficult for many relatives to understand about the patient's problems and treatment plans as they usually lack medical knowledge [12]. If the patient is deteriorating, they assume that adequate and proper care is not being provided by the medical staff. In such situations they may even show feelings of anger and rage towards them [13].

The relatives may also suffer from depression and feeling of guilt that worsen if the patient dies [146]. This feeling is expressed by an exaggerated responsibility for the traumatic event. The family members reproach and accuse themselves of the errors committed against the patient. A person, who was with the patient at the time of accident but not injured, may suffer from a feeling of survivor guilt.

Gregorio et al [147] analysed psychological repercussions in the family members of the gravely traumatized patients admitted into an ICU. The families were interviewed 48 hours after the admission. A large number of the family members showed extreme deviations in their behaviour. They manifested symptoms of being depressed, of not feeling well and hopelessness. The scores for suicidal depression and low energy depression were high. There was decrease in level of energy, feeling of tiredness in the absence of physical exercise and loss of interest in previously liked activities. Anxiety, irritability, excessive preoccupation with physical health, hallucinations of delirious ideas and difficulty in expression were also noted. The authors concluded that more than 50% of the family members showed symptoms of depression, and psychological manifestations were more pronounced in the women.

According to Hodovanic et al [148] role alterations, isolation from other family members, financial constraints, transportation problems and the fear of losing their loved one were identified as factors believed to induce family crisis and disorganization. The patient's hospitalisation presents an enormous financial strain on the family. These problems are further exaggerated when patient is an earning member.

If the patient is a child, parents have to leave siblings at home for long periods that adds to their worries and stress. De Vries et al, studying paediatric victims of traffic crashes, found 15% of the parents to be suffering from PTSD [149]. Only 20% of the affected parents sought help for themselves. Wesson et al reported a significant level of anxiety and depression in mothers of trauma patients, regardless of injury severity of the child [150]. These findings indicate towards the need to provide support to the parents while treating paediatric trauma patients.

Even after the acute phase is over, sequelae of traumatic injury in patients have a significant effect on family. Hall et al studied stressors in families of patients with traumatic brain injury. They found that financial strain and behavioural changes including withdrawal from social contacts, depression and anxiety created stressors for the family [151]. Jacobs et al reported that 28% of families exhausted all or most of their financial resources, and 24% experienced a mild to moderate financial drain after a family member experienced a traumatic brain injury [108]. Inadequate preparation for outcome and lack of support services also affect the families' ability to cope with the long-term effects of traumatic brain injury [152].

Intervention Strategies

The health care team members can intervene in a variety of areas to offer support to the family members.

In a review by Hickey [153] information was among the 10 most important needs perceived by the family members. Reassurance about patient comfort and receipt of the best possible care, a feeling of being accepted, and convenience needs e.g. food, facilities also were identified as important.

Two-way communication between clinical staff and the families is crucial [13]. Knowing what is happening to the patient, even if negative, is less frightening than not knowing at all. This reduces the feeling of anxiety, helplessness and sense of immobilization. Therefore honest information should be provided regularly in carefully chosen, simple words. However, the information must be titrated with the relatives' grief process as too much information too soon will not be retained and may further overwhelm them [154]. Regular meetings with a family representative can be scheduled in the office. In addition to this, current status of the patient and other messages can be displayed on a message board outside ICU or trauma ward.

Orientation to the ICU environment and routine is also important. Written information regarding hospital and ICU services and regulations can be made available to the relatives [145]. When the relatives are going to visit their patient for the first time in emergency room, they should be prepared mentally as to what they are going to see [11].

Another important factor in the coping ability of a family is hope for survival of their loved one [12,13]. Most families can eventually accept and deal with even worst situations if they are given some hope.

Personnel should be supportive and reassuring. They should show empathy and respect towards the relatives [145]. This can be achieved by active listening, open and honest communication, friendly approach and appropriate touch. This approach helps to build up trust in the caregivers and reduces anxiety of the relatives.

Sometimes the families are not receptive to the best efforts of the staff to comfort them. In case of demonstration of negative reactions by them, it is important to recognize the underlying psychological stress and the feelings of uncertainty and not to take these reactions personally [12]. If required, evaluation of the family members by a mental health professional may prove to be beneficial.

Jamerson et al [145] suggested some organizational changes to help family members waiting outside ICU. Ready access to fluids and nutrition by providing coffee and vending machines is important. The waiting area should be well lit and comfortable with windows and telephones. Diversionary activities such as television, magazines, puzzles or games can be provided.

The family must be counselled about the physical and psychosocial adjustments that the patient may require at home and work place after discharge from the hospital. The family members can be introduced to the relatives of other patients who have faced and found out ways of coping with similar problems. By doing so, a clinician can help some relatives avoid repeating mistakes others made and may help build up confidence [154].

When death of a patient is inevitable, it is the caregivers' duty to provide an environment in which the families can learn to cope with this unpleasant reality [155]. They should be prepared to receive the bad news by gradual information of the worsening condition. If the patient does die, the family must be provided an opportunity to see and to be alone with the deceased. If they are not allowed to see the body after death, there may be problems in accepting the death along with feelings of bitterness [156].

HEALTHCARE PROFESSIONALS CARING FOR TRAUMA PATIENTS

Constant exposure to injured patients in emergency room, ICU, operation theatre or ward presents a stressful situation for the medical personnel and makes them vulnerable to psychological problems. The sight of crying, moaning or gasping patients with blood, vomitus or excreta around them; patients with amputated limbs, burns, disfigured body parts; unconscious people; or conscious but helpless and immobile patients with cervical traction is a horrifying experience. Patients with grievous injuries die in front of caregivers. This invokes a feeling of failure and helplessness, as they cannot save their patients despite having all the treatment facilities. Repeated exposure to loss of life or body parts also reminds them of their own vulnerability.

Almost all the trauma patients suffer from pain. Physicians and nurses try to alleviate their suffering but in some unstable patients, it may not be possible to provide adequate pain relief initially. This situation can give rise to dissatisfaction not only among the patients and their relatives, but also the caregivers.

Managing patients, who are demonstrating defense mechanisms like regression, anger or anxiety is not easy. Some patients showing denial may refuse for medication or some procedures necessary for their treatment. Handling such patients is again a very stressful job.

The intensive care unit (ICU) has been described frequently as "highly stressful" [157,158]. It imposes a number of professional, environmental and interpersonal demands on ICU personnel. It has been reported to produce a variety of psychological, physiological and overt behaviour effects that can interfere with work performance [159]. Gentry and Parkes [157] identified work overload, issues of patient's death and dying, need for social support, psychological strain and staff turnover as the key ICU stressors. Exposure to death and dying may be associated with secondary stressors including a sense of responsibility for the dying patient, a perception that a patient is suffering unnecessarily or anticipation that an error will cost a patient's life, particularly if a decision is not taken rapidly [159]. Common physical environment factors such as too many interruptions, slow results from the laboratory and refusal of consent for critical care procedures can also contribute significantly to overall stress levels. Other factors affecting the healthcare professionals include threat to one's self-esteem, personal conflicts with colleagues, differences in assessment and treatment of patients and lack of accurate communication[12].

Many of the trauma cases are medico-legal in nature. In such cases, in addition to treating the patient's injuries and maintaining strict records, the responsibility of handling the police, media and legal personnel puts extra stress on the caregivers.

Besides all these factors, another stressor for the staff members caring for traumatized is their responsibility to inform and support the distraught relatives. They are required to regularly explain the risks and poor prognosis of the patient, still keeping the relatives in a hopeful and positive frame of mind. Sometimes the disturbed relatives feel that their loved one is not getting adequate care and therefore become verbally and sometimes physically abusive [158]. When a patient dies, breaking the news of death to the patient's near and dear ones is an extremely stressful experience.

Intervention Strategies

The most important requirement is good communication among physicians of different ranks and also between physicians and nursing staff. This helps to improve decision-making and patient management. Inter-personal tensions are also minimised. It is also important for the healthcare professionals to know that sharing one's thoughts and feelings about patients is a healthy approach and should not be considered as weakness or unprofessionalism[12].

In emergency room, team spirit can be enhanced by arranging meeting of the trauma team at the beginning of each shift[20]. The responsibilities of various team members, preferences for certain techniques and resources available on each shift can be discussed.

Death of a patient should not be considered by healthcare professionals as a failure or loss of self-esteem. They must learn to accept the reality of the situation in a healthy manner and move on to the next patient [12].

The working hours should not be very long. Adequate time for sleep and recreation should be provided between duties. Involvement in habits and social activities is quite rejuvenating.

Carefully planned orientation, training and on-going in-service education programmes improve decision making abilities and thus help to reduce fear of making mistakes.

Creation of support groups and presence of psychosocial support personnel are also important for the psychological well being of the staff members.

REFERENCES

[1] Blanchard EB, Hickling EJ, Taylor AE, Loos WR, Gerardi RJ. Psychological morbidity associated with motor vehicle accidents. *Behav Res Ther* 1994; 32:283-290.

[2] Brom D, Kleber RJ, Hofman MC. Victims of traffic accidents: Incidence and prevention of post-traumatic stress disorder. *J Clin Psychol* 1993; 49: 131-140.

[3] Hickling EJ, Blanchard EB. Post-traumatic stress disorder and motor vehicle accidents. *Journal of anxiety disorders* 1992; 6: 285-291.

[4] Mayou R, Bryant B, Duthie R: *Psychiatric consequences of road traffic accidents.* BMJ 1993; 307: 647-651.

[5] Mayou R, Tyndel S, Bryant B. Long-term outcome of motor vehicle accident injury. *Psychosom Med* 1997; 59:578-584.

[6] Schnyder U, Morgeli H, Nigg C et al. Early psychological reactions to life-threatening injuries. *Crit Care Med* 2000; 28: 86-92.

[7] Ozaltin M, Kaptanoglu C, Aksaray G. Acute stress disorder and posttraumatic stress disorder after motor vehicle accidents *Turk Psikiyatri Derg*. 2004;15: 16-25.

[8] Schmidt CW Jr. Psychiatric management of acute trauma. In: Zuidema GD, Rutherford RB, Ballinger WE. *The Management of Trauma* 4th ed. Philadelphia: WB Saunders Co, 1985; pp 807-814.

[9] Michaels AJ, Michaels CE, Moon CH et al .Posttraumatic stress disorder after injury: impact on general health outcome and early risk assessment. *J Trauma* 1999; 47:460-466.

[10] Wolman RL, Lutterman A. Management of pain from burn injury. *Contemp Surgery* 1988; 33(3A) suppl: 20-25.

[11] Blumenfield M, Schoeps MM. *Psychological care of the burn and trauma patients.* Baltimore: Williams and Wilkins 1993; pp1-147.

[12] Wallace-Barnhill GL. Psychological problems for patients, families and health professionals. In: Shoemaker WC, Ayres S, Grenvik A, Holbrook PR, Thompson WL. *Textbook of Critical Care.* 2nd ed. Philadelphia: WB Saunders Co. 1989; pp 1414-1420.

[13] Wallace-Barnhill GL. Understanding reactions of patient and family. In: Civetta JM, Taylor RW, Kirby RR. Critical Care. 3rd ed. *JB Philadelphia Lippincott-Raven.* 1997; pp 89-94.

[14] Baker CF. Sensory overload and noise in the ICU: sources of environmental stress. *CCQ* 1984; 6: 66-80.

[15] Kleck HG. ICU syndrome: Onset, manifestations, treatment, stressors and prevention. *CCQ* 1984; 6: 21-28.

[16] Brewer MJ. To sleep or not to sleep: the consequences of sleep deprivation. *Crit Care Nurse* 1985; 5: 35-41.
[17] Coyle MA. Transfer anxiety: preparing to leave intensive care. *Intensive Crit Care Nurs*. 2001; 17: 138-143.
[18] Titchener J. Management and study of psychological response to trauma. *J Trauma* 1970; 10: 974-980.
[19] Schnaper N. The psychological implications of severe trauma: emotional sequelae to unconsciousness. *J Trauma* 1975; 15: 94-98.
[20] Lenehan GP. Emotional impact of trauma. *Nurs Clin North Am* 1986; 21:729-740.
[21] Mieszala P. Post-burn psychological adaptation: an overview. *CCQ* 1978; 1: 93-111.
[22] Dubovsky SL. The psychophysiology of health, illness and stress. In: Simons RC, Pardes H. *Understanding human behaviour in health and illness*. Baltimore: Williams and Wilkins. 2nd ed. 1981: pp90.
[23] Engel GI, Reichsman F. Spontaneous and experimentally induced depression in an infant with a gastric fistula: a contribution to the problem of depression. *J Am Psychoanal Assoc* 1956; 4: 428.
[24] Averill JR. *Anger and aggression: an essay on emotion*. New York: Springer, 1982.
[25] Strain JJ, Grossman S. Psychological reaction to medical illness and hospitalization. In: Strain JJ, Grossman S. *Psychological care of the medically ill: a primer in liaison psychiatry*. New York: Appleton-Century-Crofts, 1975.
[26] Strain JJ. *Psychological intervention in medical practice*. New York: Appleton-Century-Crofts, 1978.
[27] Stedeford A. Facing death-patients, families and professionals. Oxford: *Heinemann Medical Books*, 1984; pp 154.
[28] Kubler-Ross E. *On death and dying*. London. Macmillan, 1969.
[29] Kessler RC. Post-traumatic stress disorder: the burden to the individual and to society. *J Clin Psychiatry* 2000; 61: 4-12.
[30] Malt UF, Olafsen OM. Psychological appraisal and emotional response to physical injury: A clinical, phenomenological study of 109 adults. *Psychiatr Med* 1992; 10: 117-134.
[31] McClelland P, Hepburn B, Warres N. Psychological management of the critically ill. In: Cowley RA, Conn A, Dunham CM. Trauma Care-Vol II Medical Management. Philadelphia: *JB Lippincott Co*. 1987 pp 198-215.
[32] Schnyder U, Malt UF. Acute stress response patterns to accidental injuries. *J Psychosom Res* 1998; 45: 419-424.
[33] Sen P, Ross N, Rogers S. Recovering maxillofacial trauma patients: the hidden problems. *J Wound Care* 2001 ;10: 53-57.
[34] Mason S, Wardrope J, Turpin G, Rowlands A. The psychological burden of injury: an 18 month prospective cohort study. *Emerg Med J* 2002; 19: 400-404.
[35] American Psychiatric Association. *Diagnostic and statistical manual of mental disorders* (4th ed) 1994.Washington, DC: American Psychiatric Association.
[36] Malt UF, Hoivik B, Blikra G. Psychosocial consequences of road accidents. *Eur Psychiatry* 1993; 8: 227-228.
[37] Kuch K, Swinson RP, Kirby M. Post-traumatic stress disorder after car accidents. *Can J Psychiatry* 1985; 30: 426-427.

[38] Harvey AG, Bryant RA. Acute stress disorder across trauma populations. *J Nerv Ment Dis* 1999; 187: 443-446.

[39] Brewin CR, Andrews B, Rose S, Kirk M. Acute stress disorder and post-traumatic stress disorder in victims of violent crime. *Am J Psychiatry* 1999; 156: 360-366.

[40] Harvey AG, Bryant RA. Dissociative symptoms in acute stress disorder. *J Trauma Stress* 1999; 12:673-680.

[41] Harvey AG, Bryant RA. Acute stress disorder after mild traumatic brain injury. *J Nerv Ment Dis* 1998; 186:333-337.

[42] Difede J, Ptacek JT, Roberts J et al. Acute stress disorder after burn injury: a predictor of posttraumatic stress disorder? *Psychosom Med* 2002; 64: 826-834.

[43] Harvey AG, Bryant RA. The relationship between acute stress disorder and posttraumatic stress disorder: a 2-year prospective evaluation. *J Consult Clin Psychol* 1999; 67: 985-988.

[44] Shalev AY, Peri T, Canetti L, Schreiber S. Predictors of PTSD in injured trauma survivors: a prospective study. *Am J Psychiatry* 1996;153: 219-225.

[45] Holbrook TL, Hoyt DB, Anderson JP. The importance of gender on outcome after major trauma: Functional and psychologic outcomes in women versus men. *J Trauma* 2001; 50: 270-273.

[46] Holbrook TL, Hoyt DB, Stein MB, Sieber WJ. Perceived threat to life predicts posttraumatic stress disorder after major trauma: Risk factors and functional outcome. *J Trauma.* 2001; 51: 287-292.

[47] Breslau N, Davis GC, Andreski P, Peterson EL, Schultz LR. Sex differences in posttraumatic stress disorder. *Arch Gen Psychiatry* 1997; 54:1044-1048.

[48] Stein MB, Walker JR, Forde DR. Gender differences in susceptibility to posttraumatic stress disorder. *Behav Res Ther* 2000; 38: 619-628.

[49] Foa EB, Cashman L, Jaycox L, Perry K. The validation of a self-report measure of posttraumatic stress disorder, the posttraumatic diagnostic scale. *Psychol assessment* 1997; 9: 445-451.

[50] Bryant RA, Harvey AG. Avoidant coping style and posttraumatic stress following motor vehicle accidents. *Behav Res Ther* 1995;33:631-635.

[51] Horowitz MJ, Wilner N, Alvarez W. Impact of event scale: A measure of subjective stress. *Psychosom Med* 1979; 41: 209-218.

[52] Weiss D, Marmar C. The Impact of Event Scale -Revised. In: Wilson J, Keane T (Eds), *Assessing psychological trauma and PTSD.* 1997. New York: Guildford.

[53] Blake DD, Weathers FW, Nagy LM et al. The development of a clinician-administered PTSD scale. *J Trauma Stress* 1995; 8:75-90.

[54] Spitzer RL, Williams JBW, Gibbon M, First MB. *Structured clinical interview for DSM-IV (SCID-IV).* Biometric Research Department, New York State Psychiatric Institute, 1994.

[55] Davidson JR, Book SW, Colket JT et al. Assessment of a new self-rating scale for post-traumatic stress disorder *Psychol Med.* 1997;27:153-160.

[56] Keane TM, Caddell JM, Taylor KL. Mississippi Scale for Combat related post-traumatic stress disorder: three studies in reliability and validity. *J Consult Clin Psychol* 1988; 56: 85-90.

[57] Vreven DL, Gudanowski DM, King LA, King DW. The civilian version of the Mississippi PTSD Scale: a psychometric evaluation. *J Trauma Stress* 1995; 8: 91-109.

[58] Cardena E, Koopman C, Classen C, Waelde LC, Spiegel D. Psychometric properties of the Stanford Acute Stress Reaction Questionnaire (SASRQ): a valid and reliable measure of acute stress. *J Trauma Stress* 2000;13:719-734.

[59] Koopman C, Classen C, Spiegel D. Predictors of posttraumatic stress symptoms among survivors of the Oakland/Berkeley, Calif., Firestorm. *Am J Psychiatry* 1994; 151: 888-894.

[60] Schnaper N, Cowley RA. Overview: Psychiatric sequelae to multiple trauma. *Am J Psychiatry* 1976; 133: 883-890.

[61] Kornfeld DS. Psychiatric view of the Intensive Care Unit. *Br Med J* 1969;1: 108-110.

[62] Christie J. What is trauma? In: Langstaff D, Christie J. *Trauma Care- a team approach.* Oxford: Butterworth Heinemann, 2000 pp 3-12.

[63] Solomon SD, Johnson DM. Psychosocial treatment of posttraumatic stress disorder: a practice-friendly review of outcome research. *J Clin Psychol* 2002; 58: 947-959.

[64] Lee GK, Beaton RD, Ensign J. Eye movement desensitization and reprocessing. A brief and effective treatment for stress. *J Psychosoc Nurs Ment Health Serv* 2003 ;41: 22-31.

[65] Shepherd J, Stein K, Milne R. Eye movement desensitization and reprocessing in the treatment of post-traumatic stress disorder: a review of an emerging therapy. *Psychol Med* 2000; 30: 863-871.

[66] Shea MT, Zlotnick C. Understanding and treating PTSD: Introduction. *J Clin Psychol* 2002; 58:869-875.

[67] Krupnick JL. Brief psychodynamic treatment of PTSD: *J Clin Psychol.* 2002; 58: 919-932.

[68] Rose S, Bisson J, Wessely S. *Psychological debriefing for preventing post traumatic stress disorder (PTSD)* (Cochrane Review). In: The Cochrane Library, Issue 3, 2004. Chichester, UK: John Wiley & Sons, Ltd.

[69] Cardena E. Hypnosis in the treatment of trauma: a promising, but not fully supported, efficacious intervention. *Int J Clin Exp Hypn* 2000; 48:225-238.

[70] Phillips M. Potential contributions of hypnosis to ego-strengthening procedures in EMDR. Eye Movement Desensitization Reprocessing. *Am J Clin Hypn* 2001; 43: 247-262.

[71] Asnis GM, Kohn SR, Henderson M, Brown NL. SSRIs versus Non-SSRIs in post-traumatic stress disorder. An update with recommendations. *Drugs* 2004; 64: 383-404.

[72] Brady K, Pearlstein T, Asnis GM et al. Efficacy and safety of sertraline treatment of post-traumatic stress disorder: a randomized controlled trial. *JAMA* 2000; 283:1837-1844.

[73] Davidson JR, Rothbaum BO, van der Kolk BA, Sikes CR, Farfel GM. Multicenter, double- blind comparison of sertraline and placebo in the treatment of posttraumatic stress disorder. *Arch Gen Psychiatry* 2001; 58:485-492.

[74] Davidson JR, Pearlstein T, Londborg P et al. efficacy of sertraline in preventing relapse of posttraumatic stress disorder: results of a 28-week, double-blind, placebo controlled study. *Am J Psychiatry* 2001; 158: 1974-1981.

[75] Tucker P, Zaninelli R, Yehuda R, Ruggiero L, Dillingham K, Pitts CD. Paroxetine in the treatment of chronic posttraumatic stress disorder: results of a placebo-controlled, flexible-dosage trial. *J Clin Psychiatry.* 2001; 62: 860-868.

[76] Marshall RD, Beebe KL, Oldham M, Zaninelli R. Efficacy and safety of paroxetine treatment for chronic PTSD: a fixed-dose, placebo-controlled study. *Am J Psychiatry* 2001; 158:1982-1988.

[77] Connor KM, Sutherland SM, Tupler LA, Malik ML. Davidson JR. Fluoxetine in post-traumatic stress disorder: randomised, double-blind study. *Br J Psychiatry* 1999; 175:17-22.

[78] Martenyi F, Brown EB, Zhang H, Prakash A, Koke SC. Fluoxetine versus placebo in posttraumatic stress disorder. *J Clin Psychiatry* 2002; 63:199-206.

[79] Londborg PD, Hegel MT, Goldstein S et al. Sertraline treatment of post-traumatic stress disorder: results of 24 weeks of open-label continuation treatment. *J Clin Psychiatry* 2001; 62: 325-31.

[80] Martenyi F, Brown EB, Zhang H, Koke SC, Prakash A. Fluoxetine vs placebo in prevention of relapse in posttraumatic stress disorder. *Br J Psychiatry* 2002; 181: 315-320.

[81] Hamner MB, Freuh BC. Response to venlafaxine in previously antidepressant treatment-resistant combat veteran with post-traumatic stress disorder. *Int Clin Psychopharmacol* 1998; 13: 233-234.

[82] Hidalgo R, Hertzberg MA, Mellman T et al. Nefazodone in post-traumatic stress disorder: results from six open-label trials. Int Clin Psychopharmacol 1999; 14: 61-68.

[83] Menza MA. Withdrawal syndrome in a depressed patient treated with trazodone. *Am J Psychiatry* 1986; 143: 1195.

[84] Hargrave R. Serotonergic agents in the management of dementia and post-traumatic stress disorder. *Psychosomatics* 1993; 34: 461-462.

[85] Connor KM, Davidson JR, Weisler RH, Ahearn E. A pilot study of mirtazapine in post-traumatic stress disorder. *Int Clin Psychopharmacol* 1999; 14: 29-31.

[86] Foa EB, Davidson JRT, Frances A. The expert consensus guideline series: treatment of post-traumatic stress disorder: The Expert Consensus Panels for PTSD. *J Clin Psychiatry* 1999; 60 suppl 16: 1-75.

[87] Ballenger JC, Davidson JRT, Lecrubier Y et al. Consensus statement on post-traumatic stress disorder. From the International consensus group on depression and anxiety. *J Clin Psychiatry* 2000; 61 suppl 5:60-66.

[88] Kosten TR, Frank JB, Dan E, McDougle CJ, Giller EL Jr. Pharmacotherapy for post-traumatic stress disorder using phenelzine or imipramine. *J Nerv Ment Dis* 1991; 179: 366-370.

[89] Davidson JR, Kudler H, Smith R et al Treatment of post-traumatic stress disorder with amitryptyline and placebo. *Arch Gen Psychiatry* 1990; 47: 259-266.

[90] Reist C, Kauffmann CD, Haier RJ et al. A controlled trial of desipramine in 18 men with post-traumatic stress disorder. *Am J Psychiatry* 1989; 146: 513-516.

[91] Hertzberg MA, Butterfield MI, Feldman ME et al. A preliminary study of lamotrigine for the treatment of post-traumatic stress disorder. *Biol Psychiatry* 1999; 45:1226-1229.

[92] Braun BP, Greenberg D, Dasberg DH, Lerer B. Core symptoms of post-traumatic stress disorder unimproved by alprazolam treatment. *J Clin Psychiatry* 1990; 51: 236-238.

[93] Gelpin E, Bonne O, Peri T, Brandes D, Shalev AY. Treatment of recent trauma survivors with benzodiazepines: a prospective study. *J Clin Psychiatry* 1996; 57: 390-394.

[94] Stahl SM, *Essential psychopharmacology: neuroscientific basis and practical applications.* 2000. 2nd Ed. Cambridge. Cambridge University Press.
[95] Fichtner CG, Crayton JW. Buspirone in combat-related post-traumatic stress disorder. *J Clin Psychopharmacol* 1994; 14: 79-81.
[96] Hamner MB. Clozapine treatment for a veteran with comorbid psychosis and PTSD. *Am J Psychiatry* 1996; 153: 841.
[97] Petty F, Brannan S, Casada J etal. Olanzapine treatment for post-traumatic stress disorder: an open-label study. *Int Clin Psychopharmacol* 2001; 16:331-337.
[98] Famularo R, Kinscherff R, Fenton T. Propranolol treatment for childhood post-traumatic stress disorder, acute type: a pilot study. *Am J Dis Child* 1988; 142: 1244-1247.
[99] Franulic A, Horta E, Maturana R, Scherpenisse J, Carbonell C. Organic personality disorder after traumatic brain injury: cognitive, anatomic and psychosocial factors. A 6 months follow-up. *Brain Inj* 2000:14: 431-439.
[100] McClelland RJ. Psychosocial sequelae of head injury- anatomy of a relationship. *Br J Psychiatry* 1988; 153: 141-146.
[101] Arciniegas D, Adler L, Topkoff J, Kawthra E, Filley CM, Reite M. Attention and memory dysfunction after traumatic brain injury: cholinergic mechanisms, sensory gating, and a hypothesis for further investigation. *Brain Inj* 1999; 13:1-13.
[102] Jennett B, Bond MR. Assessment of outcome after severe brain damage. *The Lancet* 1975; i: 480-484.
[103] Brooks DN. The head injured family. *J Clin Exp Neuropsychol 1991*; 13:155-188.
[104] Hellawell DJ, Taylor RT, Pentland B. Cognitive and psychosocial outcome following moderate or severe traumatic brain injury. *Brain Inj* 1999; 13: 489-504.
[105] van Zomeren AH , van den Burg W. Residual complaints of patients two years after severe head injury. *J Neurol Neurosurg Psychiatry* 1985; 48: 21-28.
[106] Marsh NV. Social skill deficits following traumatic brain injury: assessment and treatment. In: McDonald S, Togher L, Code C (Eds) Communication disorders following traumatic brain injury. 1999. Hove, *Psychology Press*. Pp174-210.
[107] Oddy M, Humphrey M, Uttley D. Subjective impairment and social recovery after closed head injury. *J Neurol Neurosurg Psychiatry* 1978; 41: 611-616.
[108] Jacobs HE. The Los Angeles Head injury survey: procedures and initial findings. *Arch Phys Med Rehabil* 1988; 69: 425-431.
[109] Jennett B, Snoek J, Bond MR, Brooks N. Disability after severe head injury: observations on the use of the Glasgow outcome scale. *J Neurol Neurosurg Psychiatry* 1981; 44: 285-293.
[110] Karpman T, Wolfe S, Vargo JW. The psychological adjustment of adult clients and their parents following closed head injury. *J Rehabil Counseling* 1985; 17: 28-33.
[111] Livingston MG. Assessment of need for coordinated approach in families with victims of head injury. *Br Med J* (Clin Res Ed*)* 1986; 293: 742-744.
[112] Kersel DA, Marsh NV, Havill JH, Sleigh JW. Psychosocial functioning during the year following severe traumatic brain injury. *Brain Inj* 2001; 15: 683-696.
[113] Brooks DN, McKinlay W. Personality and behavioural change after severe blunt head injury-a relative's view. *J Neurol Neurosurg Psychiatry* 1983; 46: 336-344.

[114] Rosenbaum M, Najenson T. Changes in life patterns and symptoms of low mood as reported by wives of severely brain injured soldiers. *J Consult Clin Psychol* 1976; 44: 881-888.

[115] Bornstein RA, Miller HB, van Schoor JT. Neuropsychological deficit and emotional disturbance in head-injured patients. *J Neurosurg* 1989; 70: 509-513.

[116] Bourdon SE. Psychological impact of neurotrauma in the acute care setting. *Nurs Clin North Am* 1986; 21:629-640.

[117] Eames P, Wood R. Rehabilitation after severe brain injury: a follow-up study of a behaviour modification approach. *J Neurol Neurosurg Psychiatry* 1985; 48: 613-619.

[118] Mueller AD. Psychologic factors in rehabilitation of paraplegic patients. *Arch Phys Rehabil* 1962; 43: 151-159.

[119] Nagler B. Psychiatric aspects of cord injury. *Am J Psychiatry* 1950; 107: 49-56.

[120] Kennedy P, Rogers BA. Anxiety and depression after spinal cord injury: a longitudinal analysis. *Arch Phys Med Rehabil* 2000; 81: 932-937.

[121] Brackett TO, Condon N, Kindelan KM, Bassett L. The emotional care of a person with a spinal cord injury. *JAMA* 1984; 252: 793-795.

[122] Das S. Some psychological problems of quadriplegics. *Med J Aust* 1969; 2: 562-564.

[123] Curcoll ML. Psychological approach to the rehabilitation of the spinal cord injured: the contribution of relaxation techniques. *Paraplegia* 1992; 30: 425-427.

[124] Mathew KM, Ravichandran G, May K, Morsley K. The biopsychosocial model and spinal cord injury. *Spinal cord* 2001; 39: 644-649.

[125] Parker CM. Psycho-social transitions: Comparison to loss of a limb and loss of a spouse. *Br J Psychol* 1975; 127: 204-210.

[126] Fitzpatrick MC. The psychologic assessment and psychosocial recovery of the patient with an amputation. *Clin Orthop* 1999; 361: 98-107.

[127] Grunert BK, Smith CJ, Devine CA et al. Early psychological aspects of severe hand injury. *J Hand Surg* 1988; 13B: 177-180.

[128] Ribbers G, Mulder T, Rijken R. The phantom phenomena: a critical review. *Int J Rehabil Res* 1989; 12: 175-186.

[129] Sherman RA, Ernst JL, Barja RH, Bruno GM. Phantom pain: a lesson in the necessity for careful clinical research on chronic pain problems. *J Rehabil Res Dev* 1988; 25: 7-10.

[130] Tedstone JE, Tarrier N. An investigation of the prevalence of psychological morbidity in burn-injured patients. *Burns* 1997; 23: 550-554.

[131] West DA, Shuck JM. Emotional problems of the severely burned patient. *Surg Clin North Am* 1978; 58: 1189-1204.

[132] Ptacek JT, Patterson DR, Heimbach DM. Inpatient depression in persons with burns. *J Burn Care Rehabil* 2002; 23:1-9.

[133] Jonsson CE, Schüldt K, Linder J, Björnhagen V, Ekholm J. Rehabilitative, psychiatric, functional and aesthetic problems in patients treated for burn injuries- A preliminary follow-up study. *Acta Chir Plast* 1997; 39: 3-8.

[134] Menzies V. Depression and burn wounds. *Arch Psychiatr Nurs* 2000; 14: 199-206.

[135] Patterson DR, Everett JT, Bombardier CH, Questad KA, Lee VK, Marvin JA. Psychological effects of severe burn injuries. *Psychol Bull* 1993; 113: 362-378.

[136] Andreasen NJC. Neuropsychiatric complications in burn patients. *Int J Psychiatry Med* 1974; 5: 161-171.

[137] Perry SW, Cella DE, Falkenberg J, Heidrich G, Goodwin C. Pain perception in burn patients with stress disorders. *J Pain Symptom Manage* 1987; 2: 29-33.
[138] Patterson DR, Carrigan L, Questad KA, Robinson R. Post-traumatic stress disorder in hospitalized patients with burn injuries. *J Burn Care Rehabil* 1990; 11: 181-184.
[139] Taal LA, Faber AW. Dissociation as a predictor of psychopathology following burns injury. *Burns* 1997; 23: 400-403.
[140] Goodstein RK. Burns: An overview of clinical consequences affecting patient, staff and family. *Compr Psychiatry* 1985; 26: 43-57.
[141] Bowden ML, Feller I, Tholen D, Davidson TN, James MH. Self-esteem of severely burned patients. *Arch Phys Med Rehabil* 1980; 61: 449- 452.
[142] Martin HL. Parents' and children's reactions to burns and scalds in children. *Br J Med Psychol* 1970; 43: 183-191.
[143] Wright L, Fulwiler R. Long range emotional sequelae of burns: effects on children and their mothers. *Pediatr Res* 1974; 8: 931-934.
[144] Sawyer MG, Minde K, Zuker R. The burned child- scarred for life? A study of the psychosocial impact of a burn injury at different developmental stages. *Burns Incl Therm Inj* 1983; 9: 205-213.
[145] Jamerson PA, Scheibmeir M, Bott MJ, Crighton F, Hinton RH, Cobb AK. The experiences of families with a relative in the intensive care unit. *Heart Lung* 1996; 25: 467-474.
[146] Breslau N, Staruch KS, Mortimer EA. Psychological distress in mothers of disabled children. *Am J Dis Child* 1982; 136: 682-686.
[147] Perez-San Gregorio MA, Blanco-Picabia A, Murillo-Cabezas F, Domínguez-Roldan JM, Sanchez B, Nunez-Roldan A. Psychological problems in the family members of gravely traumatised patients admitted into an intensive care unit. *Intensive Care Med* 1992; 18:278-281.
[148] Hodovanic B, Reardon D, Reese W, Hedges B. Family crisis intervention program in the medical intensive care unit. *Heart Lung* 1984; 13: 243-249.
[149] de Vries AP, Kassam-Adams N, Cnaan A, Sherman-Slate E, Gallagher PR, Winston FK. Looking beyond the physical injury: posttraumatic stress disorder in children and parents after pediatric traffic injury. *Pediatrics* 1999; 104: 1293-1299.
[150] Wesson DE, Scorpio RJ, Spence LJ et al. The physical, psychological, and socioeconomic costs of pediatric trauma. *J Trauma* 1992; 33: 252-255.
[151] Hall KM, Karzmark P, Stevens M, Englander J, O'Hare P, Wright J. Family stressors in traumatic brain injury: a two-year follow-up. *Arch Phys Med Rehabil* 1994; 75: 876-884.
[152] Resnick C. The effect of head injury on family and marital stability. *Soc Work Health Care* 1993; 18: 49-62.
[153] Hickey M. What are the needs of families of critically ill patients? A review of the literature since 1976. *Heart Lung* 1990; 19: 401-415.
[154] Montogomery V, Oliver R, Reisner A, Fallat ME. The effect of severe traumatic brain injury on the family. *J Trauma* 2002; 52:1121-1124.
[155] Civetta JM. Beyond technology: Intensive care in the 1980s. *Crit Care Med* 1981; 9: 763-767.
[156] DeLauder L. Needs of grieving parents in sudden death situations. *J Emerg Nurs* 1983: 9: 303-305.

[157] Gentry WD, Parkes KR. Psychologic stress in intensive care unit and non-intensive care unit nursing. A review of the past decade. *Heart Lung* 1982;11: 43-47.

[158] Hay D, Oken D. The psychological stresses of intensive care unit nursing. *Psychosom Med* 1972; 34:109-118.

[159] Spoth R, Konewko P. Intensive care staff stressors and life event changes across multiple settings and work units. *Heart Lung* 1987; 16: 278-284.

In: Posttraumatic Stress Disorder: New Research
Editor: Guida D. Kume, pp.115-145
ISBN 1-60021-078-3

Chapter 4

POSTTRAUMATIC STRESS: CONCEPTS, MODELS AND NEUROCHEMICAL ALTERATIONS

Regina Margis*, Carla Dalmaz and Carlos-Alberto Gonçalves
Programas de Pós-Graduação em Bioquímica e Neurociências, Instituto de Ciências Básicas da Saúde, Universidade Federal do Rio Grande do Sul, Porto Alegre, Brazil

ABSTRACT

Posttraumatic stress disorder (PTSD) is a condition that has a lifetime prevalence of approximately 7.8%. It is defined in DSM-IV as an anxiety disorder in which a person has been exposed to a traumatic event, involving either witnessing or experiencing threatened death or injury or witnessing or experiencing threat to physical integrity. The response to the traumatic event must involve fear or horror. In PTSD, the patient develops symptoms in three domains: reexperiencing the trauma, avoiding stimuli associated with the trauma and experiencing symptoms of increased autonomic arousal. Exposure to stress can have numerous pathophysiological effects. In order to understand the neurobiology of PTSD, it is important to establish animal models of PTSD, in which different aspects of this disorder may be studied. Some of these models include inescapable footshocks in a shuttle-box, exposure to a predator, underwater trauma, and early stress models. Exposure of animals to these situations may lead to behavioral changes such as maladaptive responses to stress, avoidance, and increase in responsiveness to external stimuli in a stressful context. The authors broach endocrine changes in the HPA axis, biochemical alterations in neurotrophic factors, cytokines, and neurotransmission at serotonergic, noradrenergic, glutamatergic and GABAergic synapses. The use of biochemical peripheral markers is discussed, as well as limitations and contributions of the current investigation into this psychiatric disorder.

* Corresponding author: Regina Margis, E-mail: regina.margis@terra.com.br; Fax: 55-51-3316 5534

INTRODUCTION

Mounting evidence has demonstrated that exposure to stress results in long-standing changes in biological stress response systems that underlie many symptoms of stress-related disorders, such as posttraumatic stress disorder (PTSD) [Vermetten and Bremner, 2002].

PTSD has been recognized for more than a century, but with different denominations, such as nervous shock, compensation neurosis, shell shock, or war neurosis. Nowadays, posttraumatic stress disorder (PTSD) is defined in the Diagnostic and Statistical Manual of Mental Disorders, revised fourth edition (DSM-IV-TR) [American Psychiatric Association, 2000] as an anxiety disorder in which a person has been exposed to a traumatic event (or events), such as natural disasters, road accidents, violent assault, torture or imprisonment in concentration camps. DSM-IV-TR specifies that the traumatic event involves either witnessing or experiencing threatened death or injury or witnessing or experiencing threat to physical integrity. The person's response to the traumatic event must involve fear, helplessness or horror.

In PTSD, the patient develops symptoms in three domains: reexperiencing the trauma, avoiding stimuli associated with the trauma and experiencing symptoms of increased autonomic arousal. Thus, the traumatic event is persistently reexperienced in recurrent and intrusive recollections of the event, recurrent dreams, and the patient acts as if the traumatic event is recurring and presents intense psychological distress or physiologic reactivity upon exposure to cues that symbolize or resemble the traumatic event. A person with PTSD presents persistent avoidance of stimuli associated with the trauma and numbing of general responsiveness with three or more of the following: efforts to avoid thoughts, feelings, or conversations associated with trauma, efforts to avoid activities, places or people that arouse recollections of the trauma; inability to recall an important aspect of the trauma; markedly diminished interest or participation in significant events; feelings of detachment or estrangement; restrict range of affect; and sense of foreshortened future. This subject must present persistent symptoms of increased arousal, indicated by two or more of the following: difficulty falling or staying asleep, irritability or outbursts of anger, difficulty concentrating, hypervigilance, and exaggerated startle response; these symptoms were not present before the traumatic event.

The diagnosis of PTSD is made when symptoms persist for at least one month [American Psychiatric Association, 2000]. These symptoms can develop during the first month following the trauma, or may be delayed for several months or years. PTSD is specified as acute if the duration of symptoms is less than three months; and as chronic if symptoms persist for three or more months. According to DSM-IV-TR [American Psychiatric Association, 2000], PTSD can be specified as with delayed onset when onset of symptoms is at least six months after the stressor.

PTSD is a serious and debilitating medical condition [Kessler, 2000]. Studies document high rates of psychiatric comorbidity among subjects with PTSD [Kessler et al, 1995; Kessler, 2000].Females were found to be more than twice as likely as males to have lifetime PTSD. Surveys of the general population indicate that PTSD affects approximately 15 to 24% of those exposed to traumatic events [Breslau et al, 1991; Kessler et al, 1995]. The lifetime prevalence of this disorder in the general population is approximately 8%, according to DSM-III-R criteria [Kessler et al, 1995].

PTSD symptoms may persist for years. Kluznick (1986) and Goldstein (1987) observed PTSD symptoms among survivors of imprisonment during the World War II, despite the forty-years that had passed since their traumatic experiences. Its prevalence and incidence rates vary according to individual circumstances, such as past stress history, psychiatric comorbidity and biological vulnerability [Yehuda et al, 1995; 1998a; 1999]. Some authors propose that one of the predictors of chronic PTSD is the nature of the traumatic stress [Yehuda et al, 1998]. However, it is important to note that a substantial number of subjects exposed to trauma – acute or chronic - do not develop PTSD (see Figure 1).

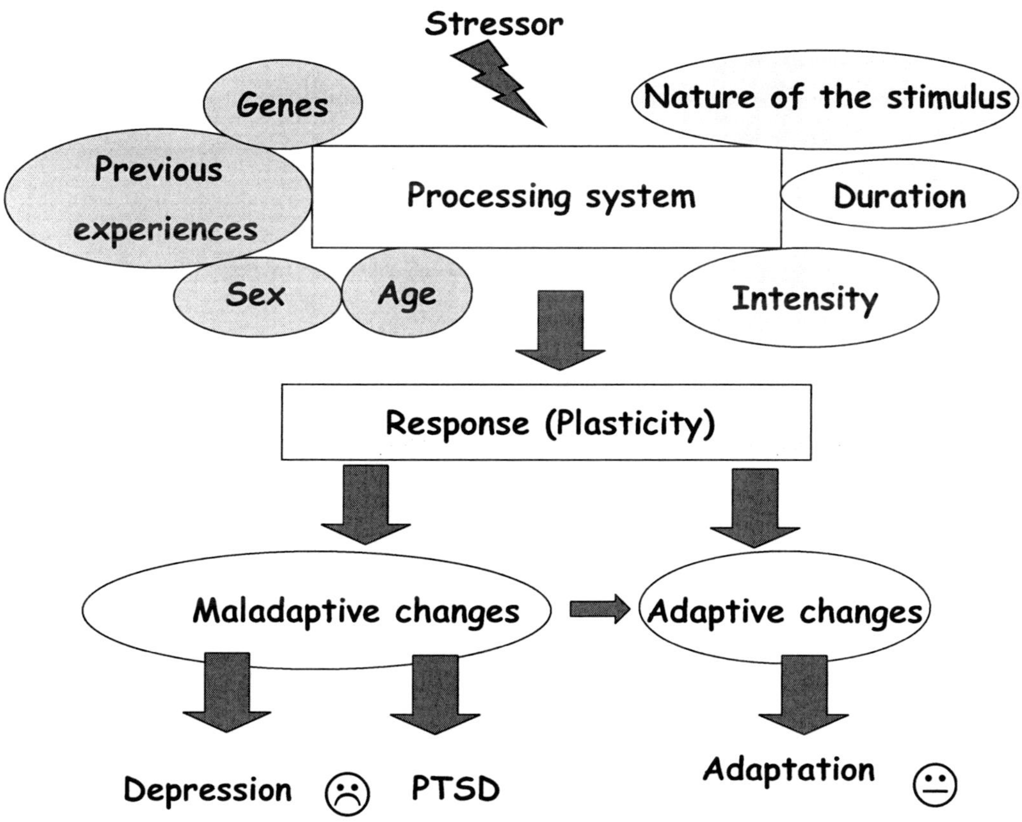

Figure 1. Evolution of a traumatic stress response. Exposure to stress transforms individuals, leading to adaptive changes that incorporate into the individual's experience, changing the nervous system (plasticity). This processing is influenced by individual vulnerability (gray balloons) and by characteristics of the stimulus (light gray balloons). The outcome may be adaptive, or maladaptive, leading to pathologies, such as PTSD and depression.

Exposure to stressors can have numerous physiological and behavioral effects. Due to the complexity of PTSD pathophysiology, it is important to understand the neurobiology of PTSD, considering neurotransmitters, hormones and cytokines involved. In fact, many studies have been carried out, but several questions remain without answer.

Animal Models of PTSD

As a consequence of exposure to a significantly severe stressor, a subject will experience a stress response, which may sometimes develop into PTSD. In order to better understand neurochemical and psychopharmacological aspects of this disorder, several laboratories have tried to establish animal models of PTSD, in which behavioral, autonomic and hormonal changes persist after the initial trauma. Although a rat model will probably not present all the complexity of this disorder in humans, it is believed that it will help the study of its mechanisms.

A number of animal models have been developed in which exposure to intense stressors results in long lasting altered responsivity to aversive challenges, which mimic many of the changes seen in PTSD. Whereas exposure to a stressor is a necessary condition for PTSD, this factor may not be sufficient to consider such a model as a posttraumatic stress disorder-animal model. It is important to determine what kind of stress will be useful to precipitate PTSD-like biochemical and behavioral symptoms, with regard to the induction of core PTSD symptoms (reexperiencing the trauma, avoidance stimuli associated with the trauma and hyperarousal). One of the limitations of animal models is the impossibility of evaluating aspects concerning intrusive symptoms. Several criteria have been proposed, which must be fulfilled by animal models of stress for them to be useful for understanding the induction of PTSD. Yehuda and coworkers (1993) proposed some aspects for evaluating the relevance of individual stress paradigms to the phenomenology of PTSD. They suggest that animals exposed to even brief stressors could present behavioral effects that may resemble PTSD symptoms (because PTSD can develop after acute or chronic traumatic stress). Therefore, these authors propose that models depending on long-lasting stressors are not relevant to the induction of PTSD. Another feature of these models is that the stressor should produce biological alterations that persist over time (because diagnosis of PTSD can only exist if core symptoms persist for at least one month - as described above). Of course, the extent to which the animal data is transferable to humans remains to be determined.

Since PTSD may occur in humans exposed chronically to stressors or after a single exposure to a traumatic event, animal models have been developed using both these situations: one exposure to an intense stressor, and paradigms in which repeated exposure to an aversive stimulus is associated with progressive intensification of a behavioral or physiologic response. It should be pointed out, however, that human patients are exposed to different life events, while an experimental animal has lived all its life in standard conditions. Furthermore, individual differences exist, and exposure to a stressor per se is not unequivocally predictive of development of PTSD. In humans, only a proportion of subjects exposed to a certain stressor will develop the disorder. This factor has been considered in some recent studies, in which the exposed animals have been separated into two groups, representing the extremes of the response spectrum, one more vulnerable (or maladapted) and another less vulnerable (or well adapted) to stress [Cohen et al, 2003; 2004; Cohen and Zohar, 2004]. We describe below some animal models of PTSD.

Several stress paradigms have been used as a stimulus to model PTSD. One of these is the exposure to a predator, which is a life-threatening experience for the animal. In these models, lasting increases in anxiety-like behavior (ALB) are observed, for example, as assessed in the elevated plus maze after 5 to 10-min exposure of a rat to a cat [Adamec et al,

1993; Margis et al, 2004] or to cat scent [Cohen and Zohar, 2004]. Rats become more anxious in the plus maze, as measured days or even weeks after the exposure [Adamec and Shallow, 1993; Adamec et al, 1997; Adamec et al, 1999; Cohen et al, 2003; 2004], and develop abnormal activity of the hypothalamic-pituitary-adrenal (HPA) axis; both lower [Cohen et al, 2000] and higher [Cohen et al, 2003; Cohen and Zohar, 2004] plasma corticosterone and ACTH levels were observed, as well as disordered physiological measures, such as increased sympathetic activity [Cohen et al, 2003]. It is important to mention that different strains of animals may exhibit different plasma corticosterone levels, both before and after exposure to this type of stressor [Adamec et al, 1997]. Another model in which the animal is exposed to a life threatening experience is underwater trauma [Cohen et al, 2004]. Using this model, significant memory deficits were observed in the water maze some weeks after the stress [Richter-Levin, 1998]; since the authors used a water maze task to evaluate memory in animals that had been submitted to a trauma involving water, it may be interesting observe the effects in some additional tasks. The animals were also observed to present high anxiety levels [Richter-Levin, 1998].

The exposure to uncontrollable stressors, such as inescapable shock, produces a set of behavioral changes such as learned helplessness, and this paradigm has been proposed to be a model of depression and of anxiety-related disorders such as PTSD [van der Kolk et al, 1989; Duffy and Malloy, 1994]. In order to maintain the initial trauma, some authors use a re-exposure to a traumatic stressor [van der Kolk et al, 1989; Ottenweller et al, 1989; Servatius et al, 1995; Garrick et al, 1997] or repeated exposures to situational reminders [Stam et al, 2000; Maier, 2001; Sawamura et al, 2004; Louvart et al, 2005], which are believed to induce re-experiencing of the aversive event. Several parameters were found to be altered, including higher anxiety levels [Louvart et al, 2005], altered locomotor activity, depending on the moment when it is measured [Ottenweller et al, 1989; Koba et al, 2001; Sawamura et al, 2004], altered social behavior [Louvart et al, 2005], exaggerated startle reflex or non-habituation of the startle response [Pynoos et al, 1996; Garrick et al, 1997; Garrick et al, 2001], opioid-mediated stress-induced analgesia [van der Kolk et al, 1989], greater avoidance performance (interpreted as the propensity to recall unpleasant events in PTSD) [Pare, 1996; Koba et al, 2001; Sawamura et al, 2004], increases in basal corticosterone [Servatius et al, 1995; Ottenweller et al, 1989), while others have observed a blunted corticosterone response to stress [Louvart et al, 2005]. These animal models appear to produce some behavioral changes analogous to those seen in patients with PTSD [Pynoos et al, 1996]. Additionally, since the amygdala becomes hyperactive in posttraumatic stress disorder [Davis et al, 1997], and amygdala kindling enhances emotionality [Kellett and Kokkinidis, 2004], a different model of PTSD has also been proposed, in which an autonomic dysfunction is induced, triggered by the laboratory model of kindling [Scaer, 2001; Kellett and Kokkinidis, 2004].

Besides inescapable shock, fear conditioning has been suggested as a model of PTSD. In a recent review [Bonne et al, 2004], the authors propose that reexperiencing symptoms in PTSD results from implementation of impaired fear conditioning-like mechanisms in response to severe stress, when even with the aversive event absent, a neutral stimulus would trigger reexperiencing in PTSD, and would evoke an emotional response similar to the unconditioned response [Bonne et al, 2004]. This procedure could lead to several of the characteristics mentioned above. Lasting disruption in sleep architecture has also been observed in this model [Pawlyk et al, 2005].

A model using stress-restress (restraint followed by a forced swim and exposure to ether vapors), a paradigm in which repeated exposure to stimuli is associated with progressive intensification of a neurophysiological, behavioral, or pharmacological response, has also been proposed as a model for PTSD [Liberzon et al, 1997; Harvey et al, 2004; Khan and Liberzon, 2004]. Rats are exposed to a single session of prolonged stress, such as the session described above, and briefly restressed seven days later. Animals showed enhanced hypothalamus-pituitary-adrenal (HPA) negative feedback in comparison to naive animals [Liberzon et al, 1997], and exaggerated acoustic startle response [Khan and Liberzon, 2004].

Several data suggest that early life experiences can affect physiology and behavior in a long-lasting manner. A putative risk factor for PTSD is early childhood experiences of abuse and neglect [McEwen, 2000; de Kloet et al, 2005]. Repeated separation of neonatal rat pups from their mother results in many long-lasting alterations in physiology and behavior [Post et al, 1998], and animal models of early life stress likely represent the biological basis of an enhanced risk for psychopathology [Bremne and Vermetten, 2001; Heim and Nemeroff, 2002]. Early stressors such as maternal separation result in lasting effects on stress-responsive neurobiological systems, including the HPA axis and noradrenergic systems. In our opinion, an animal model of maternal separation may represent a risk population, which would be more vulnerable to the development of PTSD, when exposed to a threatening experience, such as inescapable shock, stress-restress, etc.

Many of the disturbances observed in the models cited above resemble PTSD symptoms, and thus these models may be useful for studying this disorder. It should be mentioned that some animal models for psychiatric disorders, such as PTSD, lack specificity (i.e., some situations have been proposed to model different disorders). In this case, some animal models of depression are also proposed as PTSD models (e.g., inescapable shock). Therefore, it is important to carefully choose the parameters to be evaluated. For example, anhedonia is usually used as a characteristic of depression in animal models, as well as learned helplessness [Thiebot et al, 1992; Willner, 1997]. Increased startle response and freezing are examples of responses observed in models of anxiety, including PTSD [Nijenhuis et al, 1998; Khan and Liberzon, 2004; Cohen et al, 2004]. Moreover, as was mentioned above, no rat model is expected to reflect the complexity of this disorder in humans. Nevertheless, animal paradigms may lead to hypotheses that will help the study of PTSD mechanisms and help the screening for drugs with potential relevance to its treatment.

NEUROCHEMICAL ALTERATIONS IN PTSD

Neurotransmitters

Catecholaminergic System

Acute stress and fear activate locus ceruleus / noradrenaline system [for a review, see Vermetten and Bremner, 2002]. Challenge paradigms have been used to test noradrenergic reactivity in patients with PTSD. Evidence of increased catecholaminergic activity has been documented in PTSD patients [Yehuda et al, 1992 and Tanaka et al, 2000].

Noradrenergic hyperactivity has been considered as a mechanism for development of intrusive and emotional memories of trauma. In fact, preclinical and clinical research studies have found noradrenaline to be important in arousal, attention and memory [Southwick et al, 1999]. The expression of both conditioned and unconditioned fear is known to depend on the activation of amygdaloid noradrenaline [Shulz et al, 2002].

We describe below some studies evaluating catecholaminergic activity in PTSD patients, these include: the measurement of serum and cerebral spinal fluid (CSF) noradrenaline concentrations, plasma 3-methoxy-4-hydroxyphenylglycol (MHPG, a noradrenaline metabolite) levels, and urinary excretion of adrenaline, noradrenaline (NA), dopamine (DA) and homovanilic acid (HVA, a dopamine metabolite), and challenges with yoimbine (an alpha-2 antagonist) and clonidine (an alpha-2 agonist).

Heightened blood pressure, heart rate, and skin conductance have been reported in PTSD patients compared to healthy subjects and to other psychiatric patients [Southwick et al, 1993; Southwick et al, 1999]. Intravenous yohimbine was observed to induce panic attacks (70%) and flashbacks (40%) and increases in systolic blood pressure and heart rate in a subgroup of patients with PTSD. This same drug was also found to induce significant increases in core PTSD symptoms in these patients, such as intrusive traumatic thoughts, emotional numbing and grief [Southwick et al, 1993; Southwick et al, 1999]. Additionally, a study using positron emission tomography (PET) reported a significant difference in brain metabolic response to yohimbine in Vietnam combat veterans with PTSD compared with healthy subjects in prefrontal, temporal, parietal, and orbitofrontal cortice. Metabolism tended to decrease in patients with PTSD, and increase in healthy subjects following administration of yohimbine [Bremner et al,1997a].

Clonidine, which reduces noradrenergic activity, was shown to ameliorate PTSD symptoms [Kinzie and Leung, 1989; Donnelly, 2003]. Growth hormone (GH) response to clonidine was assessed to evaluate noradrenergic receptor function. This response was significantly blunted in Vietnam veterans with PTSD, displaying no depression, compared to both the depressed PTSD group and the control group [Morris et al, 2004]. Another study, however, did not find differences between PTSD subjects and healthy controls in GH basal levels nor in responses to challenge with desmethylimipramine, a NA reuptake inhibitor. These authors also observed that PTSD patients had significantly higher baseline NA levels [Yatham et al, 1996]. Some investigations using plasma measurements of adrenaline and NA have provided evidence of noradrenergic dysfunction in PTSD patients compared with controls and also following exposure to stress [McFall et al, 1990; Blanchard et al, 1991].

Under unstimulated conditions, increased levels of plasma noradrenaline (NA) were observed in PTSD subjects [Spivak et al, 1999], presenting or not a secondary depression [Yehuda et al, 1998b]. Considering receptor binding sites, a reduced total number of α2-adrenergic receptor binding sites was identified on platelets in PTSD subjects [Perry et al, 1987]. The authors suggested that this down-regulation could result from a chronic elevation of NA levels in these patients.

CSF noradrenaline concentrations were also significantly higher in combat veterans with chronic PTSD than in the healthy men, using CSF serial samples obtained over a 6-hour period through an indwelling subarachnoid catheter. Moreover, CSF NA levels strongly and positively correlated with the severity of PTSD symptoms [Geracioti et al, 2001].

Noradrenergic system activation may also be evaluated by measuring MHPG. Data demonstrate that baseline MHPG values are not significantly different in PTSD patients compared to control groups [Yehuda et al, 1998b]. However, another study observed significantly lower basal MHPG and reduced MHPG volatility to clonidine challenge

(Marshall et al 2002) in PTSD patients. Moreover, a challenge assay with yoimbine demonstrated higher plasma MHPG levels in patients with PTSD than in healthy male controls [Southwick et al, 1993].

In addition, plasma dopamine beta-hydroxylase activity, an enzyme involved in the pathway that synthesizes NA, was observed to be significantly higher in PTSD patients with psychotic features compared to patients without psychotic symptoms [Hammer and Gold, 1998], suggesting an increased noradrenergic activity. However, increased activity of an intracellular enzyme, when observed in plasma, could also be due to other causes.

Most studies have reported higher urinary excretion of adrenaline and noradrenaline in PTSD patients compared to healthy [Kosten et al, 1987] and psychiatric controls [Yehuda et al, 1992; 1998b], as well as in children with chronic PTSD [De Bellis et al, 1999], or exposed for the first time to acute trauma [Delahanty et al, 2005]; high initial urinary epinephrine levels immediately following the traumatic event, were significantly correlated with acute PTSD symptoms, mainly in boys [Delahanty et al, 2005]. On the other hand, Mellman and coworkers (1995) did not find differences in 24-hour urine excretion of noradrenaline and of MHPG, however, a significantly higher ratio of nocturnal versus daytime excretions of MHPG was found in PTSD patients.

Taking all these data together, results suggest an increased noradrenergic activity in PTSD patients, compared to healthy subjects or to other psychiatric patients. This increased activity is observed in both central and peripheral noradrenergic systems.

Some studies have evaluated the dopaminergic system in PTSD patients. Most studies have observed increased plasma and urinary DA. For example, plasma DA levels were shown to be significantly higher in CR-PTSD compared to major depressive patients and healthy control subjects [Hamner and Diamond, 1993]. DA 24-hour urinary excretion was higher in mothers of childhood cancer survivors with PTSD [Glover et al, 2003], in CR-PTSD inpatients [Yehuda et al, 1992], and in CR-PTSD outpatients [Spivak et al, 1999] compared to controls; in addition, no differences between CR-PTSD outpatients and controls have been reported in urinary DA levels [Yehuda et al, 1992]. Furthermore, mean 24-hour urinary excretion of HVA was significantly higher in PTSD patients than in control subjects and correlated significantly with total Impact of Event Scale score, particularly with avoidant symptom cluster [Spivak et al, 1999]. Finally, it is important to mention that there are also findings suggesting that genetically determined aspects in the dopaminergic system may contribute to PTSD susceptibility among trauma survivors [Comings, 1996; Segman, 2002].

Serotonergic System

Many preclinical studies suggest the involvement of serotonin (5-HT) in stress [see Vermetten and Bremner, 2002, for a review]. Serotonergic projections to locus ceruleus (LC) have been shown, and serotonergic function is believed to influence the output of the NA pathway. Similarly, there is evidence for an interaction between 5-HT and NMDA receptors; serotonin may potentiate NMDA receptor binding and activity [McEwen, 2000b].

Central serotonergic system dysfunction has been correlated with impulse control, and impulsive-aggressive behavior [Cocarro, 1989]. Low CSF 5-hydroxyindolacetic acid (a 5-HT metabolite) has been associated with suicide [Asberg et al, 1976; Mann, 1987]. This consideration is important because PTSD is an anxiety disorder with frequent suicidal behavior and high rates of comorbidities [Kessler et al, 1995; 1999].

Studies aiming to evaluate the role of serotonin receptors in CR-PTSD have used meta-chlorophenylpiperazine (m-CPP) and 31% of patients with PTSD were seen to experience m-CPP induced panic attack and 27% experienced flashbacks. In the same study, yoimbine was used to evaluate noradrenergic reactivity. Among PTSD patients, 81% develop panic attack with m-CPP or yoimbine; interestingly, patients did not experience this attack with both drugs [Southwick et al, 1997], suggesting a different underlying molecular basis for this disorder. Spivak and coworkers (1999) found significantly lower plasma 5-HT in male outpatients with untreated CR-PTSD, compared to healthy control subjects. As described above, these PTSD patients showed significantly elevated plasma NE levels, thus, the NE/5-HT ratio was higher in PTSD than in control subjects [Spivak et al, 1999].

In addition, changes in 5-HT transporters have been suggested in PTSD. Decreased [Maes et al, 1999] and increased [Arora et al, 1993] affinities of platelet binding sites to [^{3}H] paroxetine have been described. Recently, Bonne and coworkers (2005) compared 5-HT type 1A receptor ($5HT_{1A}R$) binding between PTSD patients and healthy subjects using positron emission tomography. No significant differences in $5HT_{1A}R$ were observed in midbrain raphe, anterior temporopolar cortex, posterior cingulated, anterior cingulated, anterior insula and mesiotemporal cortex. It is important note that, in this particular study, most of the patients had psychiatric comorbidities.

Clinical trials using selective serotonin reuptake inhibitors (SSRI) may also be used to evaluate a role for 5-HT in PTSD. PTSD treatment with SSRI has a beneficial effect on intrusion, avoidance and arousal symptoms, and reduces irritability and anger [Davidson et al, 2001; Marshall et al, 2001; Martenyi et al, 2002]. Some SSRI (sertraline and paroxetine) have been approved for PTSD treatment by the Food and Drug Administration.

With respect to treatment with paroxetine, a study has reported that PTSD patients showed a significant improvement in symptoms and in verbal declarative memory after paroxetine treatment during 9-12 months [Vermetten et al, 2003]; furthermore, an increase in hippocampal volume of 4.6% was observed. However, these changes in hippocampal volume were not associated with improvement in PTSD symptoms and did not present a significant relationship with memory improvement [Vermetten et al, 2003].

Although the hippocampal volume data mentioned above did not present any correlation with PTSD symptoms, these reports are important since many studies have described reduced hippocampal size during magnetic resonance imaging in adults with CR-PTSD or childhood sexual or physical abuse, when compared with healthy or trauma control subjects [Bremner et al, 1995; Gurvits et al, 1996; Stein et al, 1997; Bremner et al, 1997b]. More recently, Winter and Irle (2004) demonstrated a significantly smaller volume of the right hippocampus in adult burn patients with PTSD compared to control subjects. However, the same alteration was observed in patients without PTSD (or any other current or lifetime psychiatric diagnosis) exposed to the same trauma. Similar data were obtained in individuals who were exposed to accidents [Bonne et al, 2001].

Opioid System

Exposure to stressors is known to induce opiate-mediated effects. For example, acute exposure to stress may produce immediate analgesia [Lewis et al, 1980; Bodnar, 1986], and brain homogenates of rats submitted to inescapable shock show a decreased density of μ-opiate receptors compared to rats submitted to escapable shock [Stuckey et al, 1989]. Rats subjected to repeated restraint stress also display decreased opioid receptors density in frontal cortex, hippocampus and spinal cord [Dantas et al, 2005]. Otherwise, acute [Nikulina et al, 1999] and repeated exposure [Nikulina et al, 2005] to social defeat stress in rats induces upregulation of μ-opioid receptor mRNA expression in the ventral tegmental area.

Evidence supports the hypothesis that CRF and endogenous opioids interact in the LC to co-regulate the stress response. It has also been observed that CRF and opioids have opposing effects on LC discharge [Valentino and Van Bockstaele, 2001]. Since the LC-NA system has an alerting function, and considering PTSD symptoms, such as hyperarousal, it is important to highlight the possibility of a role for the opioid system in PTSD.

Nishith and coworkers (2002) compared symptoms and stress-induced analgesia of PTSD battered and non-battered women. An audiotape recording of the participant's assault report was made. Listening to this tape, a greater degree of analgesia was significantly associated with PTSD symptoms (mainly PTSD related arousal symptoms) and depression.

Pitman and coworkers (1990), studying Vietnam veterans, observed that naloxone (an opiate antagonist) was able to reverse analgesia induced by exposure to a combat film, while the placebo group showed a 30% decrease in reported pain intensity ratings to heat stimuli. Vietnam-veterans with combat-related PTSD demonstrated, during exposure to traumatic reminders, reduced sensitivity to pain (numbing) and this reduction was reversed by naloxone [Van der Kolk et al, 1989].

The studies reported above suggest increased activity of opiate systems in PTSD. However, Hoffman and coworkers (1989) found decreased concentrations of plasma beta-endorphin. Otherwise, Baker and coworkers (1997) did not find differences in plasma beta-endorphin levels between PTSD patients and controls. Additionally, increased CSF beta-endorphin levels were observed in PTSD patients and there was a negative correlation between these levels and intrusive and avoidant PTSD symptoms [Baker et al, 1997]. These results should be considered with caution and future studies are necessary, because many doubts persist like physiology and source of beta-endorphin in CSF and the role of the opioid activity in stress response. Therefore, further studies will help to elucidate all intricacies of opioid system activation in PTSD.

Glutamatergic and GABAergic Pathways

In 1993, Moghaddam presented evidence to show that stress increases neuronal release of excitatory amino acids in a regionally selective manner.

Glutamate acts as a neurotransmitter via several types of receptor, such as the N-methyl-D-aspartate (NMDA) receptor, non-NMDA ionotropic receptor subtypes and metabotropic receptors. Adamec et al (1999) described that blockade of NMDA receptors in rats with MK-801 (noncompetitive NMDA antagonist), given 30 min prior to exposure to a cat, promotes approaches to cats during exposure, and this behavior was eliminated by prior injection of Prazosin (alpha-1 noradrenergic receptor antagonist). This result suggests an involvement of NMDA and alpha-1 noradrenergic receptors in the mediation of anxiety-like response during exposure to a predator. Moreover, it has been shown that MK-801, and 7-amino-phosphono-heptanoic acid (AP7) or (±)-3-(2-carboxypiperazin-4-yl)-propyl-l-phosphonic acid (CPP), both competitive NMDA receptor blockers, given 30 min prior to exposure to a cat prevents the increase in anxiety-like behavior assessed 1 week later. However, MK-801 or AP7 given to a cat 30 min after exposure does not prevent the increase in anxiety-like behavior seen one week later.

In addition, it is interesting to note that animal studies show that stressful events, both acute and chronic, impair long-term potentiation (LTP) induction in the hippocampus [Garcia, 2001]. LTP induction in the hippocampus is dependent upon NMDA receptor activation [Collingridge and Bliss, 1995]. Plavides and coworkers (2002) demonstrated that exposure of rats to chronic stress produces a suppression in hippocampal LTP induction. In fact, stress may induce changes in threshold for synaptic plasticity for LTP and memory formation [Garcia, 2001].

In contrast, GABA suppresses hippocampal LTP [Douglas, 1982]. Moreover, intra-amygdala muscimol ($GABA_A$ receptor agonist) infusion in rats before uncontrollable restraint-tail shock stress blocked some stress-induced physiological and behavioral effects. Muscimol-infused stressed animals showed unimpaired spatial memory and their hippocampal slices demonstrated robust LTP comparable with unstressed rats. However, immediate post-stress infusions of muscimol into amygdala failed to interfere with stress impairments of LTP and spatial memory [Kim et al, 2005].

Still considering animal models, it has been observed that animals exposed to stressors such as footshock or forced swimming present decreased benzodiazepine receptor densities in cerebral cortices. Recently, Matsumoto and coworkers (2005) proposed that cortical $GABA_A$ receptors contribute to the response to contextual fear conditioning.

The role of benzodiazepine receptors in anxiety symptoms is well accepted; therefore, an alteration in these receptors in PTSD patients could be expected. In fact, studies in PTSD patients have reported a decreased platelet peripheral-type benzodiazepine receptor when compared to controls [Gavish et al, 1996]. A single photon emission computerized tomography (SPECT) image with (^{125}I)iomazenyl showed that CR-PTSD patients had 41% lower distribution volumes (by measurement of benzodiazepine binding) in the prefrontal cortex relative to case-matched healthy subjects [Bremner et al, 2000]. On the other hand, another study using CR-PTSD and healthy veterans in a SPECT study with [^{123}I] iomazenyl, found no difference in benzodiazepine receptors in any region [Fujita et al, 2004].

Another way to evaluate the GABAergic system is to measure plasma GABA levels. Using this approach, Vaiva and coworkers (2004) measured plasma GABA in a population of 108 road traffic accident victims on arrival at a trauma department and evaluated them for PTSD 6 weeks later. They observed that mean GABA level in the PTSD group was significantly lower compared with members of the trauma-exposed group who did not develop PTSD, providing additional support for the role of GABA system in this disorder.

Therefore, different neural circuits may be involved in PTSD. What is known is that some of its symptoms could be associated with specific neurotransmitters. However, these findings still are a fragmentary picture, and the particular role of each one of these neurotransmitters in PTSD needs to be better clarified.

Neuroendocrine Alterations

Considering the hormonal changes presented by PTSD patients, some usual observations concern increased catecholamines and HPA axis dysregulation. There is evidence of increased activity of the sympathoadrenal axis, and studies have connected posttraumatic stress disorder to increased levels of catecholamines [e.g., Young and Breslau, 2004b], and elevated blood pressures at baseline [Kellner et al, 2003]; a loss of the normal relationship between CSF noradrenaline and blood pressure has also been observed in CR- PTSD [Strawn et al, 2004].

Stress activates the HPA axis, thus, it would be expected that PTSD would be associated with activation of this axis; however, this is not usually the case. Studies have found different results when measuring cortisol levels in PTSD. Several reports have shown reduced cortisol in patients with PTSD precipitated by different traumas. These lower levels of basal cortisol are observed on awakening [Rohleder et al, 2004; Delahanty et al, 2004; Neylan et al, 2005], and also lower daytime cortisol levels have been observed [Glover and Poland, 2002; Bremner et al, 2003; Rohleder et al, 2004]. Additionally, a negative correlation has been found between plasma cortisol levels and PTSD symptoms severity [Baker et al, 1999; Bremner et al, 2003; Neylan et al, 2005]. On the other hand, there are several studies in which no changes in basal cortisol levels are observed [Baker et al, 1999; Tucker et al, 2004a, 2004b; Young and Breslau, 2004a, 2004b; Young et al, 2004; Bachmann et al, 2005]. In addition, a few reports have shown an elevation in cortisol [e.g., Young and Breslau, 2004a; 2004b]. One factor to be considered in these evaluations is the high presence of comorbidities that make the interpretation of these observations difficult.

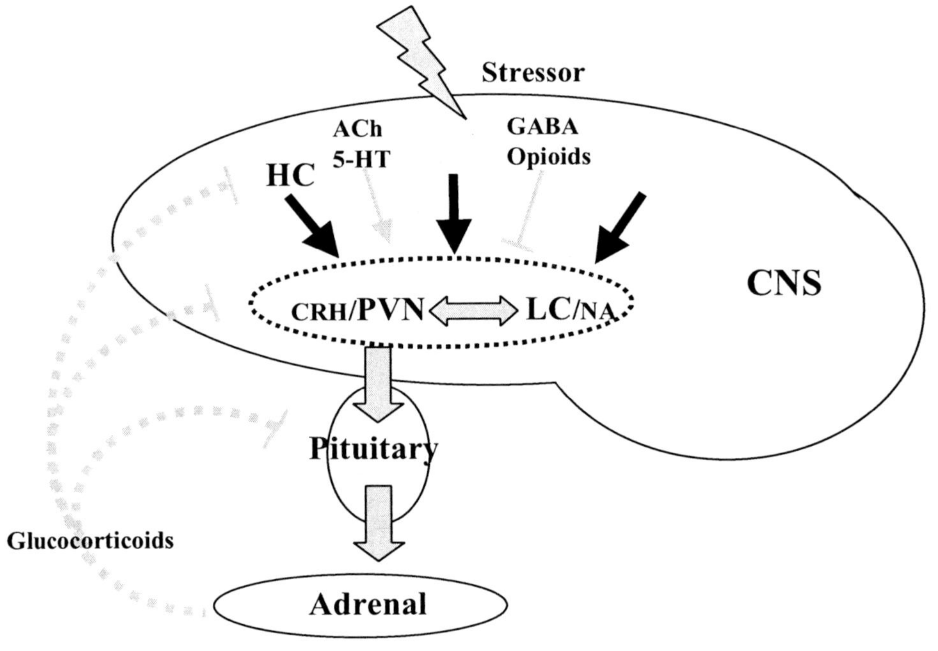

Figure 2. CNS stress responsive system. In response to a stressor, signal inputs from different brain regions (represented by black arrows) reach the hypothalamus. Locus ceruleus/noradrenaline (LC/NA) and paraventricular nucleus/ corticotrophin releasing hormone (PVN/CRH) stimulate each other. Both systems are excited by serotonergic (5HT) and cholinergic (ACh) agents and inhibited by opiates and gabaergic (GABA) agents. Glucocorticoid hormones represent the final product of the neuroendocrine activation of the HPA axis, acting on metabolic and behavioral function. The characteristic regulation of this axis is a negative feedback loop, represented by the dashed line. Glucocorticoids act through the brain (well characterized in hippocampus and hypothalamus) and the pituitary to inhibit this neuroendocrine system. Appropriate feedback in the HPA axis is, therefore, critical. This feedback is believed to be enhanced in PTSD patients. CNS = central nervous system; HC = hippocampus.

PTSD has, in many studies, reported to present a hyporesponsive HPA-system and, paradoxically, elevated corticotropin-releasing hormone (CRH) concentrations in CSF [Strohle and Holsboer, 2003]. Observed alterations in the HPA axis include different responses to HPA axis stimulation, when patients are compared to controls [Baker et al, 1999; Duval et al, 2004; Yehuda et al, 2004a; 2004d]. Evidence suggests that PTSD patients have enhanced sensitization of the HPA axis (Figure 2). Findings from dexamethasone suppression tests (DST) show significantly lower ACTH [Duval et al, 2004; Yehuda et al, 2004a, 2004d] and cortisol [Yehuda et al, 2004a] levels after dexamethasone. Additionally, PTSD patients had a significantly lower ACTH response to CRH, compared to a control group [Smith et al, 1989]. This blunted responses to dexamethasone occurring in patients with PTSD suggests increased cortisol negative feedback inhibition of ACTH secretion. These findings led to the enhanced negative feedback hypothesis, to explain lower cortisol levels in PTSD.

In agreement with this hypothesis, an increased glucocorticoid (GC) sensitivity has been reported in some studies with PTSD patients, including an increase in leukocyte glucocorticoid receptors [Yehuda et al, 2004], which has been postulated to occur also in the hippocampus. In these studies, the number of cytosolic glucocorticoid receptors was also correlated with age at exposure to the focal traumatic event [Yehuda et al, 2004b]. However, decreased [Yehuda et al, 2004c] or intact [Kellner et al, 2002] corticoid receptor responsiveness in leukocytes has also been found in PTSD patients.

It should be pointed out, however, that studies are not always in agreement with respect to the HPA axis activity in PTSD patients, and variable findings have been reported. Both normal cortisol suppression after DST [Bachmann et al, 2005] or a normal response after exposure to a physical and mental stress test [Klumpers et al, 2004] have been observed, as well as similar levels of ACTH or cortisol after CRH stimulation [Kellner et al, 2003].

Of course, these variable results may be due to different life experiences of PTSD patients. For example, timing of the stressful experience as well as the type of the trauma may influence the outcome of these evaluations. Some studies have considered time elapsed since the trauma exposure and find no correlations between ACTH and cortisol levels and time elapsed since trauma [Duval et al, 2004; Young et al, 2004]. Another important factor to be considered is the age of the patients. Cortisol levels have been observed to increase with age in depressed patients without PTSD but not in depressed patients with PTSD or in healthy volunteers [Sher et al, 2004]. In addition to the age of the patient, the age at the moment of the exposure to trauma is also important. The number of cytosolic glucocorticoid receptors is correlated with age at exposure to the focal traumatic event [Yehuda et al, 2004b]. Comparing urinary cathecolamines soon after trauma and the later development of PTSD, a correlation was observed just in boys [Delahanty et al, 2005]. Another study reported no differences between sexes in cortisol levels after DST [Duval et al, 2004] in PTSD patients. Curiously, studies evaluating hormonal measurements have not given enough attention to the sex of patients, a factor that deserves further investigation. Finally, comorbidities are commonly found with PTSD, and this factor may also influence hormonal levels [e.g., Sautter et al, 2003; Young and Breslau, 2004a; Tucker et al, 2004b; Young and Breslau, 2004b].

An interesting finding related to cortisol levels in PTSD is that prolonged administration of glucocorticoids to critically ill patients resulted in a significant reduction of PTSD symptoms later on [Schelling et al, 2004]. This protective effect of cortisol was tentatively explained by a cortisol-induced temporary impairment in traumatic memory retrieval.

An apparently paradoxical observation is the increased release of CRH, as measured in CSF [Bremner et al, 1997c; Baker et al, 1999], in PTSD, i.e., patients have hyperactive central CRH systems with underactivity of the pituitary-adrenal axis [Kasckow et al, 2001]. This peptide, besides serving as the main regulating hormone of the HPA axis, which is activated within seconds after exposure to acute stress, also acts as a neurotransmitter in numerous other brain regions involved with emotional responses. It exhibits a broad distribution throughout the brain, and is present in many brain structures that mediate stress and anxiety/fear responses, including hypothalamus, pituitary, brainstem, cerebral cortex and the amygdala [Sajdyk et al, 2004]. These higher CSF CRH concentrations in patients with PTSD possibly reflect alterations in stress-related neurotransmitter systems.

Other hormones have been found to be altered in PTSD patients. For example, plasma levels of dehydroepiandrosterone (DHEA) were increased in PTSD subjects, both basal [Boscarino, 2004], and in response to ACTH [Rasmusson et al, 2004]; elevations in thyroid hormones (total T3) have also been reported [Karlovic et al, 2004]. In addition, other hormonal alterations include serum leptin levels, which may be elevated in states of hyperarousal [Liao et al., 2004]. Central leptin infusion has been shown to activate the sympathetic nervous system in primates [Tant-Christensen et al, 1999], and leptin levels have been suggested to be a neuroendocrinologic marker for the hypervigilant state [Liao et al, 2004]. Prolactin has also been evaluated. Basal levels are not altered in PTSD patients [Davis et al, 1999]. Some other reports have observed increased [Sabioncello et al, 2000] or decreased [Sondergaard and Theorell, 2003] levels of prolactin after exposure to trauma (subjects not necessarily presenting PTSD). Additionally, evidence of serotonergic dysregulation in PTSD includes blunted prolactin response to fenfluramine or m-CPP [Davis et al, 1999]. However, some studies suggest that a blunted prolactin response to d-fenfluramine or m-CPP administration may be a consequence of trauma exposure, rather than PTSD [Rinne et al, 2000; Steiger et al, 2001; Schweitzer et al, 2004].

Although there are still many doubts concerning these hormonal levels, further research, especially taking in account different factors, such as age, sex and time from the trauma, as well as comorbidities, will help to understand the complex interactions of these stress-responsive systems.

Cytokines and Growth Factors

The relationship of the cytokines and growth factors with PTSD and other psychiatric disorders has been increasingly investigated. Cytokines and growth factors are small secreted proteins for paracrine communication, which share many activities including cell survival, proliferation, and differentiation, and even in cell death or repair when harmful stimuli are triggered. Most commonly, growth factors are cell type specific and released in non-injury situations, while cytokines have broader cell specificity and are released during injury situations. However, it is often quite difficult to distinguish growth factors from cytokines based on their release stimulus only, e.g. stressful experience, and signal transduction mechanisms often help us to distinguish them. Growth factors, in contrast to cytokines, bind to tyrosine receptor kinases (Trk). Cytokine receptors activate two main signaling pathways: JAK/STAT or NF-kappaB (Table 1).

Table 1. Release, signal transduction and alterations of BDNF, IL-1, IL-6 and S100B in stressful events

Messenger	Release modulation	Signal transduction	Stress-induced changes
BDNF	Glucorticoids, GABA, serotonin	Trk B/ERK/PI-3K[a]	Biphasic:↓[b] and ↑[c] mRNA (brain tissue) ↓ Protein (serum)[d]
IL-1	IL-1, TNF, IL-6, glucorticoids, catecholamines, glutamate, ATP, serotonin	NF-kappaB/ERK[e]	↑ Protein (serum)[f]
IL-6	IL-1, TNF, glucorticoids, catecholamines, serotonin	JAK/STAT-3/ERK[g]	↑ Protein (serum)[h]
S100B	IL-1, BDNF, ACTH, glutamate, serotonin, glucorticoids,	ERK[i]/NF-kappaB[j]	↓ Protein (serum[k] and CSF[l])

References: [a] Yamada and Nabeshima; [b] Duman, 2002; [c] De Foubert et al., 2004; [d] Hashimoto et al., 2004; [e] Hanada and Yoshimura, 2002; [f] Spivak et al., 1997; [g] Heinrich et al., 2003; [h] Maes et al., 1999; [i] Gonçalves et al., 2002; [j] Alexanian and Bamburg; [k] Scaccianoce et al., 2004; [l] Margis et al., 2004.

BDNF

BDNF is a member of the nerve growth-factor family, secreted by neurons and glial cells, often associated with plastic alterations observed in hippocampus during stress-induced disorders, PTSD or depression [Rasmusson et al, 2002]. In fact, BDNF mRNA is downregulated in the hippocampus of rats during stress by immobilization [Smith et al, 1995] or stress associated with footshock [Rasmusson et al, 2002]. It is important to mention that this does not reflect a general response to injury, since an up regulation of BDNF gene expression is found in a variety of seizure models (see [Jankowsky and Patterson, 2001] for a review). The decreased BDNF gene expression induced by stress is likely mediated by glucocorticoids [Smith et al, 1995], gabaergic receptors [Berninger et al, 1995] or serotonergic receptors [Vaidya et al, 1997; Coppell and Zetterstrom, 2003]. In addition, administration of antidepressants, such as fluoxetine, a selective serotonin reuptake inhibitor, blocks the stress-induced downregulation of BDNF gene expression [Duman, 2002].

In this context, the BDNF decrease could be modulating structural and functional changes observed in PTSD patients [Bremmer et al, 1997b], as proposed by Duman and co-workers [Rasmusson et al, 2002]. It is possible that this BDNF decrease may contribute, together with glucocorticoid augmentation, to reduced neurogenesis in hippocampal dentate gyrus and atrophy of CA3 neurons. Interestingly, this stress modification may facilitate the progression of degenerative diseases such as Alzheimer disease [Hock et al, 2000]. However, the putative protective role of antidepressants against PTSD or any stress-induced disorders has not been established. Moreover, it is not clear yet if this reduction of BDNF mRNA is associated with decreases of the content of BDNF protein. In fact, a recent study of one daily oral administration of fluoxetine in rats showed a decrease in BDNF gene expression in the first four days, without changes in BDNF protein [De Foubert et al, 2004]. Moreover, an increase of BDNF mRNA and protein was observed from 14th and 21st days on, respectively.

Additional support for the role of BDNF in stress-induced disorders comes from studies with protein infusion into the hippocampus [Shirayama et al, 2002; Radecki et al, 2005]. Apparently, spatial learning and LTP impairments, which were observed in rats stressed by immobilization, were improved after BDNF infusion [Radecki et al, 2005]. Moreover, clinical studies have shown a decrease in serum levels of BDNF in mood disorders [Hashimoto et al, 2004], and an increment in serum BDNF was found in patients receiving fluoxetine [Shimizu et al, 2003]. All these data support the hypothesis that BDNF is involved in stress-induced disorders, including PTSD. However, to our knowledge, there are no clinical data regarding BDNF changes in this disorder.

Pro-Inflammatory Cytokines

A biochemical basis for a bidirectional communication between nervous and immune systems has been established in the last two decades [Kronfol and Remick, 2000]. In this respect, pro-inflammatory cytokines have been highlighted as essential signaling molecules in this communication, particularly interleukin-1 (IL-1), tumor necrosis factor-α (TNFα) and interleukin-6 (IL-6). The immune system works as a sensory organ, informing the nervous system about physical stressors, as well as working as an effector organ when psychosocial stressors affect its activity through the nervous system. A failure in the communication between the immune and central nervous systems could be responsible for the inability to solve adequately stressful events, resulting for instance in PTSD.

Cytokines in brain tissue come from the periphery or are endogenously produced by neurons, astrocytes and microglia. Two main mechanisms are postulated to explain how they get into the CNS [see (Banks, 2005) for a review]: (i) passive transport at circunventricular sites lacking a blood-brain barrier; (ii) carrier-mediated transport. Endogenous cytokines are produced and released through stimulation by other cytokines [Kronfol and Remick, 2000] as well as by neurotransmitters and hormones (particularly related to HPA axis). It is important to emphasize that many neurotransmitters in addition to catecholamines may be involved in the modulation of cytokine expression and release (including glutamate [e.g. Aronica et al, 2005], serotonin [e.g. Lieb et al., 2005] and ATP [e.g. Marty et al., 2005]) and their cell targets include neural and non-neural cells.

Elevated central and peripheral levels of IL-1 were found in experimental animal models using many acute stressor stimuli [Nguyen et al, 1998; O'Connor et al, 2003]. Increased serum levels of IL-1 were found in patients with panic disorder [Brambilla et al, 1994] and CR PTSD [Spivak et al, 1997]. Additional studies on PTSD patients showed elevated serum levels of IL-6 and IL-6 receptors [Maes et al, 1999; Miller et al, 2001]. The evidence in the literature concerning cytokine changes in PTSD is largely correlational and it is not clear whether cytokine changes (more commonly elevation of inflammatory cytokines) are secondary to the disorder or are involved in its etiopathology.

The serum elevation of inflammatory cytokines (particularly IL-1), which are known to be inhibited by glucocorticoids, could reflect the low levels of glucocorticoids observed in PTSD patients, as mentioned above. However, a recent study with PTSD patients confirmed elevated serum levels of IL-1 without changes in cortisol [Tucker et al, 2004a]. The authors found significantly lower IL-1 levels after treatment with citalopram and sertraline, selective serotonine reuptake inhibitors. Interestingly, the placebo group also improved emotional symptoms and reduced serum IL-1, suggesting this cytokine to be a marker for improvement in this disorder. However, cytokine-mediated communication is quite complex in stressful events, and the final picture is a delicate balance between several endogenous anti-inflammatory cytokines (e.g. IL-4, IL-10), receptor antagonists (e.g. IL-1ra) and soluble receptors [Anisman et al, 2002].

S100B

S100B is an astrocyte-derived cytokine, which has only recently started to be investigated in several psychiatric disorders [Rothermundt et al, 2003]. *In vitro* S100B expression and/or secretion appears to be modulated by serotonin [Whitaker-Azmitia et al, 1990], ACTH [Suzuki et al, 1987] and glucocorticoids [Niu et al, 1997], three well-known mediators of the stress response. Moreover, a study has demonstrated that restraint stress, but not injection of corticosterone, increases serum S100B levels in control and in adrenalectomized rats [Scaccianoce et al, 2004].

In rats, we observed an increase in CSF S100B levels 1h after exposure to a cat, followed by a decrease 24 h later, without changes in hippocampal or cortical content of this protein [Margis et al, 2004]. Rats exposed to restraint stress also exhibited a similar variation in CSF S100B (R Margis, unpublished dada). CSF S100B is almost entirely released from astrocytes. These results may suggest that this CSF S100B change is due to changes in the secretion profile of S100B, or in its extracellular turnover. In fact, *in vitro* results indicate that extracellular S100B represents less than 1% of the intracellular content [Tramontina et al, 2002], signifying that changes in extracellular S100B, unlike BDNF or inflammatory cytokines, may be independent on S100B expression, and that an intracellular increase in S100B is not necessarily associated with an increase in secretion [Tramontina et al, 2002]. Moreover, it is important to mention that IL-1 and BDNF are apparently able to stimulate S100B secretion [Hinkle et al, 1998; Nishi et al, 2000].

This protein has been implicated in the underlying hippocampal mechanisms of learning and memory [Mello e Souza, 2000; Nishiyama et al, 2002]. Moreover, S100B infusion in the cerebellum of adult rats had a putative modulatory effect on extinction of acoustic startle response and conditioned fear in adult rats [Sherstnev et al, 2003]. In this context, it is important to mention that impaired fear conditioning-like mechanisms after exposure to stress has been suggested as a paradigm for the reexperiencing symptoms in PTSD [Bonne et al, 2004].

All these data could suggest a role of cytokines in PTSD. However, any specific role for cytokines in this disorder remains speculative. This is not only due to some inconsistent replication of laboratory findings, but also due to the pleiotropic nature of cytokines and to the redundancies between them and growth factors.

Additional Comments

People differ in their ability to recover from a traumatic experience. It is known that only a minority of traumatized victims develop PTSD; however, it has been shown that approximately 30% of all traumatized victims with PTSD still present PTSD symptoms after 10 years [Kessler, 1995]. The PTSD patient is affected at neuroanatomical, neuroendocrinological, neurochemical, cognitive, behavioral and social levels. Important behavioral characteristics observed in PTSD patients are fear conditioning, inability to habituate and an inability to extinguish a learned behavior; these patients present disruption of learning and memory and distortion of the appraisal process.

All aspects mentioned above are important to understand PTSD complexity, and the role of cognitive-behavioral therapy as a kind of psychotherapy proposed to PTSD patients. Cognitive therapy postulates that dysfunctional thinking pattern produces pathologic emotions that can result in the manifestation of psychiatric disorders. As an example; a dysfunctional cognition and the resultant emotion, such as anxiety, or irritability, can induce an avoidance behavior when exposed to a safe situation. In this process, the role of conditioning fear has been demonstrated. These patients present disruption of learning and memory and an inability to extinguish a learned behavior that results in impairments in coping with a situation or challenge. Thus, cognitive therapy attempts to teach the patients to identify their dysfunctional cognitions, challenge them, and replace them with realistic and functional beliefs.

It should be pointed out, however, that although cognitive-behavioral therapy may be able to affect neural plasticity, improving several PTSD symptoms, pharmacological therapy is very useful in most of the cases. Several clinical trials have been performed with antidepressives, anticonvulsivants, and antipsychotics.

It is important to emphasize that comorbidities constitute a difficulty in the clinical evaluation and diagnosis of PTSD, besides being a confusing factor in clinical trials, since around 80% of PTSD patients present some comorbidity. PTSD treatment will also improve the comorbidity, reinforcing the clinical importance of a diagnosis of this disorder.

The establishment of suitable animal models of PTSD is important for a better understanding of the pathophysiological foundations of this disorder. At this moment, there are several models proposed for PTSD. However, it is unclear if they reproduce most of the neurochemical, hormonal and behavioral characteristics of PTSD, since the models proposed have not been thoroughly studied yet. As was pointed out earlier, it will not be possible to reproduce all the complexities of PTSD in humans; despite this limitation, these studies will permit the characterization of new possible targets for pharmacological strategies for PTSD.

Research into biochemical peripheral markers, associated with neuropsychological testing and non-invasive methodological (particularly structural and functional brain imaging [Bremner et al, 1995; 1997; Bonne et al, 2001; Liberzon and Phan et al, 2003; Winter and Irle, 2004]), and sensory evoked potentials [e.g. Ghisolfi et al, 2004] will allow us to follow and understand better this psychiatric disorder. However, some present limitations must be considered in clinical and animal studies. First, most of the available data regarding peripheral markers are correlational and it is still difficult to characterize whether changes in these putative markers are cause or consequence. Secondly, a change in a putative marker must be viewed as a resulting picture, in which several components are involved and, therefore, caution is required when making wide generalizations. Thirdly, many peripheral markers (particularly serum markers) have extracerebral sources and redoubled caution is needed to interpret these results.

CONCLUSION

The changes underlying PTSD disorder are not completely understood. This is a disorder that interferes severely with the life of patients and their families. Although it is known that people have always been exposed to traumatic experiences, the increased violence in our society highlights the importance of investigating stress disorders, such as PTSD. Previous studies have improved the understanding of this disorder, but the number of subjects in most of these studies is small, and conflicting results are sometimes reported. The discussion concerning individual susceptibility is still vague, and demands a better characterization. This characterization involves the use and improvement of neuropsychological testing, biochemical peripheral markers, and non-invasive methodologies, such as brain imaging, and sensory evoked potentials. It is hoped that all these studies will allow us to understand better this psychiatric disorder and its underlying mechanisms, and to improve the quality of life of these patients.

REFERENCES

Adamec, RE; Shallow, T. Lasting effects on rodent anxiety of a single exposure to a cat. *Physiol Behav*, 1993 54, 101-109.

Adamec, A. Transmitter systems involved in neuroplasticity increased anxiety and defense following traumatic stress. *Neurosci Biobehav Rev*, 1997 21(6), 755-765.

Adamec, RE; Burton, P; Shallow, T; Budgell, J. NMDA receptors mediate lasting increases in anxiety like-behavior produced by the stress of predator exposure – implications for anxiety associated with posttraumatic stress disorder. *Physiol & Behav* 1999 65(4/5), 723-737.

Alexanian, AR; Bamburg, JR. Neuronal survival activity of s100betabeta is enhanced by calcineurin inhibitors and requires activation of NF-kappaB. *FASEB J,* 1999 13(12), 1611-1620.

American Psychiatric Association. Diagnostic and Statistical Manual of Mental Disorders, fourth edition, text revision. Washington, DC, *American Psychiatric Association*,2000.

Anisman, H; Hayley, S; Turrin, N; Merali, Z. Cytokines as a stressor: implications for depressive illness. *Int J Neuropsychopharmacol*, 2002 5, 357-373.

Aronica, E; Gorter, JA; Rozemuller, AJ; Yankaya, B; Troost, D. Activation of metabotropic glutamate receptor 3 enhances interleukin (IL)-1beta-stimulated release of IL-6 in cultured human astrocytes. *Neurosci*, 2005 130(4), 927-933.

Arora, RC; Fichtner, CG; O'Connor, FL; Crayton, JW. Paroxetine binding in blood platelets of posttraumatic stress disorder. *Life Sci,* 1993 53, 919-928.

Asberg, M; Traskman, I; Thoren, R. 5HIAA in the cerebrospinal fluid: a biochemical suicide predictor. *Arch Gen Psych*, 1976 33, 93-97.

Bachmann, AW; Sedgley, TL; Jackson, RV; Gibson, JN; Young, RM; Torpy, DJ. Glucocorticoid receptor polymorphisms and post-traumatic stress disorder. *Psychoneuroendocrinol*, 2005 30, 297-306.

Baker, DG; West, SA; Orth, DN; Hill, KK; Nicholson, WE; Ekhator, NN; Bruce, AB; Wortman, MD; Keck, PE Jr; Geracioti, TD Jr. Cerebrospinal fluid and plasma beta-endorphin in combat veterans with post-traumatic stress disorder. *Psychoneuroendocrinol*, 1997 7, 517-529.

Baker, DG; West, SA; Nicholson, WE; Ekhator, NN; Kasckow, JW; Hill, KK; Bruce, AB; Orth, DN; Geracioti, TD Jr. Serial CSF corticotropin-releasing hormone levels and adrenocortical activity in combat veterans with posttraumatic stress disorder. *Am J Psych*, 1999 156, 585-588.

Banks, WA. Blood-brain barrier transport of cytokines: a mechanism for neuropathology. *Curr Pharm Des*, 2005 11, 973-984.

Berninger, B; Marty, S; Zafra, F; da Penha Berzaghi, M; Thoenen, H; Lindholm, D. GABAergic stimulation switches from enhancing to repressing BDNF expression in rat hippocampal neurons during maturation in vitro. *Development*, 1995 121(8), 2327-2335.

Blanchard, EB; Kolb, LC; Prins, A; Gates, S; McCoy, GC. Changes in plasma norepinephrine to combat-related stimuli among Vietnam veterans with posttraumatic stress disorder. *J Nerv Ment Dis*, 1991 179(6), 371-373.

Bodnar, RJ. Neuropharmacological and neuroendocrine substrates of stress-induced analgesia *Ann NY Acad Sci*, 1986 467, 345-360.

Bonne, O; Brandes, D; Gilboa, A; Gomori, JM; Shenton, ME; Pitman, RK; Shalev, AY. Longitudinal MRI study of hippocampal volume in trauma survivors with PTSD. *Am J Psych,* 2001 158(8),1248-1251.

Bonne, O; Grillon, C; Vythilingam, M; Neumeister, A; Charney, DS. Adaptive and maladaptive psychobiological responses to severe psychological stress: implications for the discovery of novel pharmacotherapy. *Neurosci Biobehav Rev*, 2004 28(1), 65-94.

Bonne, O; Bain, E.; Neumeister A.; et al No change in serotonin type 1A receptor binding in patients with posttraumatic stress disorder *Am J Psych*, 2005 162:383-385.

Boscarino JA. Posttraumatic stress disorder and physical illness: results from clinical and epidemiologic studies. *Ann N Y Acad Sci*, 2004 1032, 141-153.

Brambilla, F; Bellodi, L; Perna, G; Bertani, A; Panerai, A; Sacerdote, P. Plasma interleukin-1 beta concentrations in panic disorder. *Psychiatry Res,* 1994 54(2),135-142.

Bremner, JD; Randall, P; Scott, TM; Bronen, RA; Seibyl, JP; Southwick, SM; Delaney, RC; McCarthy, G; Charney, DS; Innis, RB. MRI-based measurement of hippocampal volume in patients with combat-related posttraumatic stress disorder. *Am J Psych*, 1995 152(7), 973-981.

Bremner, JD; Innis, RB; Ng, CK; Staib, LH; Salomon, RM; Bronen, RA; Duncan, J; Southwick, SM; Krystal, JH; Rich, D; Zubal, G; Dey, H; Soufer, R; Charney, DS. Positron emission tomography measurement of cerebral metabolic correlates of yohimbine administration in combat-related posttraumatic stress disorder. *Arch Gen Psych*, 1997a 54 (3), 246-254.

Bremner, JD; Randall, P; Vermetten,E; Staib, L; Bronen, RA; Mazure, C; Capelli, S; McCarthy, G; Innis, RB; Charney, DS. Magnetic resonance imaging-based measurement of hippocampal volume in posttraumatic stress disorder related to childhood physical and sexual abuse—a preliminary report. *Biol Psychiatry*, 1997b 41(1),23-32.

Bremner, JD; Licinio, J; Darnell, A; Krystal, JH; Owens, MJ; Southwick, SM; Nemeroff, CB; Charney, DS. Elevated CSF corticotropin-releasing factor concentrations in posttraumatic stress disorder. *Am J Psych*, 1997c 154, 624-629.

Bremner, JD; Innis, R; Southwick, S; Staib, L; Zoghbi, S and Charney, DS. Decreased benzodiazepine receptor binding in prefrontal cortex in combat-related posttraumatic stress disorder. *Am J Psych*, 2000 157,:1120-1126

Bremner, JD; Vermetten, E. Stress and development: behavioral and biological consequences. *Dev Psychopathol*, 2001 13, 473-489.

Bremner, JD; Vythilingam, M; Anderson, G; Vermetten, E; McGlashan, T; Heninger, G; Rasmusson, A; Southwick, SM; Charney, DS. Assessment of the hypothalamic-pituitary-adrenal axis over a 24-hour diurnal period and in response to neuroendocrine challenges in women with and without childhood sexual abuse and posttraumatic stress disorder. *Biol Psychiatry*, 2003 54, 710-718.

Breslau, N; Davis, GC; Andreski, P; Peterson, E. Traumatic events and posttraumatic stress disorder in an urban population of young adults. *Arch Gen Psychiatry*, 1991 48(3),216-222.

Cocarro EF. Central serotonin and impulsive aggression. *Br J Psychiatry*, 1989 155,:52-62.

Cohen, H; Benjamin, J; Kaplan, Z; Kotler, M. Administration of high-dose ketoconazole, an inhibitor of steroid synthesis, prevents posttraumatic anxiety in an animal model. *Neuropsychopharmacol*, 2000 10,429-435.

Cohen, H; Zohar, J; Matar, M. The relevance of differential response to trauma in an animal model of posttraumatic stress disorder. *Biol Psychiatry*, 2003 53,463-473.

Cohen, H; Zohar, J. An animal model of posttraumatic stress disorder: the use of cut-off behavioral criteria. *Ann N Y Acad Sci*, 2004 1032,167-178.

Cohen, H; Zohar, J; Matar, MA; Zeev, K; Loewenthal, U; Richter-Levin, G. Setting apart the affected: the use of behavioral criteria in animal models of post traumatic stress disorder. *Neuropsychopharmacology*, 2004 29, 1962-1670.

Collingridge, GL; Bliss, TV. Memories of NMDA receptors and LTP. *Trends Neurosci*, 1995 18(2), 54-56.

Comings, DE; Muhleman, D; Gysin, R. Dopamine D2 receptor (DRD2) gene and susceptibility to posttraumatic stress disorder: a study and replication. *Biol Psychiatry,* 1996 40(5),368-372.

Coppell, AL; Pei, Q; Zetterstrom, TS. Bi-phasic change in BDNF gene expression following antidepressant drug treatment. *Neuropharmacology*, 2003 44(7), 903-910.

Dantas, G.; Torres, ILS.; Crema, L.M.; Lara, DR.; Dalmaz,C. Repeated restraint stress reduces opioid receptor binding in different rat CNS structures. *Neurochem Res,* 2005 30 (1):1-7.

Davidson, JRT; Rothbaun, BO; van der Kolk, BA; Sikes, Cr; Farfel, GM. Multicenter, double-blind comparison of Sertraline and placebo in the treatment of posttraumatic stress disorder. *Arch Gen Psych,* 2001 58(5),485-492.

Davis, M; Walker, DL; Lee, Y. Roles of the amygdala and bed nucleus of the stria terminalis in fear and anxiety measured with the acoustic startle reflex. Possible relevance to PTSD. *Ann N Y Acad Sci*, 1997 821,305-331.

Davis, LL; Clark, DM; Kramer, GL; Moeller, FG; Petty, F. D-fenfluramine challenge in posttraumatic stress disorder. *Biol Psychiatry*, 1999 45, 928-930.

De Bellis MD, Baum AS, Birmaher B, Keshavan MS, Eccard CH, Boring AM, Jenkins FJ, Ryan ND.A.E. Bennett Research Award. Developmental traumatology. Part I: Biological stress systems. *Biol Psychiatry*,.1999 45(10), 1259-1270.

De Foubert, G; Carney, SL; Robinson, CS; Destexhe, EJ; Tomlinson, R; Hicks, CA; Murray, TK; Gaillard, JP; Deville, C; Xhenseval, V; Thomas, CE; O'Neill, MJ; Zetterstrom, TS. Fluoxetine-induced change in rat brain expression of brain-derived neurotrophic factor varies depending on length of treatment. *Neuroscience*, 2004 128(3), 597-604.

de Kloet, ER; Sibug, RM; Helmerhorst, FM; Schmidt, M. Stress, genes and the mechanism of programming the brain for later life. *Neurosci Biobehav Rev*, 2005 29, 271-281.

Delahanty, DL; Bogart, LM; Figler, JL. Posttraumatic stress disorder symptoms, salivary cortisol, medication adherence, and CD4 levels in HIV-positive individuals. *AIDS Care*, 2004 16, 247-260.

Delahanty, DL; Nugent, NR; Christopher NC; Walsh M. Initial urinary epinephrine and cortisol levels predict acute PTSD symptoms in child trauma victims *Psychoneuroendocrinology* 2005 30, 121-128.

Donnelly, CL. Pharmacologic treatment approaches for children and adolescents with posttraumatic stress disorder. *Child Adolesc Psychiatr Clin N Am*, 2003 12(2), 251-269.

Douglas RM, Goddard GV, Riives M. Inhibitory modulation of long-term potentiation: evidence for a postsynaptic locus of control. *Brain Res*, 1982 240(2),259-272.

Duffy, JD; Malloy, PF. Efficacy of buspirone in the treatment of posttraumatic stress disorder: an open trial. *Ann Clin Psychiatry*, 1994 6, 33-37.

Duman, RS. Pathophysiology of depression: the concept of synaptic plasticity. Eur Psychiatry, 2002 17 (3), 306-310.

Duval, F; Crocq, MA; Guillon, MS; Mokrani, MC; Monreal, J; Bailey, P; Macher, JP. Increased adrenocorticotropin suppression after dexamethasone administration in sexually abused adolescents with posttraumatic stress disorder. *Ann N Y Acad Sci*, 2004 1032, 273-275.

Fujita, M; Southwick, SM; Denucci, CC; Zoghbi, SS; Dillon, MS; Baldwin, RM; Bozkurt, A; Kugaya, A; Verhoeff, NPLG; Seibyl, JP; Innis, RB. Central type benzodiazepine receptors in Gulf War veterans with posttraumatic stress disorder. *Biol Psych*, 2004 56, 95-100.

Garcia, R. Stress, hippocampal plasticity and spatial learning. Synapse, 2001 40,180-183.

Garrick, T; Morrow, N; Eth, S; Marciano, D; Shalev, A. Psychophysiologic parameters of traumatic stress disorder in rats. *Ann N Y Acad Sci*, 1997 821, 533-537.

Garrick, T; Morrow, N; Shalev, AY; Eth, S. Stress-induced enhancement of auditory startle: an animal model of posttraumatic stress disorder. *Psychiatry*, 2001 64, 346-354.

Gavish, M; Laor, N; Bidder, M; Fisher, D; Fonia, O; Muller, U; Reiss, A; Wolmer, L; Karp, L; Weizman, R. Altered platelet peripheral-type benzodiazepine receptor in posttraumatic stress disorder. *Neuropsychopharmacology*, 1996 14(3), 181-186.

Geracioti, TD Jr; Baker, DG; Ekhator, NN; West, SA; Hill, KK; Bruce, AB; Schmidt, D; Rounds-Kugler, B; Yehuda, R; Keck, PE Jr; Kasckow, JW. CSF norepinephrine concentrations in posttraumatic stress disorder. *Am J Psych*, 2001 158(8), 1227-1230.

Ghisolfi, ES; Margis, R; Becker, J; Zanardo, AP; Strimitzer, IM; Lara DR. Impaired P50 sensory gating in post-traumatic stress disorder secondry to urban violence. *Int J Psychophysiology* 2004 51, 209-214.

Glover, DA; Poland, RE. Urinary cortisol and catecholamines in mothers of child cancer survivors with and without PTSD. *Psychoneuroendocrinology*, 2002 27, 805-819.

Glover, DA; Powers, MB; Bergman, L; Smits, JA; Telch, MJ; Stuber, M. Urinary dopamine and turn bias in traumatized women with and without PTSD symptoms. *Behav Brain Res*, 2003 144(1-2), 137-141.

Goldstein, G; van Kammen W; Shelly, C; Miller, DJ; van Kammen, DP. Survivors of imprisonment in the Pacific Theater during World War II. *Am J Psych*, 1987 144, 1210-1213.

Gonçalves, DS; Lenz, G; Karl, J; Gonçalves, CA; Rodnight, R. Extracellular S100B protein modulates ERK in astrocyte cultures. *Neuroreport,* 2000 11(4), 807-9.

Gurvits, TV; Shenton, ME; Hokama, H; Ohta, H; Lasko, NB; Gilbertson, MW; Orr, SP; Kikinis, R; Jolesz, FA; McCarley, RW; Pitman, RK. Magnetic resonance imaging study of hippocampal volume in chronic, combat-related posttraumatic stress disorder. *Biol Psychiatry*, 1996 40(11),1091-1099.

Hamner, MB; Diamond, BI. Elevated plasma dopamine in posttraumatic stress disorder: a preliminary report. *Biol Psychiatry*, 1993 33(4), 304-306.

Hamner, MB; Gold, PB. Plasma dopamine beta-hydroxylase activity in psychotic and non-psychotic post-traumatic stress disorder. *Psychiatry Res*, 1998 77(3),175-181.

Hanada, T; Yoshimura, A. Regulation of cytokine signaling and inflammation. *Cytokine Growth Factor Rev*, 2002 13(4-5),413-421.

Harvey, BH; Oosthuizen, F; Brand, L; Wegener, G; Stein, DJ. Stress-restress evokes sustained iNOS activity and altered GABA levels and NMDA receptors in rat hippocampus. *Psychopharmacology* (Berl), 2004 175,494-502.

Hashimoto, K; Shimizu, E; Iyo, M. Critical role of brain-derived neurotrophic factor in mood disorders. *Brain Res Rev*, 2004 45(2), 104-14.

Heim, C; Nemeroff, CB. Neurobiology of early life stress: clinical studies. Semin Clin *Neuropsychiatry*, 2002 7, 147-159.

Heim, C; Owens, MJ; Plotsky, PM; Nemeroff, CB. Persistent changes in corticotropin-releasing factor systems due to early life stress: relationship to the pathophysiology of major depression and post-traumatic stress disorder. *Psychopharmacol Bull,* 1997 33, 185-192.

Heinrich, PC; Behrmann, I; Haan, S; Hermanns, HM; Muller-Newen, G; Schaper, F. Principles of interleukin (IL)-6-type cytokine signalling and its regulation. *Biochem J*, 2003 374 ,1-20.

Hinkle, DA; Harney, JP; Cai, A; Hilt, DC; Yarowsky, PJ; Wise, PM. Basic fibroblast growth factor-2 and interleukin-1 beta regulate S100 beta expression in cultured astrocytes. *Neuroscience,* 1998 82 (1), 33-41.

Hock, CH; Heese, K; Olivieri, G; Hulette, CH; Rosenberg, C; Nitsch, RM; Otten, U. Alterations in neurotrophins and neurotrophin receptors in Alzheimer's disease. *J Neural Transm Suppl,* 2000 59, 171-174.

Hoffman, L; Burges Watson, P; Wilson, G; Montgomery, J. Low plasma beta-endorphin in post-traumatic stress disorder. Aust N Z J Psychiatry, 1989 23(2), 269-273.

Jankowsky, JL; Patterson, PH. The role of cytokines and growth factors in seizures and their sequelae. *Prog Neurobiol*, 2001 63(2),125-149.

Karlovic, D; Marusic, S; Martinac, M. Increase of serum triiodothyronine concentration in soldiers with combat-related chronic post-traumatic stress disorder with or without alcohol dependence. *Wien Klin Wochenschr*, 2004 116, 385-390.

Kasckow, JW; Baker, D; Geracioti, TD Jr. Corticotropin-releasing hormone in depression and post-traumatic stress disorder. *Peptides*, 2001 22, 845-851.

Kellett, J; Kokkinidis, L. Extinction deficit and fear reinstatement after electrical stimulation of the amygdala: implications for kindling-associated fear and anxiety. *Neuroscience*, 2004 127, 277-287.

Kellner, M; Baker, DG; Yassouridis, A; Bettinger, S; Otte, C; Naber, D; Wiedemann, K. Mineralocorticoid receptor function in patients with posttraumatic stress disorder. *Am J Psychiatry*, 2002 159, 1938-1940.

Kellner, M; Yassouridis, A; Hubner, R; Baker, DG; Wiedemann, K. Endocrine and cardiovascular responses to corticotropin-releasing hormone in patients with posttraumatic stress disorder: a role for atrial natriuretic peptide? *Neuropsychobiology*, 2003 47, 102-108.

Kessler, RC; Sonnega, A; Bromet, E; Hughes, M; Nelson, CB. Posttrauamtic stress disorder in the National Comorbidity Survey. *Arch Gen Psychiatry*, 1995 52, 1048-1060.

Kessler, RC; Borges, BW; Walters, EE. Prevalence and risk factors of lifetime suicide attempts in the National Comorbidity Survey. *Arch Gen Psychiatry*, 1999 56, 617-626.

Kessler, RC. Posttraumatic stress disorder:the burden to the individual and to society. *J Clin Psych*, 2000 61(5), 4-12.

Khan, S; Liberzon, I. Topiramate attenuates exaggerated acoustic startle in an animal model of PTSD. *Psychopharmacology* (Berl), 2004 172, 225-229.

Kim, JJ; Koo, JW; Lee, HJ; Han, JS. Amygdalar inactivation blocks stress-induced impairments in hippocampal long-term potentiation and spatial memory. *J Neurosci*, 2005 25(6), 1532-1539.

Kinzie, JD; Leung, P. Clonidine in Cambodian patients with posttraumatic stress disorder. *J Nerv Ment Dis*, 1989 177(9), 546-550 .

Klumpers, UM; Tulen, JH; Timmerman, L; Fekkes, D; Loonen, AJ; Boomsma, F. Responsivity to stress in chronic posttraumatic stress disorder due to childhood sexual abuse. *Psychol Rep*, 2004 94, 408-410.

Kluznick, JC; Speed N; Van Valkenburg, C; Magraw, R. Forty-year follow-up of United States prisoners of war. *Am J Psych*, 1986 143,1443-1446.

Koba, T; Kodama, Y; Shimizu, K; Nomura, S; Sugawara, M; Kobayashi, Y; Ogasawara, T. Persistent behavioural changes in rats following inescapable shock stress: a potential model of posttraumatic stress disorder. *World J Biol Psychiatry*, 2001 2, 34-37.

Kosten, TR; Mason, JW; Giller, EL; Ostroff, RB; Harkness, L. Sustained urinary norepinephrine and epinephrine elevation in PTSD. *Psychoneuroendocrinology*, 1987 12, 13-20

Kronfol, Z; Remick, DG. Cytokines and the brain: implications for clinical psychiatry. *Am J Psychiatry*, 2000 157(5), 683-694.

Lewis, JW; Cannon, JT; Liebeskind, JC. Opioid and nonopioid mechanisms of stress analgesia *Science*, 1980 208, 623-625.

Liao, SC; Lee, MB; Lee, YJ; Huang, TS. Hyperleptinemia in subjects with persistent partial posttraumatic stress disorder after a major earthquake. *Psychosom Med,* 2004 66, 23-28.

Liberzon, I; Krstov, M; Young, EA. Stress-restress: effects on ACTH and fast feedback. *Psychoneuroendocrinology,* 1997 22, 443-453.

Liberzon, I; Phan, KL. Brain-imaging studies of posttraumatic stress disorder. *CNS Spectr*, 2003 8(9), 641-650.

Lieb, K; Biersack, L; Waschbisch, A; Orlikowski, S; Akundi, RS; Candelario-Jalil, E; Hull, M; Fiebich, BL. Serotonin via 5-HT7 receptors activates p38 mitogen-activated protein kinase and protein kinase C epsilon resulting in interleukin-6 synthesis in human U373 MG astrocytoma cells. *J Neurochem*. 2005 93(3), 549-559.

Louvart, H; Maccari, S; Ducrocq, F; Thomas, P; Darnaudery, M. Long-term behavioural alterations in female rats after a single intense footshock followed by situational reminders. *Psychoneuroendocrinology*, 2005 30, 316-324.

Maes, M; Lin ,AH; Delmeire, L; Van Gastel, A; Kenis, G; De Jongh, R; Bosmans, E. Elevated serum interleukin-6 (IL-6) and IL-6 receptor concentrations in posttraumatic stress disorder following accidental man-made traumatic events. *Biol Psychiatry*, 1999 45(7),833-839.

Maes M.; Lin AH.; Verkerk R.; et al Serotonergic and noradrenergic markers of posttraumatic stress disorder with and without major depression *Neuropsychopharmacology* 1999, 20,188-197

Maier, SF. Exposure to the stressor environment prevents the temporal dissipation of behavioral depression/learned helplessness. *Biol Psychiatry*, 2001 49,763-773.

Mann, JD. Psychobiological predictors of suicide. *J Clin Psych*, 1987 48 (2), 39-43.

Margis, R; Zanatto, VC; Tramontina, F; Vinade, E; Lhullier, F; Portela, LV; Souza, DO; Dalmaz, C; Kapczinski, F; Gonçalves, CA. Changes in S100B cerebrospinal fluid levels of rats subjected to predator stress. *Brain Res*, 2004 1028(2), 213-218.

Marshall, RD; Beebe, KL; Oldham, M; Zaninelli, R. Efficacy and safety of paroxetine treatment for chronic PTSD: a fixed-dose placebo controlled study. *Am J Psychiatry*, 2001 158, 1982-1988.

Marshall, RD; Blanco, C; Printz, D; Liebowitz, MR; Klein, DF; Coplan, J. A pilot study of noradrenergic and HPA axis functioning in PTSD vs. panic disorder. *Psychiatry Res*, 2002 110(3), 219-30.

Martenyi, F; Brown, EB; Zhang, H; Prakash, A; Koke, SC. Fluoxetine versus placebo in posttraumatic stress disorder. *J Clin Psychiatry*, 2002 63(3),199-206.

Marty, V; Medina, C; Combe, C; Parnet, P; Amedee, T. ATP binding cassette transporter ABC1 is required for the release of interleukin-1beta by P2X7-stimulated and lipopolysaccharide-primed mouse Schwann cells. *Glia*, 2005 49(4), 511-519.

Matsumoto, M; Togashi, H; Kaku, A; Kanno, M; Tahara, K; Yoshioka, M. Cortical GABAergic regulation of dopaminergic responses to psychological stress in the rat dorsolateral striatum. *Synapse*, 2005 56(2),171-121.

McEwen, BS. Allostasis and allostatic load: implications for neuropsychopharmacology. *Neuropsychopharmacology*, 2000 22,108-124.

McEwen BS. Effects of adverse experiences for brain structure and function. *Biol Psychiatry*, 2000b 48(8),721-31.

McEwen, BS. Mood disorders and allostatic load. *Biol Psychiatry*, 2003 54, 200-207.

McFall, ME; Murburg, MM; Ko, GN; Veith, RC. Autonomic responses to stress in Vietnam combat veterans with posttraumatic stress disorder. *Biol Psychiatry*, 1990 27(10),1165-1175

Mellman, TA; Kumar, A; Kulick-Bell, R; Kumar, M; Nolan, B. Nocturnal/daytime urine noradrenergic measures and sleep incombat-relatedPTSD. *BiolPsychiatry*, .1995 38(3), 174-179.

Mello e Souza, T; Rohden, A; Meinhardt, M; Gonçalves, CA; Quillfeldt, JA. S100B infusion into the rat hippocampus facilitates memory for the inhibitory avoidance task but not for the open-field habituation. *Physiol Behav*, 2000 71(1-2), 29-33.

Miller, RJ; Sutherland, AG; Hutchion, JD; Alexander, DA. C-reactive protein and interleukin 6 receptor in post-traumatic stress disorder: a pilot study. *Cytokine*, 2001 13(4), 253-255.

Moghaddam, B. Stress preferentially increases extraneuronal levels of excitatory amino acids in the prefrontal cortex: comparison to hippocampus and basal ganglia. *Journal of Neurochemistry*, 1993 60, 1650-1657.

Morris, P; Hopwood, M; Maguire, K; Norman, T; Schweitzer, I. Blunted growth hormone response to clonidine in post-traumatic stress disorder. *Psychoneuroendocrinology*, 2004 29(2), 269-278.

Neylan, TC; Brunet, A; Pole, N; Best, SR; Metzler, TJ; Yehuda, R; Marmar, CR. PTSD symptoms predict waking salivary cortisol levels in police officers. *Psychoneuroendocrinology,* 2005 30, 373-381.

Nguyen, KT; Deak, T; Owens, SM; Kohno, T; Fleshner, M; Watkins, LR; Maier, SF. Exposure to acute stress induces brain interleukin-1beta protein in the rat. *J Neurosci*, 1998 18(6), 2239-2246.

Nijenhuis, ER; Vanderlinden, J; Spinhoven, P. Animal defensive reactions as a model for trauma-induced dissociative reactions. *J Trauma Stress*, 1998 11, 243-260.

Nikulina, EM;Hammer, RP Jr; Miczek, KA; Kream, RM. Social defeat stress increases expression of mu-opioid receptor mRNA in rat ventral tegmental area. *Neuroreport*, 1999 10(14),3015-3019.

Nikulina, EM; Miczek, KA; Hammer, RP. Prolonged Effects of Repeated Social Defeat Stress on mRNA Expression and Function of mu-Opioid Receptors in the Ventral Tegmental Area of Rats. *Neuropsychopharmacology*. 2005 [Epub ahead of print].

Nishi, M; Kawata, M; Azmitia, EC. Trophic interactions between brain-derived neurotrophic factor and s100beta on cultured serotonergic neurons. *Brain Res*, 2000 868(1), 113-118.

Nishith, P; Griffin, MG; Poth, TL. Stress-induced analgesia: prediction of posttraumatic stress symptoms in battered versus nonbattered women. *Biol Psych*, 2002 51, 867-874.

Nishiyama, H; Knopfel, T; Endo, S; Itohara, S. Glial protein S100B modulates long-term neuronal synaptic plasticity. *Proc Natl Acad Sci* U S A, 2002 99(6), 4037-4042.

Niu, H; Hinkle, DA; Wise, PM. Dexamethasone regulates basic fibroblast growth factor, nerve growth factor and S100beta expression in cultured hippocampal astrocytes. *Brain Res Mol Brain Res*, 1997 51(1-2), 97-105.

O'Connor, KA; Johnson, JD; Hansen, MK; Wieseler Frank, JL; Maksimova, E; Watkins, LR; Maier, SF. Peripheral and central proinflammatory cytokine response to a severe acute stressor. *Brain Res*, 2003 991(1-2),123-32.

Ottenweller, JE; Natelson, BH; Pitman, DL; Drastal, SD. Adrenocortical and behavioral responses to repeated stressors: toward an animal model of chronic stress and stress-related mental illness. *Biol Psychiatry*, 1989 26, 829-841.

Pare, WP. Enhanced retrieval of unpleasant memories influenced by shock controllability, shock sequence, and rat strain. *Biol Psychiatry*, 1996 39, 808-813.

Pawlyk, AC; Jha, SK; Brennan, FX; Morrison, AR; Ross, RJ. A rodent model of sleep disturbances in posttraumatic stress disorder: the role of context after fear conditioning. *Biol Psychiatry*, 2005 57, 268-277.

Perry, BD; Giller, EL Jr; Southwick, SM. Altered platelet alpha 2-adrenergic bindings sites in posttraumatic stress disorder *Am J Psych* 1987 144, 1511-1512.

Pitman, RK; van der Kolk, BA; Orr, SP; Greenberg, MS. Naloxone-reversible analgesic response to combat-related stimuli in posttraumatic stress disorder. *Arch Gen Psych*, 1990 47, 541-544.

Plavides, C; Nivón, LG; McEwen, BS. Effects of chronic stress on hippocampal long-term potentiation. *Hippocampus*, 2002 12, 245-257.

Post, RM; Weiss, SR; Li, H; Smith, MA; Zhang, LX; Xing, G; Osuch, EA; McCann, UD. Neural plasticity and emotional memory. *Dev Psychopathol*, 1998 10, 829-855.

Pynoos, RS; Ritzmann, RF; Steinberg, AM; Goenjian, A; Prisecaru, I. A behavioral animal model of posttraumatic stress disorder featuring repeated exposure to situational reminders. *Biol Psychiatry*, 1996 39, 129-134.

Radecki, DT; Brown, LM; Martinez, J; Teyler, TJ. BDNF protects against stress-induced impairments in spatial learning and memory and LTP. *Hippocampus*, 2005 15(2), 246-253.

Rasmusson, AM; Shi, L; Duman, R. Downregulation of BDNF mRNA in the hippocampal dentate gyrus after re-exposure to cues previously associated with footshock. *Neuropsychopharmacology,* 2002 27(2), 133-142.

Rasmusson, AM; Vasek, J; Lipschitz, DS; Vojvoda, D; Mustone, ME; Shi, Q; Gudmundsen, G; Morgan, CA; Wolfe, J; Charney, DS. An increased capacity for adrenal DHEA release is associated with decreased avoidance and negative mood symptoms in women with PTSD. *Neuropsychopharmacology*, 2004 29, 1546-1557.

Richter-Levin, G. Acute and long-term behavioral correlates of underwater trauma--potential relevance to stress and post-stress syndromes. *Psychiatry Res*, 1998 79, 73-83.

Rinne, T; Westenberg, HG; den Boer, JA; van den Brink, W. Serotonergic blunting to meta-chlorophenylpiperazine (m-CPP) highly correlates with sustained childhood abuse in impulsive and autoaggressive female borderline patients. *Biol Psychiatry*, 2000 47(6), 548-56.

Rohleder, N; Joksimovic, L; Wolf, JM; Kirschbaum, C. Hypocortisolism and increased glucocorticoid sensitivity of pro-Inflammatory cytokine production in Bosnian war refugees with posttraumatic stress disorder. *Biol Psychiatry* 2004 55, 745-751.

Rothermundt, M; Peters, M; Prehn, JH; Arolt, V. S100B in brain damage and neurodegeneration. *Microsc Res Tech*, 2003 60(6), 614-632.

Sabioncello, A; Kocijan-Hercigonja, D; Rabatic, S; Tomasic, J; Jeren, T; Matijevic, L; Rijavec, M; Dekaris, D. Immune, endocrine, and psychological responses in civilians displaced by war. *Psychosom Med,* 2000 62, 502-508.

Sajdyk, TJ; Shekhar, A; Gehlert, DR. Interactions between NPY and CRF in the amygdala to regulate emotionality. *Neuropeptides*, 2004 38, 225-234.

Sautter, FJ; Bissette, G; Wiley, J; Manguno-Mire, G; Schoenbachler, B; Myers, L; Johnson, JE; Cerbone, A; Malaspina, D. Corticotropin-releasing factor in posttraumatic stress disorder (PTSD) with secondary psychotic symptoms, nonpsychotic PTSD, and healthy control subjects. *Biol Psychiatry* 2003 54, 1382-1388.

Sawamura, T; Shimizu, K; Nibuya, M; Wakizono, T; Suzuki, G; Tsunoda, T; Takahashi, Y; Nomura, S. Effect of paroxetine on a model of posttraumatic stress disorder in rats. *Neurosci Lett*, 2004 357, 37-40.

Scaccianoce, S; Del Bianco, P; Pannitteri, G; Passarelli, F. Relationship between stress and circulating levels of S100B protein. *Brain Res*, 2004 1004(1-2), 208-2011.

Scaer, RC. The neurophysiology of dissociation and chronic disease. *Appl Psychophysiol Biofeedback,* 2001 26,73-91.

Schelling, G; Roozendaal, B; De Quervain, DJ. Can posttraumatic stress disorder be prevented with glucocorticoids? *Ann N Y Acad Sci*, 2004 1032,158-166.

Schulz, B; Fendt, M; Schnitzler, HU. Clonidine injections into the lateral nucleus of the amygdale block acquisition and expression of fear-potentiated startle. *Eur J Neurosci*, 2002 15(1), 151-157.

Schweitzer, I; Morris, P; Hopwood, M; Maguire, K; Norman, T. Prolactin response to d-fenfluramine in combat-related post-traumatic stress disorder. *Int J Neuropsychopharmacol*, 2004 7,291-298.

Segman, RH; Cooper-Kazaz, R; Macciardi, F; Goltser, T; Halfon, Y; Dobroborski, T; Shalev, AY. Association between the dopamine transporter gene and posttraumatic stress disorder. *Molecular Psychiatry*, 2002 7(8), 903-907.

Servatius, RJ; Ottenweller, JE; Natelson, BH. Delayed startle sensitization distinguishes rats exposed to one or three stress sessions: further evidence toward an animal model of PTSD. *Biol Psychiatry* 1995 38, 539-546.

Sher, L; Oquendo, MA; Galfalvy, HC; Cooper, TB; Mann, JJ. Age effects on cortisol levels in depressed patients with and without comorbid post-traumatic stress disorder, and healthy volunteers. *J Affect Disord*, 2004 82, 53-59.

Sherstnev, VV; Storozheva, ZI; Proshin, AT; Makhmutov, RY; Puzyrev, AV. S100B protein in pro- and antiapoptotic doses produces different effects on defensive behavior in adult rats. *Bull Exp Biol Med*, 2003 136(6), 543-547.

Shimizu, E; Hashimoto, K; Okamura, N; Koike, K; Komatsu, N; Kumakiri, C; Nakazato, M; Watanabe, H; Shinoda, N; Okada, S; Iyo, M. Alterations of serum levels of brain-derived neurotrophic factor (BDNF) in depressed patients with or without antidepressants. *Biol Psychiatry,* 2003 54(1), 70-75.

Shinba, T; Shinozaki, T; Mugishima, G. Clonidine immediately after immobilization stress prevents long-lasting locomotion reduction in the rat. *Prog Neuropsychopharmacol Biol Psychiatry* 2001 25, 1629-1640.

Shirayama, Y; Chen, AC; Nakagawa, S; Russell, DS; Duman, RS. Brain-derived neurotrophic factor produces antidepressant effects in behavioral models of depression. *J Neurosci,* 2002 22(8), 3251-3261.

Smith, MA; Davidson, J; Ritchie, JC; Kudler, H; Lipper, S; Chappell, P; Nemeroff, CB. The corticotropin-releasing hormone test in patients with posttraumatic stress disorder. *Biol Psychiatry*, 1989 26, 349-355.

Smith, MA; Makino, S; Kvetnansky, R; Post, RM. Stress and glucocorticoids affect the expression of brain-derived neurotrophic factor and neurotrophin-3 mRNAs in the hippocampus. *J Neurosci* 1995 15, 1768-1777.

Sondergaard, HP; Theorell, T. A longitudinal study of hormonal reactions accompanying life events in recently resettled refugees. *Psychother Psychosom*, 2003 72, 49-58.

Southwick, SM; Krystal, JH; Morgan, CA; Johnson, D; Nagy, LM; Nicolaou, A; Heninger, GR; Charney, DS. Abnormal noradrenergic function in posttraumatic stress disorder. *Arch Gen Psychiatry*, 1993 50(4), 266-274.

Southwick, SM; Krystal, JH; Bremner, JD; Morgan, CA 3rd; Nicolaou, AL; Nagy, LM; Johnson, DR; Heninger, GR; Charney, DS. Noradrenergic and serotonergic function in posttraumatic stress disorder. *Arch Gen Psychiatry*, 1997 54, 749-758.

Southwick, SM; Bremner, JD; Rasmusson, A; Morgan, CA 3rd; Arnsten, A; Charney, DS. Role of norepinephrine in the pathophysiology and treatment of posttraumatic stress disorder. *Biol Psychiatry*, 1999 46(9),1192-1204.

Spivak, B; Shohat, B; Mester, R; Avraham, S; Gil-Ad, I; Bleich, A; Valevski, A; Weizman, A. Elevated levels of serum interleukin-1 beta in combat-related posttraumatic stress disorder. *Biol Psychiatry*. 1997 42(5), 345-348.

Spivak, B; Vered, Y; Graff, E; Blum, I; Mester, R; Weizman, A. Low platelet-poor plasma concentrations of serotonin in patients with combat-related posttraumatic stress disorder. *Biol Psychiatry*, 1999 45(7), 840-845.

Stam, R; Bruijnzeel, AW; Wiegant, VM. Long-lasting stress sensitisation. *Eur J Pharmacol*, 2000 405, 217-224.

Steiger, H; Gauvin, L; Israel, M; Koerner, N; Ng Ying Kin NM, Paris, J; Young, SN. Association of serotonin and cortisol indices with childhood abuse in bulimia nervosa. *Arch Gen Psychiatry*, 2001 58(9), 837-843.

Stein, MB; Koverola, C; Hanna, C; Torchia, MG; McClarty, B. Hippocampal volume in women victimized by childhood sexual abuse. *Psychol Med*, 1997 27(4), 951-959.

Strawn, JR; Ekhator, NN; Horn, OS; Baker, DG; Geracioti, TD Jr. Blood pressure and cerebrospinal fluid norepinephrine in combat-related posttraumatic stress disorder. *Psychosom Med* 2004 66, 757-759.

Strohle, A; Holsboer, F. Stress responsive neurohormones in depression and anxiety. *Pharmacopsychiatry*, 2003 36(3), 207-214.

Stuckey, J.; Marra, S.; Minor, T.; Insel, T. Changes in μ-opiate receptors following inescapable shock. *Brain Res*, 1989 476,167-69.

Suzuki, F; Kato, K; Kato, T; Ogasawara, N. S-100 protein in clonal astroglioma cells is released by adrenocorticotropic hormone and corticotropin-like intermediate-lobe peptide. *J Neurochem*, 1987 49(5), 1557-1563.

Tanaka, M; Yoshiba, M; Emoto, H; Ishi, H. Noradrenaline systems in the hypothalamus, amygdala and locus ceruleus ar involved in the provocation of anxiety:basic studies. *Eur J Pharmacol,* 2000 405, 397-406.

Tang-Christensen, M; Havel, PJ; Jacobs, RR; Larsen, PJ; Cameron, JL. Central administration of leptin inhibits food intake and activates the sympathetic nervous system in rhesus macaques. *J Clin Endocrinol Metab*, 1999 84,711-717.

Thiebot, MH; Martin, P; Puech, AJ. Animal behavioural studies in the evaluation of antidepressant drugs. *Br J Psychiatry*, 1992 15,44-50.

Tramontina, F; Conte, S; Goncalves, D; Gottfried, C; Portela, LV; Vinade, L; Salbego, C; Gonçalves, CA. Developmental changes in S100B content in brain tissue, cerebrospinal fluid, and astrocyte cultures of rats. *Cell Mol Neurobiol*, 2002 22(3),373-378.

Tucker, P; Beebe, KL; Burgin, C; Wyatt, DB; Parker, DE; Masters, BK; Nawar, O. Paroxetine treatment of depression with posttraumatic stress disorder: effects on autonomic reactivity and cortisol secretion. *J Clin Psychopharmacol*, 2004 24,131-140. (b)

Tucker, P; Ruwe, WD; Masters, B; Parker, DE; Hossain, A; Trautman, RP; Wyatt, DB. Neuroimmune and cortisol changes in selective serotonin reuptake inhibitor and placebo treatment of chronic posttraumatic stress disorder. *Biol Psychiatry*, 2004 56, 121-128. (a)

Vaidya, VA; Marek, GJ; Aghajanian, GK; Duman, RS. 5-HT2A receptor-mediated regulation of brain-derived neurotrophic factor mRNA in the hippocampus and the neocortex. *J Neurosci,* 1997 17(8), 2785-2795.

Vaiva, G; Thomas, P; Ducrocq, F; Fontaine, M; Boss, V; Devos, P; Rascle, C; Cottencin, O; Brunet, A; Laffargue, P; Goudemand, M. Low posttrauma GABA plasma levels as a predictive factor in the development of acute posttraumatic stress disorder. *Biol Psychiatry*, 2004 55(3), 250-254.

Valentino, RJ; Van Bockstaele, E. Opposing regulation of the locus coeruleus by corticotropin-releasing factor and opioids. Potential for reciprocal interactions between stress and opioid sensitivity. *Psychopharmacology,* 2001 158(4), 331-342.

van der Kolk, BA; Greenberg, MS; Orr, SP; Pitman, RK. Endogenous opioids, stress induced analgesia, and posttraumatic stress disorder. *Psychopharmacol Bull*, 1989 25(3), 417-421.

Vermetten, E; Bremener, D. Circuits and systems in stress. I preclinical studies. *Depress and Anxiety*, 2002 15, 126-147.

Vermetten, E; Vythilingam, M.; Southwick, SM; Charney, DS; Bremner, JD. Long-term treatment with paroxetine increases verbal declarative memory and hippocampal volume in posttraumatic stress disorder. *Biol Psych*, 2003 54, 693-702.

Whitaker-Azmitia, PM; Murphy, R; Azmitia, EC. Stimulation of astroglial 5-HT1A receptors releases the serotonergic growth factor, protein S-100, and alters astroglial morphology. *Brain Res*, 1990 528(1), 155-158.

Willner, P. Validity, reliability and utility of the chronic mild stress model of depression: a 10-year review and evaluation. *Psychopharmacology* (Berl), 1997 134, 319-329.

Winter, H; Irle, E. Hippocampal volume in adult burn patients with and without posttraumantic stress disorder. *Am J Psych*, 2004 161, 2194-2200.

Yamada, K; Nabeshima, T. Brain-derived neurotrophic factor/TrkB signaling in memory processes. *J Pharmacol Sci*, 2003 91(4), 267-270.

Yatham, LN; Sacamano, J; Kusumakar, V. Assessment of noradrenergic functioning in patients with non-combat-related posttraumatic stress disorder: a study with desmethylimipramine and orthostatic challenges. *Psychiatry Res,* 1996 63(1), 1-6.

Yehuda, R; Southwick, S; Giller, EL; Ma, X; Mason, JW. Urinary catecholamine excretion and severity of PTSD symptoms in Vietnam combat veterans. *J Nerv Ment Dis*, 1992 180(5), 321-325.

Yehuda, R; Antelman, SM. Criteria for rationally evaluating animal models of posttraumatic stress disorder. *Biol Psychiatry*, 1993 33, 479-486.

Yehuda, R; Kahana, B; Schmeidler, J; Southwick, SM; Wilson, S; Giller, EL. Impact of cumulative lifetime trauma and recent stress on current posttraumatic stress disorder symptoms in holocaust survivors. *Am J Psychiatry*, 1995 152(12),1815-1818.

Yehuda, R; Siever, LJ; Teicher, MH; Levengood, RA; Gerber, DK; Schmeidler, J; Yang, RK. Plasma norepinephrine and 3-methoxy-4-hydroxyphenylglycol concentrations and severity of depression in combat posttraumatic stress disorder and major depressive disorder. *Biol Psychiatry*, 1998 44(1), 56-63.

Yehuda, R; MC Farlane, A; Shalev AY. Predicting the development of posttraumatic stress disorder from the acute response to a traumatic event. *Biol Psych*, 1998 44, 1305-1313.

Yehuda, R. Biological factors associated with susceptibility to posttraumatic stress disorder. *Can J Psychiatry*, 1999 44(1), 34-39.

Yehuda, R; Golier, JA; Halligan, SL; Meaney, M; Bierer, LM. The ACTH response to dexamethasone in PTSD. *Am J Psychiatry*, 2004 161,1397-1403. (a)

Yehuda, R; Golier, JA; Yang, RK; Tischler, L. Enhanced sensitivity to glucocorticoids in peripheral mononuclear leukocytes in posttraumatic stress disorder. *Biol Psychiatry*, 2004 55, 1110-1116. (b)

Yehuda, R; Halligan, SL; Golier, JA; Grossman, R; Bierer, LM. Effects of trauma exposure on the cortisol response to dexamethasone administration in PTSD and major depressive disorder. *Psychoneuroendocrinology,* 2004 29,:389-404. (d)

Yehuda, R; Yang, RK; Golier, JA; Tischler, L; Liong, B; Decker, K. Effect of topiramate on glucocorticoid receptor mediated action. *Neuropsychopharmacology*, 2004 29(2), :433-439. (c)

Young, EA; Breslau, N. Saliva cortisol in posttraumatic stress disorder: a community epidemiologic study. *Biol Psychiatry*, 2004a 56(3):205-209.

Young, EA; Breslau, N. Cortisol and catecholamines in posttraumatic stress disorder: an epidemiologic community study. *Arch Gen Psychiatry*, 2004b 61(4), 394-401.

Young, EA; Tolman, R; Witkowski, K; Kaplan, G. Salivary cortisol and posttraumatic stress disorder in a low-income community sample of women. *Biol Psychiatry*, 2004 55, 621-626.

In: Posttraumatic Stress Disorder: New Research
Editor: Guida D. Kume, pp.147-166
ISBN 1-60021-078-3

Chapter 5

FOCUSING ON TRAUMA AND PTSD IN GENERAL PSYCHIATRIC SERVICES – COULD OUTCOME BE IMPROVED?

***Suad Al-Saffar*[1] *and Per Borgå*[2]**
[1]Section for Psychiatry, Neurotec Department, Karolinska Institutet, Stockholm,
Unit of Mental Health, Stockholm Center of Public Health, Stockholm County Council
[2]Karolinska Institutet Danderyd Hospital, Psychiatric Clinic, Danderyd

ABSTRACT

This chapter deals with trauma and PTSD in general outpatient psychiatry, its prevalence and aetiology, the long-term consequences of unrecognised PTSD and the benefits of focusing on trauma in treatment.

INTRODUCTION

History of Trauma in Psychiatry

One of the key issues concerning psychopathology is its causes. With few exceptions, this search for causes has been less successful in psychiatry. However, the significance of trauma in the development of psychopathology was recognised long before the development of modern classification systems. Oppenheim, quoted by Kraepelin, named anxiety as a response to various stress "traumatic neuroses" *(Kraepelin, 1896)*. Freud's original theory implied that hysteria had a traumatic origin *(Breuer & Freud, 1973)*. While the psychoanalytic school regarded both early traumas of a developmental origin and external stresses experienced in childhood as critical determinants of adult psychopathology, it overlooked the possibility that extreme stresses in adulthood could be equally destabilising in their own right to the individual's psychological functioning *(Yehuda & McFarlane, 1995)*.

Trauma and its psychiatric consequences normally gain attention in times of war and national disaster only to fall into relative oblivion during the intervening periods. World War I and II were accompanied by descriptions of sequels to mental trauma under different names: shell shock syndrome, war sailor syndrome and KZ syndrome. The latter was described amongst survivors of the Nazi death camps, when they came as refugees to the Nordic countries *(Eitinger 1961; Eitinger 1965)* and has been used as a concept to our days. Characteristic for this condition was a nervous, excessive irritability as well as concentration difficulties and impaired memory. The KZ syndrome was initially interpreted as being caused by nutrition deficiency and it was only gradually recognised that psychological trauma had given rise to the condition.

Posttraumatic Stress Disorder in the DSM-system

After the Vietnam War the need for diagnosing traumatic sequelae was again addressed. The entry of the PTSD diagnosis in DSM-III *(American Psychiatric Association, 1980)* resulted in increasing number of studies to date, which have shown that different groups exposed to life threatening events develop the condition to a high degree *(Goenjian, et al. 2000; Fox and Tang, 2000; Harvey and Bryant, 1998; Epstein et al. 1998; Ursano et al. 1999; Wang et al. 2000; Wolfe et al. 1999; Wagner et al. 1998).* In line with its previous history, PTSD was linked to an event "outside the range of normal human experience". This was considered the A-criterion of the diagnosis. The B-criterion was intrusive memories of the traumatic event, the C-criterion avoidance of anything that could trigger the memories – leading to a circumscribed life - and the D-criterion hyper-arousal, an excessive irritability showing itself by e.g. concentration difficulties, disturbed sleep or an exaggerated startle response.

Different treatment centres, specialised in the treatment of specific traumas like war, torture, or sexual violence developed over time. In western European countries, refugees were taken care of at such centres, whilst in the USA those treatment centres predominated that were geared to the services of Vietnam veterans.

Trauma was initially conceptualised in singular, but the question was eventually raised whether childhood trauma could facilitate the development of PTSD when the person was later, in adult life, exposed to a subsequent trauma. Several studies have shown that the combination of childhood and adult trauma increased the risk of developing PTSD *(Davidson 1991; Bremner, Southwick et al. 1993; Zaidi and Foy 1994; Breslau, Chilcoat et al. 1999).* Recent studies show that multiple exposures to traumatic events, either of the same or of different kind, are associated with higher risk of developing PTSD *(Amir and Sol 1999; Breslau, Peterson et al. 1999; Green, Goodman et al. 2000). Dougall* et al have reported that individuals exposed to different kinds of traumas run a higher risk of developing PTSD than those exposed to the same type of event *(Dougall, Herberman et al. 2000).*

As population surveys revealed that traumas and PTSD were more prevalent than earlier thought (see below) the qualifying trauma could no longer be considered as "outside the range of normal human experience". DSM-IV revised the A-criterion to mean, having been exposed to a traumatic event involving actual or threatened death, serious injury or a threat to the physical integrity that evoked intense fear, helplessness or horror *(Association 1994).* Thus extreme trauma in everyday life came more into focus. Such traumas could be directed towards oneself or others. While the DSM system generally claims to be neutral in relation to etiologic theories, PTSD is one exception defined by an etiologic factor, i.e. exposure to an extreme traumatic event.

Earlier systems of classification, before the DSM-III, tended to assume that symptoms as a response to trauma would be time limited unless some pre-existing character pathology was present that would contribute to their maintenance *(Green, Lindy et al. 1985)*. According to DSM-I *(American 1952)*, "gross stress reaction" disorder would resolve rapidly unless perpetuated by premorbid personality pathology. DSM-II *(American 1968)* had a similar view and categorized the effect of traumatic events under the diagnosis "transient situational disturbance" if the symptoms were short-lived, and would then use the category of "Anxiety neurosis" for more enduring symptoms. This implied that the stress response was transitory in nature unless the individual had some particular vulnerability. DSM-III *(Association 1980)* emphasised the significance of extreme trauma for the development of an enduring, disabling condition, irrespective of the person's vulnerability. Extremely traumatic events "outside the range of normal human experience" could produce a chronic clinical disorder in previously healthy individuals *(Horowitz 1987)*. The view emphasised was that PTSD involved a natural process of adaptation to extraordinarily adverse situations and that the pattern of symptoms did not depend on a constitutional vulnerability. In DSM-III, PTSD, as a normative and adaptive response to trauma, addressed a social and political issue as well as a mental health one. It was thereby linked to Eitinger's view on survivors from the concentration camps, who had been victims of barbaric nazism *(Eitinger 1961; Eitinger 1965; Breslau, Chilcoat et al. 1999)* but also to views expressed by opponents of the Vietnam War.

Through the shift of focus, from the vulnerability of the individual to extreme external events, victims of traumatic experiences have received diagnostic clarity without being burdened by, or ashamed of, their own reactions as signs of weakness. This new socio-political perspective on human reactions to trauma has contributed to developing the subject of human rights, e.g. through organisations against torture, political and social oppression. This view is also reflected in the work of the United Nation and World Health Organisation (WHO 2002).

However, the debate concerning how trauma versus vulnerability should be weighed in the aetiology of PTSD, is an ongoing one. In the latest versions in the DSM-system, there is again an increasing interest in the role of the premorbid personality for the development of PTSD. Many life event researchers hold the view that the individual is subjected to traumatic events due to his own premorbid personality. The individual's mental state during the course of events is the primary reason for being victimised. Life event researchers who emphasise the role of the personality for the development of PTSD seek support in studies reporting that irrespective of the intensity of the trauma, seldom more than 50 percent of a subjected population will qualify for the PTSD diagnosis *(Green, Lindy et al. 1985)*.

In contrast, there are different studies showing that, as intensity of exposure increases, the proportion of victims who develop PTSD increases progressively *(Horowitz, Weine et al. 1995)*. There are a number of studies showing that a history of an earlier traumatic event with which the person has not come to terms may increase the risk of developing PTSD when later subjected to a further trauma *(Breslau, Davis et al. 1991; Davidson 1991; Zaidi and Foy 1994)*.

Table 1. Diagnoses for traumatic stress according to the DSM system, 1952 to 1999.

DSM SYSTEM	Short-lived (seen as normal reaction in all DSM manual)	Chronic or delayed
DSM-I (1952)	Gross stress reaction	Premorbid personality pathology
DSM-II (1968)	Transient situational disturbance	Anxiety neurosis, Premorbid personality pathology
DSM-III (1980)	Posttraumatic stress disorder, acute (duration< 6 months)	Posttraumatic stress disorder Normal reaction
DSM-III-R (1987)	Posttraumatic stress disorder, acute (duration< 1month)	Posttraumatic stress disorder Normal reaction
DSM-IV (1994)	PTSD-acute (duration < 1 month)	Posttraumatic stress disorder Normal reaction / Premorbid personality pathology
DSM-VI-TR (1999)	PTSD-acute (duration < 3 months)	Posttraumatic stress disorder Normal reaction / Premorbid personality pathology

Prevalence of Trauma and PTSD in the General Population

Most prevalence studies of exposure to traumas and PTSD have been carried out in the USA, which means that we lack knowledge of the situation in large parts of the world where the population may be considered as being at high risk. As there are indications that violence is on the increase world-wide, it is an important aspect of mental health in the population to focus on trauma and the consequences of trauma *(WHO, 2002*). According to recent population surveys in the USA around 60% have experienced one trauma that probably fulfil the A-criterion according to DSM-IV *(Kessler, Sonnega et al. 1995; Green, Goodman et al. 2000; Flett, Kazantzis et al. 2002)*. A considerable minority, 25% of females and 34% of males have experienced multiple events (Kessler, Sonnega et al. 1995).

Breslau found that more than one third of respondents already had experienced at least one traumatic event by the beginning of early adulthood *(Breslau, Davis et al. 1991)*. In these surveys, traumas to a relative or close friend are sometimes included, but rarely accounted for separately, following the DSM-IV assumption that they contribute to the development of PTSD, also when they are not directly witnessed.

Recent surveys, using DSM-IV criteria, indicate that 7-10% in general populations have a PTSD syndrome (Breslau, Davis et al. 1991; Kessler, Sonnega et al. 1995). Such figures seem considarable when compared to the limited numbers of patients catered for at treatment centres specialised in the treatment of specific traumas. The question then arises:

How does general psychiatric practice reflect those high prevalence figures?

Trauma and PTSD are Underestimated in General Psychiatric Services

It appears that general psychiatric units do not consistently apply a trauma perspective focusing on PTSD *(Davidson and Smith, 1990; Zimmerman and Mattia, 1999)*. Although trauma experiences may be prevalent, this is seldom reflected in diagnoses and treatment given (21.Tucker W).

This deficient focusing on trauma and PTSD is partly connected with the resistance that the patient, but also the treatment staff *(Jacobson and Richardson, 1987; Simpson et al. 1994; Bryer et al. 1987),* can feel when it comes to uncovering trauma. According to Jakobson and Richardson only about one tenth of the patients' traumas are known to the therapist.

Another reason for underestimation is that the majority of patients who fulfil the criteria for PTSD also fulfil criteria for at least one other diagnosis *(Brady, 1997; Brady et al. 2000; Davidsson and Foa, 1991; Kulka et al. 1990; Mueser et al. 1998; Kidson et al. 1993).* Without sufficient knowledge about PTSD, or a strategy for regularly focusing on trauma, treatment staff will allow a more established diagnosis to come to the forefront, thus overlooking the trauma component in the pathogenesis.

Is it Therapeutic to Focus on Trauma in Treatment?

Re-experiencing and reworking of traumatic memories has since long been the rule at institutions specialising in trauma and this has been supported by different therapeutic traditions *(Rachman 1980; Bady 1985; Nichols and Efran 1985).* It has been seen as essential to create a supportive environment, in which the patient can feel confidence, to enable him or her to open up to, and at the same time not get overwhelmed by the traumatic memories. If the anxiety is not triggered the patient has an opportunity to make use of his cognitive abilities in working through his memories. Recent studies show that both exposure therapy and cognitive behavioural therapy are effective for PTSD *(Paunovich and Öst 2001; Rothbaum and Schwartz 2002).* It seems that in Eye Movement Desensitisation Restructuring therapy (EMDR), regular eye movements effectively block the triggering of anxiety while recalling and thinking about the most fearful memories.

However, in everyday clinical work, the view is common among treatment staff that it may be distressing and even harmful for the patient to be reminded about horrifying traumas. The argument seems to be that at least when specialist trauma-therapeutic skills are missing, amnesia is the best to hope for.

Also these views have got support in scientific literature. Thus there are diverging opinions as to whether traumatic experiences should be addressed and re-experienced in therapy. "There is no evidence that just talking about the trauma is in itself sufficient" *(Kinzie and Boehnlein 1993).* Other authors suggest that re-experiencing painful emotions in an unstructured fashion may in fact be harmful and point out that the benefit of focusing on trauma in treatment is not evidence based *(Mac Farlane 1994; Litrell 1998).* Recent meta-analyses show that single session debriefing after major traumas has not proved efficient in long-term outcome *(van Emmerik, Kamphuis et al. 2002; Rose, Bisson et al. 2003),* which could also be seen as a support for this view.

In spite of the controversy there is no study focusing on the question of whether outcome differs when trauma was addressed in treatment or not, i.e. When a trauma has been acknowledged and attended to according to the patient's view, regardless of therapeutic methods.

Research Questions and Aims

Important questions are: How prevalent is PTSD in general psychiatry populations? What are the etiological events? What is the role of relatives' traumas for the development of PTSD? What role do multiple traumas play in comparison to a single event? Does the diagnosis have any significance for treatment and outcome? Do socio-demographic factors affect the outcome in PTSD? Is PTSD a diagnosis mainly to be considered for certain risk groups with known traumas, like refugees and war combatants, or is it relevant for general psychiatric services? Does the long-term outcome differ between patients who report that their traumas were recognised and sufficiently addressed in the course of treatment, and those who report that they were not? If it does, what are the factors influencing whether traumas are sufficiently addressed or not?

The aim of this chapter is to address these research questions, focusing a general psychiatry outpatient clinic in a multiethnic suburban living area in the neighbourhood of Stockholm.

The Living Area, the Psychiatric Clinic and the Study Population

The investigated area is a suburb of Stockholm with a total population of 43,870. It was erected in the sixties and seventies to meet the housing needs of Stockholm's growing population. Multi-family blocks of flats predominated the municipality.

The adult population, 18 years and above, was 31,155 at the time of the survey. The proportion of children and teenagers was somewhat higher than the average of Stockholm county, but the most striking difference was that the proportion of foreign born inhabitants was considerably higher: 48 percent. Among those who had arrived early as labour migrants were Turks. Later migrant groups had a considerable proportion of refugees, such as Iranians and other groups from the Middle East. The number of different nationalities was, however, large.

Psychiatric services were supplied by an outpatient clinic that could also reply on some inpatient facilities in a more centrally situated psychiatric inpatient clinic. The outpatient clinic had not been given any extra facilities due to the multiethnic composition of its catchment area. Like other psychiatric clinics in Stockholm, it had adopted the "team psychiatry model". The team responsible for this catchment area comprised psychiatrists, psychologists, nurses, social workers and mental nursing auxiliaries, sometimes also an occupational therapist. There was no special trauma focus at the clinic, and the level of psychotherapeutic training was ordinary.

Contrary to most other outpatient facilities at the time the clinic maintained an outpatient register where patient and treatment data were entered at the end of the year or when treatment was finalised. Assessments of the patients, such as diagnoses according to DSM-III R and a global assessment of improvement/deterioration were also made by the staff. The register gave a good overview of the patients and helped to select the study population. It also served as a tool for comparing the dropouts from respondents. As the main focus of the study was on trauma and PTSD two foreign born groups with a presumed high exposure to traumas were chosen: patients born in Iran and in the Arab-speaking countries of the Middle East. A group of Swedes with similar age and gender distribution as these two groups was selected.

Finally all patients born in Turkey were included. Although they shared the exile situation with the previous two groups they were presumed to have a lower prevalence of trauma, as they had come to Sweden mainly as labour migrants and relatives of labour migrants.

The Questionnaire Study

The questionnaire contained standard instruments as well as items especially constructed for this study.

130 patients, belonging to the four ethnic groups, who during a period of one year had visited the psychiatric outpatient clinic, completed a questionnaire 3-4 years later. None of them had been diagnosed with PTSD at the clinic.

The self-rating instrument for posttraumatic stress disorder (SRIP) was used, measuring symptoms of intrusion, avoidance and hyper-arousal according to the DSM-system, but with no reference to a specific trauma *(Hovens 1994)*. Traumas experienced were recorded separately, thus enabling to study the relationship between trauma and PTSD outcome. A trauma questionnaire that enquired about traumas experienced by the individual himself, and by relatives and close friends, separately was included. Traumas mentioned, among others covered traffic accidents, physical assault and traumas related to political persecution and war such as imprisonment and torture. There was for both categories (own trauma and relative's trauma) a free report of any other event the respondent had found equally traumatic. Freely reported replies were assessed by the researchers whether they belonged to the type of trauma DSM-IV is referring to. Questions were posed whether trauma had been mentioned in treatment and if so, had it been addressed. Self-rated health (SRH) (Bjørner JB 1996), HSCL-25, the depression sub-scale from SCL-90 and social and work adaptation measured outcome. In this respect patients with and without PTSD were compared, likewise patients who reported that trauma(s) had been satisfactorily addressed in the course of treatment and those who stated that it had not.

All variables were summarised using standard descriptive statistics, such as mean (M), standard deviation (SD), and frequencies (n and %). Differences between groups, e.g. PTSD vs. non-PTSD, in continuous variables were analysed with parametric Student's t-test (approximately normally distributed variables) or non-parametric Mann-Whitney U-test (skewed distributions). In case of more than two groups, one-way ANOVA or Kruskal-Wallis H-test was used. For discrete variables the χ^2-test (Fisher's exact test when an expected cell frequency was below 6) was used. A significance level of 5 percent (two-tailed) was applied.

In order not to over-interpret the relationships by using common variance in more than one comparison, stepwise logistic regression analyses (forward) were performed on dichotomised variables. This analysis was, thus, used to study independent relationships between key variables, such as having a trauma sufficiently addressed and probable PTSD, and e.g. ethnicity and clinical ratings, and not for prediction.

Results and Discussion

Prevalence of Trauma and PTSD

Of all respondents, 89 % reported being exposed to any traumatic event and 77 % to multiple events. There were no gender differences in the total number of traumas. The event of having been imprisoned was more frequent among male patients [$\chi^2(1)= 7.8$, $p<0.01$]. Forty-nine percent of women vs. 30% of men reported own traumas in the free report [χ^2 (1)=4.03, $p<0.05$]. The responses given included unexpected deaths in the family, the birth of a severely handicapped child, severe illness (own and close relative's), suicide attempt by a relative, threatened extradition from the country and having lost custody of a child to a partner in another country without possibility of keeping contact.

Ethnic minorities generally had higher number of own traumas as compared to Swedish-born patients, mean 3.51± 2.53 vs. 1.6± 1.55 (z=4.49, $p<0.001$). Traumas reported involving relatives' were 3.03±3.16 vs. 1.78±1.96 (z=1.41, p=0.16). Traumas related to war, both own trauma those involving relatives', were more frequent among patients from Arabian and Iranian groups than among Swedes and Turks, 67% vs. 1% [χ^2 (1)= 59.21, $p<0.001$] and 35% vs. 9% [$\chi^2(1)=11.93$, $p<0.01$].

Amongst Swedish patients the free report was the item most frequently answered affirmatively (45%).

Of those 115 subjects who responded satisfactorily to the PTSD symptomatic instrument, 53 (46%) patients fulfilled the symptom criteria for PTSD and were, assessed as PTSD, whereas 62 (54%) patients were regarded as being non-PTSD. Of Swedish patients 29% fulfilled PTSD criteria. The corresponding figure for Arabs was 59%, for Iranians 69% and for Turks 53% [χ^2 (3)= 11.18, $p<0.01$].

The high prevalence in this study is partly due to an overrepresentation of ethnic minorities with a refugee background, but regarding the Swedish patients still in line with some recent studies of outpatient populations (Kessler, Sonnega et al. 1995; Rosenberg, Rosenberg et al. 2000).

There are several reasons why rates of trauma exposure and PTSD in previous studies of clinical populations may often be underestimated. Self-reporting instruments normally give higher prevalence of different disorders compared to those based on interviews, but not necessarily less accurate. Another reason is that most previous PTSD instruments link the A-criterion (the trauma) to the diagnostic PTSD-instrument. When the A-criterion is asked for in the diagnostic process, there is a risk is that exclusively symptoms pertaining to one trauma will be exhibited. Solomon et al point at the risk of underreporting symptoms especially amongst multiple traumatised patients, when the symptom is not related to a specific identified event (Solomon, Keane et al 1996). This may result in the exclusion of true PTSD cases. Similarly, not linking the A-criterion to items concerning symptoms (B, C and D criteria) probably opened up for revealing more symptoms, than if these had been enquired about in relation to a specific traumatic event. The multiple trauma aetiology for PTSD demonstrated in this and other studies, speaks in favour of a less closed way of asking about symptoms.

Separately asking for specific traumas, besides including a free report, captured the multiplicity of traumas in our sample. The results show that most patients with probable

PTSD had gone through a multiplicity of traumas in line with earlier findings (Amir and Sol 1999).

Background and Treatment amongst PTSD and Non-PTSD Patients

PTSD and non-PTSD patients were similar in all socio-demographic variables, except for the fact that more PTSD patients were reared in an urban area and had a higher proportion of widows. Concerning original diagnoses given at the outpatient clinic, there were no significant difference between PTSD and non-PTSD groups, with the only exception that fewer PTSD patients had diagnosis deferred on Axis I (2%vs.11%, Fisher's exact test $p<0.05$). No patient had received a PTSD diagnosis. With regard to medication the PTSD patients received anti-depressants more often than non-PTSD patients did [$\chi^2(1)=8.95, p<0.01$]. Immediate treatment outcome (at the end of the year or at the end of treatment) did not differ between PTSD- and non-PTSD patients according to the assessment of staff.

The Aetiology of PTSD

Naturally trauma exposure differed between PTSD- and non-PTSD patients. Patients who fulfilled PTSD criteria had a higher number of own traumas 3.3 ± 0.4 compared to 1.6 ± 0.3 for non-PTSD patients ($p<0.001$). Similarly, relatives of PTSD-patients had more traumas as compared to non-PTSD-patients, 3.7 ± 0.03 vs. 1.8 ± 0.3 ($p<0.001$).

Certain traumas, like a serious accident, physical assault, torture and war trauma, were significantly related to fulfilling PTSD criteria. Nearly all examples of traumas to a relative or close friend were related to PTSD development.

As both traumas directed towards the patient and her or his relatives and close friends contribute to the development of symptomatic PTSD, Figure 1 illustrates how the total number of different traumas (own and relative's added together) is associated with the prevalence of PTSD in our sample. Patients, who had not been exposed to any trauma, never fulfilled the SRIP-based, symptomatic diagnosis of PTSD [$\chi^2(1)=15.9$, $p< 0.001$]. This lends empirical support to the linkage between trauma and the symptomatic syndrome in the definition of PTSD (Association 1980; Association 1987; Association 1994).

On the other hand, 74 % of those who recorded 10 or more traumatic events fulfilled diagnostic criteria for PTSD (Fig1). The figure clearly demonstrates an increasing proportion of patients fulfilling PTSD criteria with increasing number of traumas.

In order to analyse what factors were independently associated with the development of PTSD we used a stepwise logistic regression analysis, with PTSD as the dependent variable. As independent variables were included: number of own traumas dichotomised (<3or ≥ 3 traumas) and number of traumas to relatives and close friends dichotomised (<3or ≥ 3 traumas), ethnic minority (yes/no), gender and childhood rearing area (urban/rural). Three variables were independently associated with whether the patient exhibited PTSD or not; multiplicity of relatives' traumas (≥ 3), multiplicity of own traumas (≥ 3) and belonging to an ethnic minority. Together these variables correctly identified 75 percent of the patients. Gender did not pass the inclusion criteria.

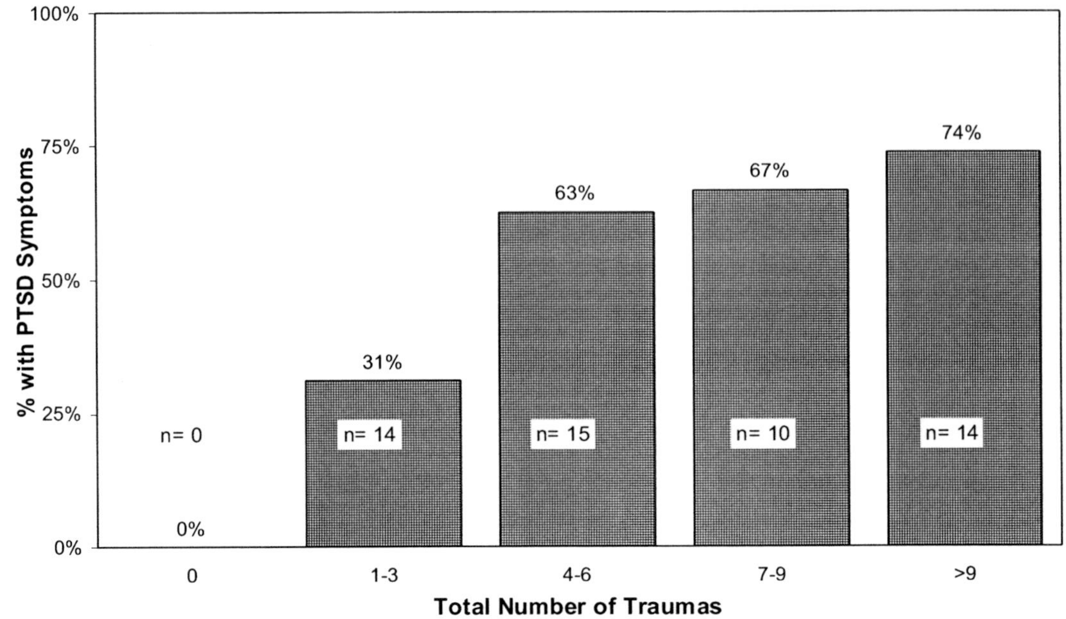

Figure 1. The proportion of PTSD in patient groups exposed to varying number of traumas

Due to collinearity between some kinds of events and low frequency of some events it was not possible to study the contribution of each type of event for the development of symptomatic PTSD.

Contrary to our expectations, reported traumas of relatives and close friends contributed as much as did the patients' own traumas to the development of PTSD. The agony caused by traumas to relatives or close friends may be perceived as more painful than a trauma targeting the individual himself, especially as the powerlessness may be experienced as greater when somebody else is victimised. The findings point at the interdependence we have with our close relatives and challenge the predominating individual perspective in psychiatric practice. Evidently, clinical practice ought to be influenced by this finding in such a way that traumas, not only of the individual himself but also of family and friends, should be mapped in history taking in order to see the patient's total trauma panorama.

Differences in Outcome between PTSD and Non-PTSD Patients

As the study's other aim was to compare the long-term outcome it may be noted that the clinic's assessment of immediate treatment outcome did not differ between patients who were assessed as PTSD and non-PTSD patients. However, the assessments by patients themselves at time of follow-up (3-4 years after the index year) give another picture (Table 2).

Table 2. Outcome at time of follow-up in PTSD and non-PTSD patients

	Total (n=115)	PTSD (n=53)	Non-PTSD (n=62)	df	Chi²=/p<
Self-rated health					z = 5.93/0.001*
Very good health	8.8%	2.0%	14.5%		
Quite good health	23.9%	5.9%	38.7%		
Fair	24.8%	19.6%	29.0%		
Pretty poor	23.9%	41.4%	9.7%		
Poor	18.6%	31.4%	8.1%		
Worried about health					z = 1.59/n.s*
Very worried	25.7%	41.2%	12.9%		
For the most part	24.8%	13.7%	33.9%		
Aware	30.1%	23.5%	35.5%		
Not concerned	19.5%	21.6%	17.7%		
How do you feel now compared with when you first made contact?					z = 4.12/0.001*
Much better	34.5%	19.2%	47.5%		
Little better	36.3%	34.6%	37.7%		
Little worse	12.4%	15.4%	9.8%		
Much worse	16.8%	30.8%	4.9%		
Working	40.4%	28.3%	50.8%	1	5.97/0.05
Work relevant to education/professional experience	54.5%	28.6%	66.7%	1	5.58/0.05
Has relatives, friends and a close friend	47.8%	38.5%	55.7%		3.35/n.s
Socialises with relatives and friends	63.7%	56.4%	69.2%	2	7.16/0.05
Active in political, union or voluntary organisation	25.2%	15.1%	33.9%	1	5.34/0.05

* Mann-Whitney's test

Thirty-one per cent of those with PTSD experienced that their health had significantly deteriorated compared to when they had first visited the clinic, as opposed to only 5 percent in the control group. Patients with PTSD also assessed their health as significantly poorer at the follow-up. It is difficult to know the extent to which the patient's and the treatment staff's different views are due to differing perspectives or to differences in the time of the assessment. If the therapist treated the patient, for example, from the diagnosis of depression, which is a common co-morbidity to PTSD (Kidson *et al.* 1993), rather than from underlying trauma, it is possible that a temporary improvement was observed. However, this improvement was not abiding, according to the patient at follow-up. This would then point to the importance of connecting the symptoms to underlying trauma in treatment.

Despite the fact that the groups did not differ regarding education, the PTSD patients were employed to a lesser extent (Table 2). Only 29 percent of those who had work found that it was on a level with their education and previous professional experience. The corresponding figure for the controls was 67 percent. However, this difference was due to the collaborating effect of ethnicity and PTSD, indicating that consequences of PTSD may be especially severe among ethnic minorities.

Outcome Variables for Patients with Trauma Sufficiently Addressed vs. not Sufficiently Addressed

In the next stage we compared patients who considered that their trauma(s) had been satisfactorily addressed in the course of treatment with those who considered that it had not. All patients who confirmed that they had mentioned their trauma(s) during treatment were included, irrespective of whether they fulfilled PTSD criteria. The basis of the division was the question whether the patient assessed that trauma(s) mentioned in treatment had been sufficiently addressed. 51 patients who considered that their trauma(s) were sufficiently addressed during treatment were compared with 39 patients who considered that it was not.

Table 3. Self-rated health and psychosocial outcome at time of follow-up amongst patients with trauma sufficiently addressed (n= 51) vs. not sufficiently addressed (n= 39).

	Trauma addressed n (%)	Trauma not addressed n (%)	Mann-Whitney z	p
Self-rated health			3.34	0.001
Very good health	6 (12)	0 (0)		
Quite good health	14 (28)	5 (13)		
Fair	14 (28)	9 (22)		
Pretty poor	10 (20)	12 (31)		
Poor	6 (14)	13 (33)		
Worried about health			0.39	ns
Very worried	15 (29)	10 (26)		
For the most part	10 (20)	11 (28)		
Aware	17 (33)	7 (18)		
Not concerned	9 (18)	11 (28)		
Improvement after contact			-3.10	0.01
Much better	20 (40)	7 (18)		
Little better	20 (40)	12 (32)		
Little worse	6 (12)	8 (21)		
Much worse	4 (8)	11 (29)		
Confidence in staff			4.39	0.001
Always	29 (57)	7 (18)		
Often	12 (24)	9 ((24)		
Sometimes	9 (18)	14 (36)		
Rarely	0 (0)	1 (3)		
Never	1 (2)	8 (21)		
Social network (passive)			1.47	ns
0	2 (4)	3 (8)		
1	8 (16)	9 (24)		
2	13 (26)	11 (29)		
3	27 (54)	15 (40)		
Social network (active)			1.77	ns
0	2 (5)	5 (16)		
1	12 (29)	9 (29)		
2	17 (41)	14 (45)		
3	11 (26)	3 (10)		

If trauma(s) had been sufficiently addressed in the view of the patients, several variables demonstrated better outcome. Trauma-addressed patients had fewer symptoms related to PTSD and depression (Table 4). The better outcome for those who had their trauma addressed could not be accounted for by other treatment variables, like medication or professional background of main therapist. The fact that patients with non-addressed trauma(s) were more often referred to a physiotherapist suggests more somatic expression in this group. There was no significant difference in the total number of visits, but patients whose trauma had been addressed had waited longer before making contact with the psychiatric care unit ($z = 2.53$, $p < 0.05$), and less often had terminated their contact at the time of follow-up ($\chi^2 = 6.31$, $p < 0.05$). Swedes had their trauma sufficiently addressed to a higher degree than ethnic minorities ($\chi^2 = 6.33$, $p < 0.05$) There was no difference in the utilisation of an interpreter amongst those who had their trauma(s) addressed and those who had not ($\chi^2 = 0.597$, ns).

Table 4. Symptomatic outcome amongst patients with trauma sufficiently addressed (n= 51) vs. not sufficiently addressed (n= 39).

	Trauma addressed		**Trauma *not* addressed**		p
	Mean	SE	Mean	SE	
HSCL-25	1.15	0.108	1.62	0.119	0.01
SCL depression subscale	1.17	0.113	1.65	0.131	0.01
Theorell's psychosomatic scale	1.05	0.106	1.37	0.109	0.05
SIP – PTSD	0.56	0.042	0.71	0.053	0.05

Table 5. Odds ratios for outcome variables, i.e. ratings of confidence in staff and symptom ratings, in a stepwise logistic regression analysis independently related to having trauma(s) sufficiently addressed.

Variables in the Equation*	**B**	**S.E.**	**Wald**	**df**	**Sign.**	**Odds ratio**
Confidence in staff	-1.978	0.554	12.760	1	0.000	7.227
Self-rated Health	-2.083	0.765	7.410	1	0.006	8.026
Self-rating for Posttraumatic Stress Disorder	-2.045	0.913	5.018	1	0.025	7.728
Depression Subscale	-1.105	0.721	2.350	1	0.125	3.020
Constant	3.615	1.054				

* Variables with no significant contribution to the regression equation: Hopkin's Symptom Check List—25, Symptom Changes during Treatment, and Psychosomatic Symptom Scale.

A stepwise logistic regression analysis of outcome variables is shown in Table 5. Of seven tested independent variables, four passed the inclusion criteria (cf. *Statistical analysis*). Confidence in staff (High), Self-rated health (High), Self-rating for Posttraumatic Stress Disorder (Low), and the Depression Scale (Low) were independently related to the fact that a trauma had been addressed and could correctly identify 74 per cent of the patients. Thus, patients who had had their traumas addressed had more confidence in the staff, higher self-rated health, and lower ratings of posttraumatic stress disorder and depression. There were no significant correlation between the outcome variables confidence in staff and self-rated health. Whereas self-rated health was correlated to all other outcome variables, confidence in staff was only significantly correlated to Improvement during treatment.

This stage of our study shows that patients with trauma sufficiently addressed had in a significant respect better outcome—had better self-rated health and fewer symptoms of PTSD and depression and had greater confidence in staff—as compared to patients who considered traumas were insufficiently addressed.

The three variables: Improvement during treatment, HSCL-25 and the Psychosomatic Symptoms' Scale did not make any independent contribution to whether or not trauma was sufficiently addressed.

The study was conducted at a general outpatient clinic with no special trauma focus and with only general therapeutic skills available. Formal psychotherapy was rare.

Despite formal similarities in treatment between the groups, a positive response to the question of whether trauma was sufficiently addressed singles out one group of patients who have a better outcome. It seems as if addressing the trauma in a clinical setting has a therapeutic effect *per se*. The results contradict the view of Kinzie's and Boehnlein that just talking about the trauma is not sufficient (Kinzie & Boehnlein). Certainly, some qualities in the talking - like empathy and respect - are preconditions for a positive outcome. The act of sufficiently addressing trauma probably has to do with acknowledging the trauma and its relevance for the present condition. This would encourage the patient to talk about it and share his experiences, e.g. through exploratory follow-up questions. The therapist's ability to address trauma seems to have little to do with his or her basic training, nor with the type of therapy applied. To verify such suppositions about the content of sufficiently addressing, it would be necessary to interview patients and therapists in a qualitative study.

The fact that those patients with trauma sufficiently addressed had waited longer before making contact with the clinic might indicate that certain latency is helpful for the patients to focus on trauma. This could be in line with the negative results of debriefing immediately following a traumatic event (van Emmerik et al, Rose et al).

Background Variables for Patients with Trauma Sufficiently Addressed vs. not Sufficiently Addressed

Patients who had not had their traumas sufficiently addressed reported a greater number of traumas, both their own (4.10 ± 0.33 vs. 2.73 ± 0.33, $z = 3.36$, $p = 0.001$) and traumas concerning a relative or close friend (3.74 ± 0.46 vs. 2.80 ± 0.40, $z = 1.68$, $p < 0.01$).

Particular types of traumas were significantly more frequent among those whose trauma had not been sufficiently addressed in treatment. These traumas were: having lost a close relative through accident or violence ($\chi^2 = 4.03$, $p<0.05$), having been physically assaulted ($\chi^2 = 11.78$, $p< 0.001$) or subjected to torture ($\chi^2 = 9.95$, $p<0.01$) or having had a relative or close friend subjected to torture ($\chi^2 = 4.66$, $p< 0.05$).

In a stepwise logistic regression analysis, all socio-demographic background variables (e.g. gender, ethnicity, and education) and multiplicity of trauma were included. Due to a high degree of collinearity between own and relatives' traumas, the sum of all traumas was chosen as the variable for logistic regression analysis. Two variables were independently associated with the fact that trauma(s) had been addressed (Table 6). These were low number of traumas and being Swedish. The prospect of having trauma addressed was almost five times as high if the patient had less than five traumas, and twice as high if the patient was a Swede (Table 5). Together these two variables correctly identified 75 per cent of the patients.

Table 6. Odds ratios for sociodemographic background variables and multiplicity of trauma experience in a stepwise logistic regression analysis independently related to having trauma(s) sufficiently addressed.

Variables in the Equation*	B	S.E.	Wald	df	Sig.	Odds ratio
Swedish-born	0.855	0.519	2.715	1	0.099	2.350
< 5 different traumas	1.536	0.515	8.905	1	0.003	4.645
Constant	-2.684	0.488				

* Variables with no significant contribution to the regression equation: Gender, Arab, Persian, Turkish, Swedish or Turkish, Childhood area, Education, Employed, and Age.

In order to control if these two background variables influenced the outcome variables' association with trauma addressed, < 5 traumas and ethnic Swede were included in a stepwise logistic regression analysis together with the outcome variables according to Table 4. Notwithstanding, confidence in staff and Self-rated health showed independent and significant relationships with trauma addressed.

This study, carried out at a general outpatient clinic in a multiethnic area, demonstrates neglect of addressing trauma in treatment. Forty-three per cent of the patients in our study, who mentioned a trauma in the treatment contact, perceived that the trauma had not been sufficiently addressed.

Patients who did not have their trauma sufficiently addressed had been exposed to a greater number of different traumas. In fact, if the total number of different traumas exceeded four, the prospect of having trauma sufficiently addressed was little more than one-fifth compared with patients with fewer traumas (cf. Table 5). The patients who did Irrespective of the number of traumas, patients born outside Sweden less often perceived that their traumas were sufficiently addressed. The utilisation of an interpreter did not influence whether or not traumas were addressed. It is possible that treatment staff regarded cultural difference as an obstacle for addressing the patient's trauma. Similarly, cross-cultural communication could also restrict the patients. A few patients, when completing the questionnaire, disclosed the view that, "Swedish staff cannot understand what we have gone through anyhow ". Patients who perceived their traumas as not sufficiently addressed, more often had been given an Axis IV diagnosis of "cultural conflict" or "exile existence" according to the patient register. This fact raises the suspicion that if trauma is not enquired about in a structured fashion, patients from ethnic minorities run the risk of having their difficulties misinterpreted as "cultural" or being attributed to their exile situation. To summarise, cultural prejudice rather than language problems threaten to prevent traumas from being sufficiently addressed.

Clinical Implications

One way of improving clinical practice would be to systematically screen for traumas by using a questionnaire. Apart from detecting traumas, such questionnaires listing different traumas could help both patient and therapist to talk about and evaluate the contribution of each trauma to the present condition of the patient. It was noted that some patients in our study felt relieved when asked about their extreme traumas, following the questionnaire. One explanation of this reaction might be that the pre-formulated questions told them that their experience was not unique and that the interviewer felt comfortable discussing such issues. To give therapists the confidence to approach and deal with horrifying and multiple traumas, supervision is helpful and sometimes necessary. The need of addressing trauma also ought to be stressed in curricula and training. The high prevalence of traumas in general psychiatry, emphasises the need of disseminating the knowledge and experience gathered at specialised treatment institutions dealing with specific traumas (e.g. torture or sexual abuse) to general psychiatric services. Cultural differences should not be seen as a legitimate reason to avoid addressing traumas. Human similarities, in spite of cultural differences, ought to be in focus during training and supervision.

Conclusion

Establishing Post-traumatic stress disorder (PTSD) as a psychiatric diagnosis has only marginally increased awareness of traumatic experiences in general psychiatry. PTSD is mostly dealt with at specialised treatment centres, e.g. for war, torture or rape where its aetiology may seem self-explanatory. In general psychiatric services, traumas are inconsistently recorded in initial psychiatric histories and, when observed, rarely reflected in the primary diagnosis and treatment. Although a number of epidemiological studies show high prevalence of both traumas and PTSD in general population, this finding has thus not affected the practice of general psychiatric services.

The prevalence of traumatic experiences is high in psychiatric outpatient populations. Trauma is frequently overlooked in general psychiatric settings and PTSD is underestimated. The aetiology of PTSD is mainly related to multiple traumas including traumas to relatives. Compared to other psychiatric outpatients in general, fulfilling diagnostic criteria for PTSD implies worse long-term outcome regarding SRH and participation in working life. When trauma had been satisfactorily addressed in treatment (irrespective of diagnosis), outcome was improved regarding SRH, PTSD and depressive symptomatology, and patients had high confidence in treatment staff. In summary, the findings indicate that a primary focus should be placed on trauma and PTSD in general psychiatric services. Special attention should be paid to patients of ethnic minorities, as they are more likely to be traumatised, more vulnerable to trauma, and less likely to get their traumatic experiences addressed in treatment.

Acknowledgements

The study on which this chapter is based was supported through grants from the Swedish Council for Planning and Co-ordination of Research, and the Research and Development Department at Stockholm County Council. We are grateful to the staff of the Psychiatric Outpatient Department for their involvement in this study and for supplying the outpatient data. We are also grateful to Social Psychiatry and Psychiatric Epidemiology and Nordic Journal of Psychiatry for letting us use some of the material previously published or accepted for publication (Al-Saffar, Borgå et al. 2002, 2003, 2003, 2003)

REFERENCES

Al-Saffar, S., Borgå, P., Edman, G., Hällström, T. The aetiology of posttraumatic stress Disorder in four ethnic groups in outpatient psychiatry. *Soc Psychiatry Psychiatr Epidemiol (2003) 38:457-462.*

Al-Saffar, S., Borgå, P., Hällström, T. Long-term consequences of unrecognised PTSD in general outpatient psychiatry. *Soc Psychiatry Psychiatr Epidemiol (2002) 37:580-585.*

Al-Saffar, S., Borgå, P., Hällström T. (2003). The influence of the patients′ ethnicity, sociodemographic conditions and strain on psychiatric diagnoses. *Nordic Journal of Psychiatry, (In press).*

Al-Saffar, S., Borgå, P., Lawoko, S., Edman, G., Hällström, T. (2003) The significance of addressing trauma in outpatient psychiatry – an observational study. *Nordic Journal of Psychiatry. (In press)*

American, P., Association. (1952). *Diagnostic and Statistical Manual of Mental Disorders (DMS I)*. Washington, DC.

American, P., Association. (1968). *Diagnostic and Statistical Manual of Mental disorders (DMS-II)*. Washington, DC.

Amir, M., & Sol, O. (1999). Psychological impact and prevalence of traumatic events in a student sample in Israel: the effect of multiple traumatic events and physical injury. *J Trauma Stress, 12*(1), 139-154.

Association, A. P. (1980). *Diagnostic and Statistical Manual of Mental Disorders (DSM III)*. Washington, DC: American Psychiatric Press.

Association, A. P. (1987). *Diagnostic and Statistical Manual of Mental Disorders (DSM-III-R)* (Vol. Third Edition - Revised). Washington, DC: American Psychiatric Press.

Association, A. P. (1994). *Diagnostic and Statistical Manual of Mental Disorders (DSM-IV)*. Washington D.C.: American Psychiatric Press.

Bady, S. L. (1985). The voice as a curative factor in psychotherapy. *Psychoanalytic Review, 72*, 479-490.

Bjørner, J. B., Søndergaard Kristensen, T., Orth-Gomér, K., Tibblin, G., Sullivan, M., & Westerholm, P. (1996). Self-rated health. A useful concept in research, prevention and clinical medicine. *Stockholm, FRN report, 96:9.*

Brady, K. T. (1997). Posttraumatic stress disorder and comorbidity: recognizing the many faces of PTSD. *Journal of Clinical Psychiatry, 58*(suppl 9), 12-15.

Brady, K. T., Killeen, T. K., Brewerton, T., & S., L. (2000). Comorbidity of psychiatric disorder and posttraumatic stress disorder. *Journal of Clinical Psychiatry, 61*(suppl 7).

Bremner, J. D., Southwick, S. M., Johnson, D. R., Yehuda, R., & Charney, D. S. (1993). Childhood physical abuse and combat-related posttraumatic stress disorder in Vietnam veterans. *Am J Psychiatry, 150*(2), 235-239.

Breslau, N., Chilcoat, H. D., Kessler, R. C., & Davis, G. C. (1999). Previous exposure to trauma and PTSD effects of subsequent trauma: results from the Detroit Area Survey of Trauma. *Am J Psychiatry, 156*(6), 902-907.

Breslau, N., Chilcoat, H. D., Kessler, R. C., Peterson, E. L., & Lucia, V. C. (1999). Vulnerability to assaultive violence: further specification of the sex difference in post-traumatic stress disorder. *Psychol Med, 29*(4), 813-821.

Breslau, N., Davis, G. C., Andreski, P., & Peterson, E. (1991). Traumatic events and posttraumatic stress disorder in an urban population of young adults. *Arch Gen Psychiatry, 48*(3), 216-222.

Breslau, N., Peterson, E. L., Kessler, R. C., & Schultz, L. R. (1999). Short screening scale for DSM-IV posttraumatic stress disorder. *Am J Psychiatry, 156*(6), 908-911.

Breuer, J., & Freud, S. (1973). *Studies of Hysteria physical mechanism of hysteria.* New York: Penguin.

Bryer, J. B., Nelson, B. A., Miller, J. B., & Kroll, P. A. (1987). Childhood sexual and physical abuse as factors in adult psychitric illness. *The American Journal of Psychiatry, 144*, 1426-1430.

Davidson, J. (1991). Post-traumatic stress disorder in the community: an epidemiological study. *Psychological Med, 21*, 713-721.

Davidson, J., & Smith, R. (1990). Traumatic experiences in psychiatric outpatients. *Journal of Traumatic Stress, 3*, 459-475.

Davidson, J. R. T. (1991a). Diagnostic issues in posttraumatic stress disorder: consideration for the DSM-IV. *J Abnorm Psychol, 100*, 346-355.

Davidson, J. R. T. (1991b). Diagnostic issues in posttraumatic stress disorder: considerations for the DSM-IV. *Journal of Abnormal Psychology, 100*, 346-355.

Dougall, A. L., Herberman, H. B., Delahanty, D. L., Inslicht, S. S., & Baum, A. (2000). Similarity of prior trauma exposure as a determinant of chronic stress responding to an airline disaster. *J Consult Clin Psychol, 68*(2), 290-295.

Eitinger, L. (1961). Pathology of the concentration camp syndrome. *Archives of General Psychiatry, 5*, 371-379.

Eitinger, L. (1965). *Concentration camp survivors in Norway and Israel.* Oslo: Universitetsforlaget.

Flett, R. A., Kazantzis, N., Long, N. R., MacDonald, C., & Millar, M. (2002). Traumatic events and physical health in a New Zealand community sample. *J Trauma Stress, 15*(4), 303-312.

Fox, S. H., & Tang, S. S. (2000). The Sierra Leonean refugee experience. *Journal of Nervous and Mental Disease, 188*, 490-495.

Goenjian, A. K., Steinberg, A. M., Najarian, L. M., Fairbanks, L. A., Tashjian, M., & Pynoss, R. S. (2000). Prospective study of posttraumatic stress, anxiety and depressive reactions after earthquake and political violence. *The American Journal of Psychiatry, 157*, 911-916.

Green, B. L., Goodman, L. A., Krupnick, J. L., Corcoran, C. B., Petty, R. M., Stockton, P., & Stern, N. M. (2000). Outcomes of single versus multiple trauma exposure in a screening sample. *J Trauma Stress, 13*(2), 271-286.

Green, B. L., Lindy, J., & Wilson, J. (1985). *Trauma and its Wake: The study and Treatment of Post-Traumatic Stress Disorder*. New York: Bruner/Mazel: USA.

Harvey, A. G., & Brytan, R. A. (1998). The relationship between acute stress disorder and posttraumatic stress disorder: a prospective evaluation of motor vehicle accident survivors. *Journal of Consulting and Clinical Psychology, 66*, 507-512.

Horowitz, K., Weine, S., & Jekel, J. (1995). PTSD symptoms in urban adolescent girls: compounded community trauma. *J Am Acad Child Adolesc Psychiatry, Oct 34(10)*, 1353-1361.

Horowitz, M. J. (1987). *Stress response syndromes*. New York: Jason Aronson.

Hovens, J. E. (1994). *Research into the psychodiagnostics of posttraumatic stress disorder.* CW Delft: Eburon Press.

Jacobson, A., & Richardson, B. (1987). Assault experiences of 100 psychiatric inpatients: evidence of the need for routine inquiry. *American Journal of Psychiatry, 144*, 908-913.

Kessler, R. C., Sonnega, A., Bromet, E., Hughes, M., & Nelson, C. B. (1995). Posttraumatic stress disorder in the national comorbodity survey. *Archives of General Psychiatry, 52*, 1048-1060.

Kidson, M. A., Douglas, J. C., & Holwill, B. J. (1993). Post traumatic stress disorder in Australin World War II veterans attending a psychiatric outpatient clinic. *The Medical Journal of Australia, 158*, 563-566.

Kinzie, J. D., & Boehnlein, J. K. (1993). Psychotherapy of the victims of massive violence; countertransference and ethical issues. *Am J Psychotherapy, 47*, 90-102.

Kraepelin, E. (1896). *Psychiatrie* (Vol. Vol. 5). Leipzig: Barth.

Kulka, R. A., Schlenger, W. E., Fairbank, J. A., Hough, R. L., Jordan, B. K., Marmar, C. R., & Weiss, D. S. (1990). The prevalence of other psychiatric disorders and nonspecific distress. *In: Trauma and the Vietnam war generation. Report of findings from the national Vietnam veterans readjustment study, pp*, 86-138.

Litrell, J. (1998). Is the reexperience of painful emotion therapeutic? *Clinical Psychology Review, 18*, 71-102.

Mac Farlane, A. C. (1994). Individual psychotherapy for post-traumatic stress disorder. *Psychiatric Clinics in North America, 17*, 393-408.

Mueser, K. T., Salyers, M., Rosenberg, S. D., Ford, J. D., Fox, L., & Carty, P. (2001). Psychometric evaluation of trauma and posttraumatic stress disorder assessments in persons with severe mental illness. *Psychological Assessment, 13*(1), 111-1117.

Nichols, M. P., & Efran, J. S. (1985). Catharsis in psychotherapy: A new perspective. *Psychotherapy, 22*, 46-58.

Paunovich, N., & Öst, L. G. (2001). Cognitive behavior therapy vs exposure therapy in the treatment of PTSD in refugees. *Behavior Reserach and Therapy, 39*, 1183-1197.

Rachman, S. (1980). Emotional processing. *Behav Res & Therapy, 18*, 51-60.

Rose, S., Bisson, J., & Wessely, S. (Eds.). (2003). *Psychological debriefing for preventing post traumatic stress disorder (PTSD) (Cochrane Review).* Oxford: Update Software.

Rosenberg, H. J., Rosenberg, S. D., Wolford, G. L., Manganiello, P. D., Brunette, M. F., & Boynton, R. A. (2000). The relationship between trauma, PTSD, and medical utilization in three high risk medical populations. *Int J Psychiatry Med, 30*(3), 247-259.

Rothbaum, B. O., & Schwartz, A. C. (2002). Exposure therapy for posttraumatic stress disorder. *American Journal of Psychotherapy, 56*, 59-75.

Simpson, T. L., Westerberg, V. S., Little, L. M., & M., T. (1994). Screening for childhood physical and sexual abuse among outpatient substance abusers. *Journal of Substance Abuse Treatment, 11*, 347-358.

Solomon, S. D., Keane, T. M., Newman, E., & Kaloupek, D. G. (1996). *Chosing self-report measures and structured interviews.* Maryland: Sidran.

Ursano, R. J., Fullerton, C. S., Epstein, R. S., Crowley, B., Kao, T.-C., Vance, K., Craig, K. J., Dougall, A. L., & Baum, A. (1999). Acuta and chronic posttraumatic stress disorder in motor vehicle accident victims. *The American Journal of Psychiatry, 156*, 589-595.

Wagner, D., Heinrichs, M., & Ehlert, U. (1998). Prevalence of symptoms of posttraumatic stress disorder in German professional firefighters. *The American Journal of Psychiatry, 155*, 1727-1732.

van Emmerik, A. A., Kamphuis, J. H., Hulsbosch, A. M., & Emmelkamp, P. M. (2002). Single session debriefing after psychological trauma: a meta-analysis. *Lancet, 360*(9335), 766-771.

Wang, X., Gao, L., Shinfuku, N., Zhang, H., Zhao, C., & Shen, Y. (2000). Longitudinal study of earthquakerelated PTSD in a randomly selected community sample in North China. *The American Journal of Psychiatry, 157*, 1260-1266.

Wolfe, J., Erickson, D. J., Sharkansky, E. J., King, D. W., & King, L. A. (1999). Course and predictors of posttraumatic stress disorder among gulf war veterans: A prospective analysis. *Journal of Consulting and Clinical Psychology, 67*, 520-528.

Yehuda, R., &Mc Farlane, A.C. (1995). The conflict between current knowledge avout PTSD and its original conceptual basis. *American Journal of Psychiatry, 152*, 1705-1713.

Zaidi, L., & Foy, D. (1994). Childhood abuse experiences and combat-related PTSD. *J Trauma Stress, 7*, 33-42.

Zimmerman, M., & Mattia, J. I. (1999). Is posttraumatic stress disorder underdiagnosed in routine clinical settings? *Journal of Nervous and Mental Disease, 187*, 420-428.

In: Posttraumatic Stress Disorder: New Research
Editor: Guida D. Kume, pp.167-187
ISBN 1-60021-078-3

Chapter 6

POSTTRAUMATIC STRESS AMONG VICTIMS OF TRAIN DISASTERS

Man Cheung Chung
University of Plymouth, Plymouth, UK
University of Plymouth, Clinical Psychology Teaching Unit, Faculty of Health and Social Work, School of Applied Psychosocial Studies, Drake Circus, Plymouth, PL4 8AA, UK

ABSTRACT

This chapter aims to review existing literature on posttraumatic stress following train disasters. It is organized according to primary, secondary and quaternary victims, with emphasis placed on the latter. Following their exposure to a train disaster, the link between quaternary victims' subjective experience of the train disaster, death anxiety, personality traits, coping styles, posttraumatic stress reactions and general health problems will be described. The chapter will end with some suggestions on future research on victims exposed to train disasters.

INTRODUCTION

It has been suggested that psychological responses to traumatic events vary depending on the type of victim (e.g. primary victim) and the type of disaster (e.g. technological) that the victims have experienced (Ursano, McCaughey, & Fullerton, 1994; Weisaeth, 1994). This chapter aims to review existing literature pertaining to posttraumatic stress responses among primary and secondary victims who have been exposed to the technological disaster of a train collision (train collisions fall into this category due to the fact that they could result from failure of humanly made products (Weisaeth, 1994)). In addition, this chapter will summarize general findings from recent studies of ours which examined the posttraumatic stress responses of quaternary victims who have been exposed to train disasters.

Back to Victorian times, one can find narrative recorded on posttraumatic stress reactions following train disasters (Harrington, 1996; van der Kolk, Weisaeth, & van der Hart, 1996; Trimble, 1981). As a result of train disasters, people may manifest psychiatric disorders, persistent somatic disorders, be involved in drug use or feel a need to seek psychological counselling or support (Lundin, 1991). Yet, to compare with recent research focusing on other types of disasters or traumatic human experiences, research into technological disasters has not been forthcoming (Blake, Albano, & Keane, 1992).

Primary Victims of Train Disasters

By primary victims, we mean those with maximal exposure to a traumatic event (Figley and Kleber, 1995). In the case of train disasters, primary victims would include, for example, the passengers on the train. Over the last 25 years, several studies have been done to examine primarily the posttraumatic stress responses of passengers who survived different train disasters. For example, in 1977, in Australia, the Granville train disaster occurred in which an early morning commuter train came off the rails and demolished a bridge stanchion. As a result, a massive concrete span came down and crashed into two train carriages. Eighty-three people were killed. One study showed that following the disaster, the primary victims (i.e. passengers) initially manifested the traumatic responses of numbness, and detached and unreal feelings which later changed to uncontrollable crying and extreme fear. They also displayed avoidance behaviour, anxiety, irritability, insomnia, nightmares, depression, fear of train travelling and unforeseen sound and survivor guilt. They also showed a strong urge to share with others about what had happened and to find out information about the disaster (Boman, 1979).

Then, in 1987 in Lerum, Sweden, two trains collided which resulted in 9 deaths and more than 100 injured. One study showed that during the 2 month period following the collision, passengers experienced a high level of intrusive thoughts, avoidance behaviour, sleeping difficulties, nightmares, feeling a need to cry and depression. This made it difficult for them to carry out daily tasks. Some found themselves having to re-live the disaster which, however, also served as an important coping process. That is, they coped by integrating this disaster into the important events in their lives. Female passengers seemed to have been more preoccupied with thoughts and feelings about the disaster and to display more avoidance behaviour than male passengers. Twenty-four percent of the passengers in this study, who felt that their lives were threatened during the disaster, tended to experience more psychological problems than those who did not experience a threat to their lives. The degree of passengers' personal injury was also found to be associated with increased psychological symptoms and difficulties in coping. Further analyses in this study revealed that older people (over 65) were more preoccupied with the disaster, displayed more avoidance behaviour, experienced more intrusive thoughts, sleeping difficulties and crying spells than younger adults (ages 45-64). Interestingly, people aged 18 and 24 were similar to older people in terms of their symptom profiles, apart from sleeping difficulties and crying spells. This implies that one should not expect a linear relationship between age and posttraumatic stress symptoms (Hagström, 1995)

One year later, in the United Kingdom, the Clapham rail crash occurred. A passenger train crashed into the back of another train which was stationary because the driver was reporting a faulty set of signals. A few seconds later, a train which was empty crashed into the wreckage (Burns & Hollins, 1991; Stevens & Partridge, 1990). Thirty-three people died and over 100 were injured. Ten to 22 months after the disaster, the passengers in one study showed a high level of intrusion and avoidance behaviour, especially those (30%) who were at closest proximity to the focus of the disaster. These posttraumatic stress symptoms were associated with risk of death, witness of death and passengers' feelings of being trapped. Posttraumatic stress symptoms were also associated with severity of physical injury in that 30% of those with moderate or severe injury showed high levels of intrusion or avoidance symptoms. Twenty-seven percent of passengers were thought to be psychiatric cases according to General Health Questionnaire (Selley, King, Peveler, Osola, Martin, & Thompson, 1997).

Train disasters such as the above can have long term psychological effects on surviving passengers. For example, one study looked at the posttraumatic stress responses of young adult passengers who experienced a bus-train collision 7 years previously (they were adolescents at the time of the crash). The results revealed that after 7 years, passengers with the highest level of exposure reported the highest levels of somatic problems, depression, phobia, anxiety, and psychoticism and reported more posttraumatic stress symptoms than those with medium and low levels of exposure. Passengers with the highest level of exposure also sought help from mental health clinics more often than those with medium and low levels of exposure. The former also reported engaging in less coping activities than the latter. Acute stress symptoms and people's fearful reactions immediately after the disaster were associated with long-term maladjustment. One important implication from this study is that in order to investigate the long-term adjustment after disasters, victims' levels of exposure to disasters and personal factors such as their psychological reactions immediately after the disaster are variables which cannot be ignored (Tyano, Iancu, Solomon, Sever, Goldstein, Touviana, & Bleich, 1996).

A follow-up study also revealed that following the bus-train disaster, these passengers showed certain specific beliefs that they had about the world, other people and themselves. The passengers with the highest level of exposure tended to believe less in the benevolence of the world, the justice of the world and their personal luck. These cognitive schema were, on the whole, associated with increased posttraumatic stress symptoms, increased general psychiatric symptoms, psychological impairment and difficulties in functioning. Also, their belief in randomness was associated with depression, obsessive-compulsive symptoms and interpersonal sensitivity. Low sense of self-worth was associated with poor mental health in terms of psychiatric symptoms, posttraumatic stress and general psychological functioning (Solomon, Iancu & Tyano, 1997).

In some cases, train disasters may create a whole group of primary victims who were not necessarily the passengers. Community residents may become primary victims, as the following shows. In 1991, a freight train derailed in Northern California. Then, a railroad tank car containing the toxic pesticide metam sodium fell into a river. The tank car ruptured and leaked about 18,000 gallons of the chemical into the river. Most residents who lived around the river were not aware of the spill and consequently affected and experienced acute symptoms of toxicity. In other words, these community residents became primary victims as a result of the chemical spill resulting from the train accident. One study showed that the spill residents experienced significantly more hypochondriasis, depression, hysteria, psychasthenia and schizophrenia than the control group. They also experienced more tension, depression, anger, fatigue and confusion and less vigor than the control. They also worried more about the environment and perceived much lower social support than the control. Also, the spill residents had higher blood pressure and less fluctuation of cortisol levels than the control (Bowler, Mergler, Huel, & Cone, 1994).

SECONDARY VICTIMS OF TRAIN DISASTERS

Several studies have been carried out to examine the posttraumatic reactions of secondary victims exposed to train disasters. To adopt the definition from Figley and Kleber (1995), secondary victims include the significant others (e.g. family members, spouses or children) of primary victims. In the Granville train disaster mentioned above, attention was paid to the posttraumatic stress reactions of the bereaved relatives and families as secondary victims. In terms of the level of functioning and psychological well-being, 15 to 18 months following the disaster, research showed that bereaved spouses were better than bereaved parents, widowers were better than widows, people with a supportive network were better than those without, and those who saw the bodies of the deceased were better than those who did not. Research also showed the benefit of bereavement counselling in that the high risk families who received bereavement counselling improved in well-being more than those who did not receive such intervention (Singh & Raphael, 1981).

Secondary victims also include crisis and rescue workers and psychotherapists. Research has well established the idea that the emotions, cognition, motivation, behaviour and interpersonal relationship of these workers can be affected, due to their involvement with the disaster (Hodgkinson & Stewart, 1991; Shepherd & Hodgkinson, 1990). One month after the Granville disaster, research showed that 77 of the 95 crisis helpers involved in the disaster experienced extreme distress resulting from their feeling of helplessness, witnessing the magnitude of destruction, witnessing the suffering of the injured people, witnessing the anguish and extreme distress of relatives, experiencing the sight and smell of mutilated bodies, and having to work under a great deal of pressure. Their level of anxiety increased, and they developed depression and sleeping difficulties. Focusing on 13 helpers, one year later, 4 of them scored between 6 and 20 on the General Health Questionnaire. Taking a score of 4/5 as the cutoff, this meant that these people were considered to be psychiatric cases (Raphael, Singh, & Bradbury, 1980; Raphael, Singh, Bradbury, & Lambert, 1983-1984).

Reinforcing the above findings, one study focused on the secondary victims of social workers involved in the Clapham rail crash and other disasters. It also found that these victims displayed significantly more somatic problems, obsessive compulsive disorder, interpersonal sensitivity, depression and anxiety than the ordinary population. This high level of psychological problems seemed to be persistent over a long period of time (i.e. a 12 month period) (Hodgkinson & Shepherd, 1994). Another study focusing on a major train disaster in 1988 near the city of Soro on Zeeland in Denmark also revealed a high level of posttraumatic stress responses among the crisis workers involved in this disaster. This disaster occurred as a result of the derailment of an intercity train while taking a curve at high speed. The study showed that 18% and 10% were thought to be psychiatric cases and suffer from posttraumatic stress disorder according to the results of the General Health Questionnaire (GHQ) and the

Impact of Event Scale (IES), respectively. These people's GHQ and IES scores tended to increase from 3 to 7 months (Andersen, Christensen & Petersen, 1991).

QUATERNARY VICTIMS

Given the above literature, one thing worth noting is that with respect to victims exposed to train disasters, research has thus far been mainly restricted to passengers, bereaved relatives and families and rescue or crisis workers. However, we know that disasters, particularly large-scale ones, can affect the whole community from the bereaved friends and families of the deceased to the infrastructure of service providers, and those from social organisations or authorities who had minimal exposure to the disaster (Wright, Binney & Kunkler, 1994; Wright, Ursano, Bartone, & Ingraham, 1990). Community residents who have minimal exposure to a disaster can also experience anxiety, anger, sadness, despair, helplessness and guilt. In other words, they cannot be ignored but need to be educated about possible traumatic reactions. Subsequent psychosocial care may be necessary in some cases (Raphael, 1977; Raphael, 1986; Raphael, 1979-80; Raphael & Meldrum, 1993; Raphael & Middleton, 1987). The cognitive processes of these community residents may change following different degrees of exposure to train disasters. The directly exposed residents, for example, may display more intrusion-based reasoning (i.e. the tendency to interpret distressing intrusions themselves as evidence that danger is impending, regardless of objective danger information) than those who were indirectly exposed. Such reasoning was associated with both acute and chronic posttraumatic stress symptoms (Engelhard, Macklin, McNally, van den Hout, & Arntz, 2001; Engelhard, van den Hout, Arntz, & McNally, 2002). In a report following an aircraft disaster, Taylor and Frazer (1981) raised awareness of the traumatic effects that aircraft disasters can have upon these community residents by defining the affected local community residents as quaternary victims.

In order to demonstrate the idea of posttraumatic stress among local community residents as quaternary victims, a couple of studies have been carried out. These studies, however, focus on victims exposed to disasters other than train disasters. For example, in 1989, the Hillsborough Football Stadium disaster occurred in the U.K. in which 95 spectators were crushed to death at a match. A study was carried out to examine the local community residents who lived within half a mile of the stadium. Despite the fact that they were not at the match and knew no friends or relatives who died in the disaster, the study found that 22% of these community residents suffered from acute posttraumatic stress disorder. The same percentage were also thought to be psychiatric cases according to the General Health Questionnaire (Wright, Binney & Kunkler, 1994). Another study looked at the traumatic effect of the 1986 Challenger space shuttle explosion (the Challenger exploded in mid air shortly after take-off in 1986) upon the children living in local communities. Children were found to experience feelings of shock or disbelief, sadness, anxiety and empathy toward the families of the deceased (Levitt & Leventhal, 1986). Male students seemed to be affected and to recall the impact of the event more than female students (Gould & Gould, 1991). A sense of impersonal regret and attenuated affect was more characteristic of boys than girls (Wright, Kunkel, Pinon, and Huston, 1989). One year after the disaster, some children still felt concerned about the explosion and would often recall the impact of the disaster (Gould & Gould, 1991; Zeece, 1986).

Quaternary Victims of a Train Disaster in the U.K.

Literature to date on posttraumatic stress among community residents as quaternary victims exposed to train disasters is virtually non-existent. However, in 1996, in Stafford, U.K., a train disaster occurred, providing an opportunity for us to shed light on the posttraumatic stress responses of a group of local community residents as quaternary victims exposed to the train disaster. We carried out a study in due course and below is a summary of the results. Details on statistical analyses and findings will not be reported here but can be found in a series of published articles (see Chung, Werrett, Farmer, Easthope & Chung, 2000; Chung, Farmer, Werrett, Easthope & Chung, 2001; Chung, Werrett, Easthope, Farmer & Chung, 2002; Chung, Easthope, Farmer, Werrett & Chung, 2003).

On the 8th March, 1996 at 2308 hours, in Rickerscote, Stafford, U.K., a freight train, carrying 8 liquid carbon dioxide tank wagons, derailed due to the complete fracture of an axle fitted to one of the wagons. The derailed wagons subsequently blocked the adjacent line and were hit by a post office train travelling in the opposite direction. Only the driver was on the freight train and 21 employees, including the driver, were on the post office train. The driver of the freight train did not appear to be injured, while all of the employees in the post office train were injured. One was killed in the gangway area between the first and second coaches which had been most damaged during the disaster (Health & Safety Executive, 1996). On both sides of the site where the collision occurred there lived local community residents. They were, in this study, considered quaternary victims exposed to a train disaster. They were not primary victims since they were not the passengers or workers on the trains. They did not sustain any injury or experience any damage to their properties. Neither were they secondary victims since they were not the relatives, families or significant others or the dead or injured. They were not involved in any way in the rescue operation.

The study that we carried out primarily aimed to ascertain:

1. the subjective experience of the disaster at the time and during the aftermath of the disaster
2. the extent to which these community residents, as quaternary victims, experienced posttraumatic stress responses, general health problems and death anxiety.
3. the factors which may predict the foregoing variables. In particular, we were interested in whether personality factors and coping strategies would predict posttraumatic stress responses, general health problems and death anxiety.

We commenced the study approximately 7 months after the disaster. For the study, we designated an area of the housing estate, which comprised houses on both sides of the track and was between 30 and 100 feet away from the crash site. In this area, there were 90 households to which we distributed letters explaining the purpose of the research. Fifteen residents refused to participate in the study; 8 residents were not at home when visited and revisited two or three times. One had moved out. The remaining 66 were interviewed which yielded the response rate of 73%. Community residents were asked to describe some of their initial and aftermath posttraumatic responses. We recorded their responses using a self-constructed questionnaire, namely, the Stafford Train Disaster Questionnaire. They were also interviewed using the Impact of Event Scale (IES) (Horowitz, Wilner & Alvarez, 1979), the General Health Questionnaire (GHQ) (Goldberg & Hillier, 1979), the Death Anxiety Scale (DAS) (Templer, 1970), the Eysenck Personality Questionnaire-R Short Scale (EPQ-R) (Eysenck & Eysenck, 1991) and the Ways of Coping Checklist (WOC) (Folkman & Lazarus, 1988).

POSTTRAUMATIC STRESS AND GENERAL HEALTH AMONG QUATERNARY VICTIMS OF A TRAIN DISASTER

The 66 community residents (M=23, F=43) who participated in the study were all Caucasian and were, on average, 54 years old (range: 22 to 91). Almost 50% were married and 31% were widows or widowers. The rest were single or divorced. Forty-four percent were retired and 3% were unemployed. Otherwise, they worked as administrators, factory workers, or educators. The average length of residence in the community was 7 years (range: 9 months to 30 years).

Reporting the results from the Impact of Event Scale (IES), in terms of intrusive thoughts, 32% of the community residents often had waves of strong feeling about the disaster. Twenty-nine percent said that when trains went passed or when they saw the rail tracks, they were often reminded of the disaster. About 20% said that they often found themselves thinking about the disaster when they did not mean to. Just over 20% also said that pictures about the disaster often popped into their minds. Fifteen percent said that they often had sleeping problems after the crash but most people did not have dreams about it.

In terms of avoidance behaviour, 29% reported that they often tried to remove the image of the disaster from memory. Just under 20% said that they tried to avoid letting themselves get upset when they thought about or were reminded of the disaster. In fact, they were trying not to think about it or talk about it, and yet were aware that they still had a lot of feelings about it that had not been dealt with. Eleven percent often felt that the crash was not real and about 10% said that they felt numb. Most residents did not, however, try to stay away from reminders of it such as the rail tracks. After all, they lived so close to them that it would have been difficult not to see the tracks.

To estimate the levels of severity of intrusive thoughts and avoidance behaviour, we compared the IES intrusion and avoidance mean scores with those of Horowitz's standardized stress clinic patient samples. These patients attended the clinic for treatment of stress response syndromes, due to having experienced bereavement, accident, violence, illness or surgery. We found that the present community residents experienced significantly less severe intrusion and avoidance behaviour than the patient samples. We then compared our scores with Horowitz's second standardized samples. These samples were medical students who experienced their first confrontation with cadaver dissection. The results showed that the present community residents' intrusion and avoidance were more severe than the medical students'.

We were aware of the fact that the distance between where the community residents lived and where the collision occurred could have bearing on the impact of the disaster that they experienced. Thus, further analyses were carried out to examine the impact of the disaster according to two groups, those who lived nearer to the crash site (between 30 and 60 feet) and those who lived further away from it (more than 60 feet). We found that the two groups were similar in intrusive thoughts and avoidance behaviour.

In terms of general health problems, 35% of the 66 community residents were thought to be psychiatric cases. Anxiety seemed to be more problematic for these community residents, followed by somatic problems. Social dysfunction and depression did not bother them. The community residents who lived nearer to the crash site were similar to those who lived further away from the crash site in terms of general health problems. Correlation results also revealed a significant association between both intrusion and avoidance and general health problems.

Subjective Experience of Quaternary Victims of a Train Disaster

Out of the 66 community residents, 17 were not present on the housing estate when the disaster occurred. In other words, they did not experience the immediate impact of the disaster even though they did witness its aftermath. To fulfil aim 1 of the study, we focused only on those (N=49) who were present on the housing estates when the disaster occurred. On the basis of the Impact of Event Scale, we distinguished the 49 community residents into low/medium (N=21) and high (N=28) levels of posttraumatic stress symptom groups. Comparing the level of symptoms with that of the standardized patient samples from Horowitz's stress clinic, the high symptom group was no different from these standardized patient samples in terms of intrusion and avoidance scores. On the other hand, the low/medium symptom group was significantly lower than the standardized patient samples in terms of intrusion and avoidance. Sixty-four percent of the high symptom group were thought to be psychiatric cases, according to the General Health Questionnaire, while 10% from the low/medium group were thought to be so.

At the time of the collision, there were significantly more residents of the high symptom group awake engaging in different activities (e.g. watching TV, having refreshments, writing or entertaining friends) than those of the low/medium symptom group. The high symptom group was significantly more aware of the signs preceding the disaster (e.g. the sound of the approaching train or the vibration) than the low/medium symptom group. When the collision occurred, the high symptom group reported significantly more shocking and terrifying feelings than those in the low/medium symptom group. Most of the residents in both groups did not think that they would be killed in the disaster.

In the aftermath of the collision, most residents in the two groups felt quite helpless, apart from those who called the emergency services. Subsequently, some carried on doing what they had been doing before the collision; some went to talk to neighbours while others went out to see what had happened. Next morning, when all of the residents saw the wreckage, over 50% of the two groups described themselves as shocked and terrified. Most of them did not expect such a disaster. One resident from the high symptom group received counselling and one was prescribed medication by a general practitioner. No residents from the low/medium group received counselling but one resident was prescribed medication. Most of the residents in the two groups thought that Railtrack was to blame for the disaster. In order to prevent a similar disaster happening again, the high symptom group felt more strongly than the low/medium symptom group that something needed to be done (e.g. regular safety checks of trains). There were significantly more residents in the high symptom group who felt anxious or were worried about their own safety, felt nervous when trains were passing and felt angry about what happened to them, than in the low/medium symptom group.

POSTTRAUMATIC STRESS RESPONSES, GENERAL HEALTH PROBLEMS AND DEATH ANXIETY AMONG QUATERNARY VICTIMS OF A TRAIN DISASTER

One may question the rationale behind looking into the link between posttraumatic stress disorder and death anxiety (aim 2). In death anxiety research, the link between death anxiety, psychological well-being and exposure to life-threatening events or illnesses has been established. For example, death anxiety has been found to be associated with exposure to such traumatic or life-threatening events as civil disturbance in Northern Ireland (Lonetto, Fleming, & Mercer, 1979; Lonetto, Mercer, Fleming, Bunting & Clare, 1980) and the Buffalo Creek disaster (Lifton & Olson, 1976). It was also found to be associated with such illnesses as cancer (Dougherty, Templer, & Brown, 1986; Gibbs & Achterberg-Lawlis, 1978; Sinha & Nigan, 1993), cardiac arrest (Sabom, 1982), HIV (Hintze, Templer, Cappelletty & Frederick, 1994) and near-death experiences (Flynn, 1986; Gallup & Proctor, 1982; Greyson, 1994; Noyes, 1980; Ring, 1980).

To many victims of disasters, the disaster is composed of two elements: trauma and life-threat. For the primary victims mentioned above, the train disaster is both traumatic and directly and personally life-threatening. Death anxiety research indicates that this would likely have implications for death anxiety. For the secondary and quaternary victims, although the train disaster may not be an event directly threatening their own lives, it represents trauma and the degree of death anxiety that they experience may consequently be heightened, especially as the train disaster occurred so close to home. The quaternary victims in Stafford may experience heightened death anxiety knowing that someone died in the incident, that it could have been them travelling on the train, and that the train wreckage could have come over the embankment and crashed into their houses. All of these issues could have reminded them of their mortality, and raised their awareness of their own death. Thus, it seems reasonable to consider the link between posttraumatic stress and death anxiety. However, in posttraumatic stress research, little has been done to look into this link. The second aim of our research intended to fill this gap in our knowledge.

Our study showed that just over 60% said that they were not at all afraid to die. Sixty percent reported that the thought of death had never bothered them. Over 65% reported that the thought of death seldom entered their minds. In fact, over 85% said that the subject of life after death did not trouble them greatly. Sixty-five percent said that they felt that the future held nothing for them to fear but sixty-eight percent said that they often thought about how short life really was.

Over 70% said that they did not shudder when they heard people talking about a World War III and that when people talked about death, they did not become nervous. Sixty percent did not dread the thought of having to have an operation and just over half said that they were not particularly afraid of getting cancer. Over 65% said that they were not really scared of having a heart attack and that the sight of a dead body was not horrifying to them. Just over half said that they were not often distressed by the way time flies so very rapidly and that they were not fearful of dying a painful death.

We then compared the mean scores of the community residents with those of the standardized samples of apartment house residents and psychiatric patients. The former were residents of an upper-middle-class apartment building in metropolitan New Jersey, while the latter were psychiatric patients in a hospital in Kentucky (Templer, Ruff & Franks 1971). The results showed that the community residents experienced significantly higher death anxiety than the apartment house residents. Comparing with the psychiatric patients, the community residents experienced similar death anxiety levels.

Contrary to our expectations, correlation results revealed no association between death anxiety and the impact of the disaster (intrusion and avoidance) and general health problems. Seemingly, death anxiety was a separate psychological reaction from posttraumatic stress reactions and general health problems. This is an interesting finding for both posttraumatic stress and death anxiety researchers. For the posttraumatic stress researchers, this finding basically suggests that although, as was mentioned earlier, one's exposure to disasters implies trauma and life-threat which, in turn, have implications for death anxiety, people seem to employ two separate psychological mechanisms in manifesting the traumatic effects of the life-threatening events and manifesting death anxiety. The way in which these two mechanisms distinguish themselves may well be a worthwhile project to pursue in future research.

For death anxiety researchers, the apparent lack of any association between death anxiety and posttraumatic stress and general health problems tells us something quite specific. It has been postulated that degree of death anxiety is determined by two factors, i.e. a two-factor model of death anxiety, one is general psychological health and the other is life experiences concerning the topic of death (Gilliland & Templer, 1985-1986; Lonetto & Templer, 1986). That is, the degree of death anxiety is associated with our pervasive psychopathological condition (people who suffer from, for example, depression or anxiety disorders may suffer from a high degree of death anxiety) or with, for example, life-threatening experiences (people who have experienced life-threatening events may suffer from increased death anxiety). The present finding basically suggests that while it could be true that the degree of death anxiety is associated with psychopathological condition, it does not mean that it is associated with "any" psychopathological condition. For example, according to the present findings, it is not associated with posttraumatic stress disorder. That is, people who suffer from posttraumatic stress disorder may not suffer from a high degree of death anxiety. Also, as was made explicit earlier, people who have experienced life-threatening events (directly or indirectly) such as train disasters may not suffer from increased death anxiety.

Having said the above, one needs to remember that this so far applies only to quaternary victims. One could argue that if death anxiety were examined among, for example, primary victims, the two psychological mechanisms (one manifests traumatic effects of life-threatening events and the other manifests death anxiety) may not be as separate. In other words, the link between trauma, life-threat and death anxiety could possibly be stronger among primary victims. In that case, the two-factor model of death anxiety may still hold in that primary victims who suffer from posttraumatic stress disorder may suffer from a high degree of death anxiety, and primary victims who have experienced life-threatening events may suffer from increased death anxiety.

POSTTRAUMATIC STRESS RESPONSES, GENERAL HEALTH PROBLEMS AND PERSONALITY AMONG QUATERNARY VICTIMS OF A TRAIN DISASTER

It has been postulated that personality can determine how people perceive and cope with stress and can affect their psychological well-being (Costa & McCrae, 1990; McCrae, 1990; Lazarus & Folkman, 1984; Miller, 2003; Moos & Schaefer, 1993). In posttraumatic stress research, some scholars are precisely concerned with how personality affects the way in which people manifest and cope with posttraumatic stress symptoms (Clark, Watson, & Mineka, 1994; Mikulincer & Florian, 1996; Zeidner & Saklofske, 1996). People with a high level of personality hardiness (Maddi & Kobasa, 1984), for example, tend to adapt to chaotic disastrous situations a lot better than those with a lower level of personality hardiness. They are also more likely to confront challenges and see them as opportunities for growth. They tend to be more able to find meaning in their work, to make sense of ambiguously defined roles and to exercise personal control over things. They are also more ready to make decisions and more able to make a kind of optimistic retrospective appraisal of traumatic experiences (Bartone, Ursano, Wright & Ingraham, 1989).

In the third aim of our study, we set out to identify the role that personality factors can play in posttraumatic stress responses among these community residents as quaternary victims. The results showed that, compared with Eysneck's standardized samples, the present community residents were significantly more introverted but less neurotic. To establish the association between posttraumatic stress and personality variables of extroversion, neuroticism and psychoticism, we found that neuroticism was the only personality variable associated with intrusion, avoidance and general health problems. This finding is consistent with other studies focusing on victims of different disasters. For example, other studies also showed associations between neuroticism and posttraumatic stress reactions among secondary victims of fire-fighters (McFarlane, 1984, 1988a, 1988b, 1989), police officers involved in body recovery work (Thompson & Solomon, 1991), and primary victims of hijack survivors, transportation accidents, war, terrorism, violent crime, and industrial and domestic accidents (Charlton & Thompson, 1996; Thompson, 1991). Veterans with combat-related posttraumatic stress tend to be more neurotic than those without it and to have personality disorders, antisocial disorders and psychopathic tendency associated with neuroticism (e.g. Hyer, Braswell, Albrecht, Boyd, Boudewyns & Talbert, 2003; O'Toole, Marshall, Schureck & Dobson, 1998; Schnurr, Friedman & Rosenberg, 1993). One study also showed that among peacekeepers, neuroticism measured before their deployment was a significant predictor to posttraumatic stress symptoms following peacekeeping duties (Bramsen, Dirkzwager & Van der Ploeg, 2000). High neuroticism was also found to be associated with posttraumatic stress symptoms among victims of natural disasters (Morgan, Matthews & Winton, 1995). The association between neuroticism and posttraumatic stress symptoms and diagnoses has been shown to last as long as three years after the rescue for some fire-fighters (McFarlane, 1992), six months following accidents for motor vehicle victims (Holeva & Tarrier, 2001), and twelve months following discharge from hospital for burns (Fauerbach, Lawrence, Schmidt, Munster & Costa, 2000). It has also been postulated that neuroticism is a variable which would predict a lifetime diagnosis of posttraumatic stress among young adults in an urban area (Breslau, Davis, Andreski & Peterson, 1991).

Interestingly, apart from neuroticism, our study identified no relationships between posttraumatic stress and any other personality variables. Other associations have been suggested elsewhere, in that, for example, introversion was associated with posttraumatic stress responses among fire-fighters (McFarlane, 1984, 1988a, 1988b, 1989); psychoticism and extroversion were also associated with social dysfunction and depression among police officers (Thompson & Solomon, 1991); introversion-thinking and introversion-seeing-thinking were associated with posttraumatic stress responses in 64.5% and 48.9% of the veterans respectively (Dalton, Aubuchon, Tom, Pederson, & McFarland, 1993). Introversion was also associated with posttraumatic stress diagnoses, four and twelve months following discharge from hospital for burns (Fauerbach, Lawrence, Schmidt, Munster & Costa, 2000) and with posttraumatic stress symptoms three months after an aircraft crash (Carlier & Gersons, 1997).

Posttraumatic Stress Responses, General Health Problems and Coping among Quaternary Victims of a Train Disaster

In posttraumatic stress research, coping strategies have been examined among victims of war-related trauma (e.g. Fairbank, Hansen, & Fitterling, 1991; Solomon, Regier, Burke, 1989; Zeidner & Ben-Zur, 1994), natural and technological trauma (e.g. Collins, Baum, & Singer, 1983; Freedy, Shaw, Jarrell, & Masters, 1992; Hicks, Marical, & Conti, 1991; North, Smith, McCool, & Lightcap, 1989; Stuhlmiller, 1994) and interpersonal and personal loss (e.g. Mikulincer & Florian, 1996). There are different ways of coping with the effects of disasters, such as monitoring and blunting (e.g. Solomon, Mikulincer, Arad, 1991), and personality hardiness (e.g. Bartone, Ursano, Wright, & Ingraham, 1989; Hodgkinson & Shepherd, 1994; Moran & Britton, 1994). Problem-focused and emotion-focused ways of coping are certainly the most widely discussed, though it is not always easy to categorize different strategies neatly into problem or emotion-focused coping (Folkman & Lazarus, 1988; Schwarzer & Schwarzer, 1996). Problem-focused coping refers to efforts undertaken to manage or alter the troubled person-environment relationship that is the source of stress, while emotion-focused coping refers to efforts undertaken to regulate stressful emotions.

As part of aim 3 in our study, we also examined the relationship between problem-focused coping, emotion-focused coping and posttraumatic stress among the community residents as quaternary victims. We found that the community residents used distancing as a coping strategy the most followed by self-controlling and seeking social support. The degree to which they used confrontive, escape-avoidance, planful problem solving and positive reappraisal coping strategies was similar. They used the least the coping strategy of accepting responsibility. To compare the results with the standardized samples from Folkman and Lazarus (1988), the results showed that the degree to which the community residents used confrontive and escape-avoidance coping strategies was somewhat similar. However, the community residents used significantly less self-controlling, seeking social support, accepting responsibility, planful problem solving and positive reappraisal coping strategies.

The results also revealed that intrusive thoughts were associated with the coping strategies of distancing, seeking social support, accepting responsibility and escape-avoidance. Avoidance behaviour was associated with escape-avoidance. The above coping strategies were all emotion-focused. This means that emotion-focused coping was strongly associated with posttraumatic stress reactions. This finding was indeed consistent with the literature. For example, emotion-focused coping was associated with posttraumatic stress among veterans from the Lebanon war (Mikulincer & Solomon, 1989) and from the Persian Gulf War (Zeidner & Ben-Zur, 1994; Zeidner & Hammer, 1992). The Israelites, who used emotion-focused coping in order to cope with the threat of missile attack during the Gulf War, tended to experience anxiety, physical and somatic symptoms, and pessimism (Zeidner & Ben-Zur, 1993). Also, veterans who received treatments for posttraumatic stress disorder tended to be those who used emotion-focused coping (Blake, Cook, & Keane, 1991). Similarly, emotion-focused coping also predicted severe psychological distress among victims of transportation accidents, industrial and domestic accidents, terrorism and violent crime in one study (Charlton and Thompson, 1996). Emotion-focused coping measured at two to three weeks and four months after some military training accidents predicted PTSD symptoms at 12 months (Eid, 2003).

Specifically, escape-avoidance, one type of emotion-focused coping strategy, is often associated with posttraumatic stress. For example, in order to cope with war memories, veterans predominantly use escape-avoidance strategies which are associated with posttraumatic stress severity (Hyer, McCranie, Boudewyns & Sperr, 1996). Similarly, in order to cope with the traumatic effects of their involvement in the rescue operation, disaster personnel have been known to use escape-avoidance or emotional distancing, which are associated with high levels of posttraumatic stress (e.g. McCarroll, Ursano, Wright & Fullerton, 1993; Marmar, Weiss, Metzler, & Delucchi, 1996). In addition to disaster personnel, escape-avoidance has also been shown to predict severe posttraumatic stress for victims of accidents, terrorism and crime (Charlton & Thompson, 1996), acute stress reactions (i.e. 2-3 weeks) for victims following fatal training accidents (Eid, 2003) and shipwreck (Eid, Johnsen & Thayer, 2001). Problem-focused coping strategies, on the other hand, have been found to moderate the detrimental effects of emotion-focused coping on mental health (Solomon, Mikulincer, & Arad, R, 1991).

In contrast, however, emotion-focused coping was thought not to be associated with avoidance for some boat sinking victims (Joseph, Williams, & Yule, 1992). One study found that all coping strategies were equally associated with the presence of PTSD. They included problem-focused coping, wishful thinking, detachment, seeking social support, focusing on positive things, self-blame, tension reduction, and keeping to oneself (Spurrell & McFarlane, 1993).

FUTURE RESEARCH

It is beyond the scope of this chapter to provide a comprehensive list of possible future studies on victims exposed to train disasters. However, a few pointers are worth mentioning here. First, focusing on future research on primary and secondary victims exposed to train disasters, while research so far on the posttraumatic stress responses of these victims has informed us mainly about the range of symptoms that people experience following disasters, little is known about the ways in which these victims cope with posttraumatic stress. These coping styles would probably be influenced by the kind of primary victim (e.g. passenger) or secondary victim (e.g. body handler). When train disasters occur, passengers are often passive recipients of the impact of the disaster. There is usually nothing they can do in order to avoid the occurrence of the disaster. As a result, they may, for example, cope with the traumatic effects by blaming others as opposed to themselves, finding information on who is responsible for the disasters, expressing anger towards those who are deemed to be responsible for the disasters and the like. On the other hand, body handlers may use more emotional distancing coping strategies by means of humour or treating the dead bodies as scientific experiments (Taylor and Frazer, 1982). It seems that to tease out, through systematic studies, the coping strategies of specific types of primary or secondary victims is important because in so doing, one can proceed to identify the coping strategies which are potentially maladaptive for particular types of victims and the coping strategies which can potentially buffer against traumatic stress for particular types of victims. Such studies would serve to help people relinquish maladaptive coping strategies and adopt more helpful ones.

Second, it seems that studies into psychological treatments such as psychotherapy may have a role to play in helping (both primary and secondary) victims to cope with posttraumatic stress resulting from train disasters. Studies should aim to tease out which type of psychotherapy is more appropriate or beneficial for a particular type of victim. The aforementioned studies on coping would probably provide useful information for psychotherapists. However, one must not undermine the difficulty involved in setting up psychotherapy services and psychotherapy research for victims, in particular, secondary victims such as policemen or fire-fighters. After all, many of these professionals, despite their suffering, would find it difficult to come forward and receive treatment, since many of them believe that their professional training should have prepared them for the traumatic effects of, for example, handling dead bodies.

Third, related closely to the notion of coping is the notion of personality. As was mentioned previously, personality can determine how people perceive and cope with stress and can affect their psychological well-being. Thus, systematic studies looking into the role that personality plays in the posttraumatic stress of primary and secondary victims exposed to train disasters are important.

Fourth, future research on all types of victims exposed to train disasters should look into the one aforementioned study which examined primary victims' (i.e. passengers) change of schema or beliefs about the world, other people and themselves. Indeed, research into the shattering of long-held cognitive schemata or world assumptions is increasingly important (Janoff-Bulman & Frieze, 1983) because it helps us understand the relationship between the self and the world (Fiske & Taylor, 1991). Future research on train disasters should try to increase our understanding of the relationship between the shattering of world assumptions and posttraumatic stress among different types of victim (be they primary, secondary or quaternary). One would speculate that the degree to which world assumptions are shattered and its association with traumatic stress would probably be influenced by a range of factors including the typology of the victim, the severity of one's exposure to the disaster, and even personality.

Fifth, focusing on future research on quaternary victims exposed to train disasters, our study has thus far been structured in order to test the additive model of personality and coping (i.e. personality and coping make independent and unique contributions to posttraumatic stress). It would be interesting to look into the mediational model of personality and coping (i.e. personality determines particular coping strategies which may result in posttraumatic stress) and the interactive model (i.e. personality interacts with coping strategies in maintaining or generating posttraumatic stress) (Hewitt & Flett, 1996). In fact, looking at the relationship between personality, coping and posttraumatic stress in terms of the foregoing three models would also be relevant in studies based on primary and secondary victims exposed to train disasters or, for that matter, other disasters.

Sixth, as was mentioned, since our study on quaternary victims exposed to train disasters revealed that death anxiety was a separate psychological reaction from posttraumatic stress, the way in which these two mechanisms distinguish themselves should be investigated further. Also, just because the link between death anxiety and posttraumatic stress has not been established among quaternary victims, this does not mean to say that such a relationship could not exist among other types of victim exposed to train disasters. Thus, the link between death anxiety and posttraumatic stress should be examined among other types of victim.

The final comment is a general one about future research into victims of train disasters. We find useful the idea of classifying people into types of victims, not because we wish to pathologize people but because such classification helps us see the range of people who could become affected as a result of train disasters and who might otherwise be overlooked. For example, in additional to primary, secondary and quaternary victims, Taylor and Frazer (1982) also identified sesternary victims who, but for chance, would have been primary victims or who have led others to take a course of action which results in their becoming primary victims. In fact, we have recently carried out a study which precisely aimed to look at this group of victims exposed to aircraft disasters (Chung, Easthope, Chung & Clark-Carter, 2001). One would imagine that train disasters could also produce sesternary victims. Thus, future investigations into train disasters may find this classification helpful as a way of identifying who is in need, hence, identifying the size of the population affected.

REFERENCES

Andersen, H.S., Christensen, A.K., & Petersen, G.O. (1991). Post-traumatic stress reactions amongst rescue workers after a major rail accident. *Anxiety Research*, 4, 245-251.

Bartone, P.T., Ursano, R.J., Wright, K.M., & Ingraham, L.H. (1989). The impact of a military air disaster on the health of assistance workers: a prospective study. *Journal of Nervous and Mental Disease*, 177(6), 317-328.

Blake, D.D., Albano, A.M., & Keane, T.M. (1992). Twenty years of trauma: Psychological abstracts 1970 through 1989. *Journal of Traumatic Stress*, 5(3), 477-484.

Blake, D.D., Cook, J.D., & Keane, T.M. (1991). Post traumatic stress disorder and coping in veterans who are seeking medical treatment. *Journal of Clinical Psychology*, 48(6), 695-704.

Boman, B. (1979). Behavioural observations on the Granville train disaster and the significance of stress for Psychiatry. *Social Science & Medicine*, 13A, 463-471.

Bowler, R.M., Mergler, D., Huel, G., & Cone, J.E. (1994). Psychological, psychosocial and psychophysiological sequelae in a community affected by a railroad chemical disaster. *Journal of Traumatic Stress*, 7(4), 601-624.

Bramsen, I., Dirkzwager, A.J.E., & Van der Ploeg, H.M (2000). Predeployment personality traits and exposure to trauma as predictors of posttraumatic stress symptoms: A prospective study of former peacekeepers. *American Journal of Psychiatry*, 157, 1115-1119.

Breslau, N., Davis, G.C., Andreski, P., & Peterson, E (1991). Traumatic events and posttraumatic stress disorder in an urban population of young adults. *Archive of General Psychiatry*, 48, 216-222.

Burns, T.P., & Hollins, S.C. (1991). Psychiatric response to the Clapham rail crash. *Journal of the Royal Society of Medicine*, 84, 15-19.

Carlier, I.V.E., & Gersons, E.P.R (1997). Stress reactions in disaster victims following the Bijlmermeer plane crash. *Journal of Trauma Stress*, 10(2), 329-335.

Charlton, P.F.C., & Thompson, J.A. (1996). Ways of coping with psychological distress after trauma. *British Journal of Clinical Psychology*, 35, 517-530.

Chung, M.C., Easthope, Y., Chung, C., & Clark-Carter, D. (2001) Traumatic stress and coping strategies of sesternary victims following an aircraft disaster in Coventry. *Stress and Health*, 17, 67-75.

Chung, M.C., Easthope, Y., Farmer, S., Werrett, J., & Chung, C. (2003) Psychological sequelae: posttraumatic stress reactions and personality factors among community residents as secondary victims. *Scandinavian Journal of Caring Sciences*, 17, 265-270.

Chung, M.C., Farmer, S., Werrett, J., Easthope, Y., & Chung, C. (2001) Traumatic stress and ways of coping of community residents exposed to a train disaster. Australian and New *Zealand Journal of Psychiatry*, 35, 528-534.

Chung, M.C., Werrett, J., Easthope, Y., Farmer, S., & Chung, C. (2002) Traumatic stress and death anxiety among community residents exposed to a train crash. Omega: *Journal of Death and Dying*, 45(2), 133-147.

Chung, M.C., Werrett, J., Farmer, S., Easthope, Y., & Chung, C. (2000). Responses to traumatic stress among community residents exposed to a train collision. *Stress Medicine*, 16, 17-25.

Clark, L.A., Watson, D., & Mineka, S (1994). Temperament, personality, and the mood and anxiety disorders. *Journal of Abnormal Psychology*, 103, 103-116.

Collins, D.L., Baum, A., & Singer, J.E. (1983). Coping with chronic stress at Three Mile Island: psychological and biochemical evidence. *Health Psychology*, 2, 149-166.

Costa, P.T. & McCrae, R.R. (1990). Personality: Another "hidden factor" in stress research. *Psychological Enquiry*, 1, 22-24.

Dalton, J.E., Aubuchon, I.N., Tom, A., Pederson, S.L., & McFarland, R.E. (1993). MBTI profiles of Vietnam veterans with post-traumatic stress disorder. *Journal of Psychological* Type, 26, 3-8.

Dougherty, K., Templer, D.I., & Brown, R. (1986). Psychological states in terminal cancer patients as measured over time. *Journal of Consulting Psychology*, 33, 357-359.

Eid, J (2003). The course of PTSD symptoms following military training accidents and brief psychosocial interventions. *Personality and Individual Differences*, 35(4), 771-783.

Eid, J., Johnsen, B.H., & Thayer, J.F. (2001). Posttraumatic stress symptoms following shipwreck of a Norwegian navy frigate—An early follow-up. *Personality and Individual Difference,* 30(80), 1283-1295.

Engelhard, I.M., Macklin, M.L., McNally, R.J., van den Hout, M.A., & Arntz, A, (2001). Emotion and intrusion-based reasoning in Vietnam veterans with and without chronic posttraumatic stress disorder. *Behaviour Therapy and Therapy*, 39(11), 1339-1348.

Engelhard, I,M., van den Hout, M.A., Arntz, A., & McNally, R.J (2002). A longitudinal study of "intrusion-based reasoning" and posttraumatic stress disorder after exposure to a train disaster. *Behaviour Research and Therapy*, 40(12), 1415-1434.

Eysenck, H.G., & Eysenck, S.B.G. (1991). *EPS Manual of E.P.Scale* (EPS-Adult). London: Hodder & Stoughton

Fairbank, J.A., Hansen, D.J., & Fitterling, J.M. (1991). Patterns of appraisal and coping across different stressor conditions among former prisoners of war with and without posttraumatic stress disorder. *Journal of Consulting and Clinical Psychology*, 59, 274-281.

Fauerbach, J.A., Lawrence, J.W., Schmidt, C.W., Munster, A.M., & Costa, P.T (2000). Personality predictors of injury-related posttraumatic stress disorder. *Journal of Nervous and Mental Disease*, 188, 510-517.

Figley, C.R., & Kleber, R.J. (1995). Beyond the "victim": Secondary traumatic stress. In R.J.Kleber., C.R.Figley., & B.P.R.Gersons (ed.) *Beyond trauma*. New York: Plenum press.

Fiske, S.T., & Taylor, S.E. (1991). *Social cognition*. New York: McGraw-Hill.

Flynn, C.P. (1986) *After the beyond: Human transformation and the near-death experience.* Englewood Cliffs, NJ: Prentice-Hall.

Folkman, S., & Lazarus, R.S. (1988). Manual for the Ways of Coping Questionnaire. Palo Alto, CA: *Consulting Psychologist Press*.

Freedy, J.R., Shaw, D.L., Jarrell, M.P., Masters, C.R. (1992). Towards an understanding of the psychological impact of natural disasters: An application of the conservation resources stress model. *Journal of Traumatic Stress*, 5(3), 441-454.

Gallup, G., & Proctor, W (1982). *Adventures in immortality: A look beyond the threshold of death.* New York: McGraw-Hill.

Gibbs, H.W., & Achterberg-Lawlis, J. (1978). Spiritual values and death anxiety: Implications for counseling with terminal cancer patients. *Journal of Counseling Psychology,* 25, 563-569.

Gilliland, J.C., & Templer, D.I (1985-1986). Relationship of death anxiety scale factors to subjective states. *Omega*, 16, 155-167.

Goldberg, D.P., & Hillier, V.F. (1979). A scaled version of the General Health Questionnaire. *Psychological Medicine*, 9, 139-145.

Gould, B.B., & Gould, J.B. (1991). Young people's perception of the space shuttle disaster: case study. *Adolescence*, 26(102), 295-303.

Greyson, B. (1994) Reduced death threat in near-death experiencers. In R.A.Neimeyer (Ed.) *Death Anxiety Handbook*. Washington: Taylor & Francis.

Hagström, R. (1995). The acute psychological impact on survivors following a train accident. *Journal of Traumatic Stress*, 8(3), 391-402.

Harrington, R. (1996). The "railway spine" diagnosis and Victorian responses to PTSD. *Journal of Psychosomatic Research*, 40(1), 11-14.

Health and Safety Executive (1996). *Railway accident at Rickerscote*. London: HSE Books.

Hewitt, P.L., & Flett, G.L. (1996) Personality traits and the coping process. In M.Zeidner & N.S.Endler (eds) *Handbook of coping*. New York: John Wiley & Sons.

Hicks, R.A., Marical, C.M., & Conti, P.A. (1991). Coping with a major stressor: differences between habitual short- and longer-sleepers. *Perceptual and Motor Skills*, 72, 631-636.

Hintze, J., Templer, D.I., Cappelletty, G.G., & Frederick, W. (1994). Death depression and death anxiety in HIV-Infected males. In R.A.Neimeyer (Eds) *Death Anxiety Handbook*. Washington: Taylor & Francis.

Hodgkinson, P.E., & Shepherd, M.A. (1994). The impact of disaster support work. *Journal of Traumatic Stress*, 7(4), 587-600.

Hodgkinson, P.E., & Stewart, M. (1991). *Coping with catastrophe. A handbook of disaster management*. London: Routledge.

Holeva, V., & Tarrier, N (2001). Personality and peritraumatic dissociation in the prediction of PTSD in victims of road traffic accidents. *Journal of Psychosomatic Research*, 51, 687-692.

Horowitz, M., Wilner, N., & Alvarez, W. (1979). Impact of Events Scale: A measure of subjective stress. *Psychosomatic Medicine*, 41(3), 209-218.

Hyer, L., McCranie, E., Boudewyns, P.A., & Sperr, E (1996). Modes of long-term coping with trauma memories: Relative use and associations with personality among Vietnam veterans with chronic PTSD. *Journal of Traumatic Stress*, 9(2), 299-316.

Hyer, L., Braswell, L., Albrecht, B., Boyd, S., Boudewyns, P., & Talbert, S (2003). Relationship of NEO-PI to personality styles and severity of trauma in chronic PTSD victims. *Journal of Clinical Psychology*, 59(12), 1295-1304.

Janoff-Bulman, R., & Frieze, I.H. (1983). A theoretical perspective for understanding reactions to victimization. *Journal of Social Issues*, 39, 1-17.

Joseph, S., Williams, R., & Yule, W. (1992). Crisis support, attributional style, coping style, and post-traumatic symptoms. *Personality and Individual Differences*, 13(11), 1249-1251.

Lazarus, R.S., & Folkman, S (1984). *Stress, appraisal and coping*. New York: Springer.

Levitt, L., & Leventhal, G. (1986). Technological catastrophe: reactions to the space shuttle disaster. *Perceptual and Motor Skills*, 63, 670.

Lifton, R.J., & Olson, E. (1976) The human meaning of total disaster: The Buffalo Creek experience. *Psychiatry*, 39, 1-18.

Lonetto, R., Fleming, S., & Mercer, G.W. (1979). The structure of death anxiety: A factor analytic study. *Journal of Personality Assessment*, 43, 388-392.

Lonetto, R., Mercer, G.W., Fleming, S., Bunting, B., & Clare, M. (1980). Death anxiety among university students in Northern Ireland and Canada. *Journal of Psychology*, 104, 75-82.

Lonetto, R., & Templer, D.I (1986). *Death anxiety*. Washington, DC: Hemisphere Publishing Corp; 1986.

Lundin, T. (1991). Train disaster survivors: Long-term effects on mental health and well-being. *Stress Medicine*, 7:87-91.

Maddi, S.R., & Kobasa, S.C. (1984). The *hardy executive: Health under stress*. Homewood, IL: Dow Jones-Irwin.

Marmar, C.R., Weiss, D.S., Metzler, T.J., & Delucchi, K (1996). Characteristics of emergency services personnel related to peritraumatic dissociation during critical incident exposure. *American Journal of Psychiatry*, 153(Suppl), 94-102.

McCarroll, J., Ursano, R., Wright, K., & Fullerton, C (1993). Handling bodies after violent death: strategies for coping. *American Journal of Orthopsychiatry*, 63(2), 209-214.

McCrae, R.R. (1990). Controlling neuroticism in the measurement of stress. *Stress Medicine*, 6, 237-241.

McFarlane, A.C. (1984). Life events, disasters and psychological distress. *Mental Health in Australia*, 1(13), 4-6.

McFarlane, A.C. (1988a). The aetiology of post-traumatic stress disorders following a natural disaster. *British Journal of Psychiatry*, 152, 116-121.

McFarlane, A.C. (1988b). The longitudinal course of posttraumatic morbidity. The range of outcomes and their predictors. *The Journal of Nervous and Mental Disease*, 176(1), 30-39.

McFarlane, A.C. (1989). The aetiology of post-traumatic morbidity: predisposing, precipitating and perpetuating factors. *British Journal of Psychiatry*, 154, 221-228.

McFarlane, A.C. (1992) Avoidance and intrusion in posttraumatic stress disorder. *Journal of Nervous and Mental Disease,* 180, 439-445.

Mikulincer, M., & Florian, V. (1996). Coping and adaptation to trauma and loss. In M.Zeidner., & N.S.Endler (ed.) *Handbook of Coping*. New York: John Wiley & Son.

Mikulincer, M., & Solomon, Z. (1989) Causal attribution, coping strategies and combat-related post-traumatic stress disorder. *European Journal of Personality*, 3(4), 269-284.

Miller, M.W. (2003). Personality and the etiology and expression of PTSD: A three-factor model perspective. *Clinical Psychology: Science and Practice*, 10(4), 373-393.

Moos, R.H., & Schaefer, J.A (1993). Coping resources and processes: Current concepts and measures. In: Goldberger, L Breznitz, S, editors. *Handbook of stress: Theoretical and clinical aspects.* New York: Free Press.

Moran, C., & Britton, N.R. (1994). Emergency work experience and reactions to traumatic incidents. *Journal of Traumatic Stress*, 7(4), 575-585.

Morgan, I.A., Matthews, G., & Winton, M. (1995). Coping and personality as predictors of posttraumatic intrusions, numbing, avoidance and general distress: A study of victims of the Perth flood. *Behavioural and Cognitive Psychotherapy*, 23(3), 251-264.

North, C.S., Smith, E.M., McCool, R.E., & Lightcap, P.E. (1989). Acute postdisaster coping and adjustment. *Journal of Traumatic Stress*, 2, 353-360.

Noyes, R. (1980). Attitude change following near-death experiences. Psychiatry, 43, 234-242.

O'Toole, B.I., Marshall, R.P., Schureck, R.J., & Dobson, M (1998). Risk factors for posttraumatic stress disorder in Australian Vietnam veterans. Australian and New Zealand *Journal of Psychiatry*, 32, 21-31.

Raphael, B. (1977). The Granville train disaster: Psychological needs and their management. *The Medical Journal of Australia*, 1, 303-305.

Raphael, B. (1979-80) A primary prevention action programme: Psychiatric involvement following a major rail disaster. *Omega*, 10(3), 211-226.

Raphael, B. (1986) *When disaster strikes*. London: Unwin Hyman.

Raphael, B., & Meldrum, L. (1993) The evolution of mental health responses and research in Australian disasters. *Journal of Traumatic Stress*, 6, 65-89.

Raphael, B., & Middleton, W. (1987) Mental health responses in a decade of disasters: Australia, 1974-1983. *Hospital and Community Psychiatry*, 38, 1331-1337.

Raphael, B., Singh, B., & Bradbury, L. (1980). Disaster: The helper's perspective. *The Medical Journal of Australia,* 2, 445-447.

Raphael, B., Singh, B., Bradbury, L., & Lambert, F. (1983-1984). Who helps the helpers? The effects of a disaster on the rescue workers. *Omega*, 14(1), 9-20.

Ring, K. (1980) *Life at death: A scientific investigation of the near-death experience.* New York: Coward, McCann & Geoghegan.

Sabom, M.B. (1982). *Recollections of death: A medical investigation.* New York: Harper & Row.

Selley, C., King, E., Peveler, R, Osola, K., Martin, N., & Thompson, C. (1997) Post-traumatic stress disorder symptoms and the Clapham rail accident. *British Journal of Psychiatry*, 171, 478-482.

Schnurr, P.P. Friedman, M.J., & Rosenberg, S.D (1993). Premilitary MMPI scores as predictors of combat-related PTSD symptoms. *American Journal of Psychiatry*, 150, 479-483.

Schwarzer, R., & Schwarzer, C. (1996). A critical survey of coping instruments. In M.Zeidner., & N.S.Endler (ed.) *Handbook of Coping*. New York: John Wiley & Son.

Shepherd, M., & Hodgkinson, P. (1990) The hidden victims of disaster: Helpers stress. *Stress Medicine*, 6, 29-35.

Singh, B., & Raphael, B. (1981). Postdisaster morbidity of the bereaved: A possible role for preventive psychiatry? *The Journal of Nervous and Mental Disease*, 169(4), 203-212.

Sinha, S.P., & Nigan, M. (1993). Stress and death anxiety. *Indian Journal of Clinical Psychology*, 20, 78-81.

Solomon, Z., Iancu, I., & Tyano, S. (1997). World assumptions following disaster. *Journal of Applied Social Psychology*, 27(20), 1785-1798.

Solomon, Z., Mikulincer, M., Arad, R. (1991). Monitoring and blunting: Implications for combat-related post-traumatic stress disorder. *Journal of Traumatic Stress*, 4(2), 209-221.

Solomon, S.D., Regier, D.A., Burke, J.D. (1989). Role of perceived control in coping with disaster. *Journal of Social and Clinical Psychology*, 8(4), 376-392.

Spurrell, M.T., & McFarlane, A.C. (1993). Post-traumatic stress disorder and coping after a natural disaster. *Social Psychiatry and Psychiatric Epidemiology*, 28, 194-200.

Stevens, K.L.H., & Partridge, R. (1990). The Clapham rail disaster. *Injury*, 21, 37-40.

Stuhlmiller, C.M. (1994). Occupational meanings and coping practices of rescue workers in an earthquake disaster. *Western Journal of Nursing Research*, 16(3), 268-287.

Taylor, A.J.W., & Frazer, A.G. (1981). *Psychological sequelae of operation overdue following the DC10 aircrash in Antarctica.* Publication from Victoria University of Wellington.

Taylor, A.J.W., and Frazer, A.G. (1982). The stress of post-disaster body handling and victim identification work. *Journal of Human Stress*, 8(4), 4-12.

Templer, D.I. (1970). The construction and validation of a Death Anxiety Scale. *Journal of General Psychology*, 82, 165-177.

Templer, D.I., Ruff, C.F., & Franks, C.M. (1971). Death anxiety: age, sex, and parental resemblance in diverse populations. *Developmental Psychology*, 4, 108.

Thompson, J. (1991). Kuwait airways hijack: psychological consequences for survivors. *Stress Medicine*, 7, 3-9.

Thompson, J., & Solomon, M. (1991) Body recovery teams at disasters: trauma or challenge? *Anxiety Research*, 4, 235-244.

Trimble, M.R. (1981). *Post-traumatic neurosis*. Chichester: John Wiley & Sons.

Tyano, S., Iancu, I., Solomon, Z., Sever, J., Goldstein, I., Touviana, Y., & Bleich, A. (1996). Seven-year follow up of child survivors of a bus-train collision. *Journal of American Academic Child and Adolescence Psychiatry*, 35(3), 365-373.

Ursano, R.J., McCaughey, B.G., & Fullerton, C.S. (1994) *Individual and community responses to trauma and disaster.* Cambridge: Cambridge University Press.

van der Kolk, B.A., Weisaeth, L., & van der Hart, O. (1996). History of trauma in psychiatry. In B.A.van der Kolk., A.C.McFarlane & L.Weisaeth (Eds.). *Traumatic stress*. New York: The Guilford Press.

Weisaeth, L. (1994) Psychological and psychiatric aspects of technological disasters. In R.J.Ursano., B.G.McCaughey., & C.S.Fullerton (ed.) *Individual and Community Responses to Trauma and Disaster*. Cambridge: Cambridge University Press.

Wright, J.C., Binney, V., & Kunkler, J. (1994) Psychological distress in the local Hillsborough or `host' community following the Hillsborough football stadium disaster. *Journal of Community & Applied Social Psychology*, 4, 77-89.

Wright, J.C., Kunkel, D., Pinon, M.F., & Huston, A.C. (1989). How children reacted to televised coverage of the space shuttle disaster. *Journal of Communication*, 39(2), 27-45.

Wright, K.M., Ursano, R.J., Bartone, P.T., & Ingraham, L.H. (1990). The shared experience of catastrophe: an expanded classification of the disaster community, *American Journal of Orthopsychiatry*, 60(1), 35-42.

Zeece, P.D. (1986) Young children's understanding of the shuttle disaster. *Journal of Psychology*, 124(5), 591-593.

Zeidner, M., & Ben-Zur, H. (1993). Coping with a national crisis: The Israeli experience with the threat of missile attacks. *Personality and Individual Differences*, 14(1), 209-224.

Zeidner, M., & Ben-Zur, H. (1994) Individual differences in anxiety, coping and post-traumatic stress in the aftermath of the Persian Gulf War. *Personality and Individual Differences*, 16(3), 459-476.

Zeidner, M., & Hammer, A.L. (1992). Coping with missile attack: resources, strategies and outcomes. *Journal of Personality*, 60(4), 709-746.

Zeidner, M., & Saklofske, D (1996). Adaptive and maladaptive coping. In: Zeidner, M., Endler, N (eds), *Handbook of Coping*. New York: John Wiley & Sons

INDEX

D

E

F

G

H

I

J

K

L

M

N

O

P

Q

R

S

T

U

V

W

Y